Hotels, Motels, and Restaurants

Valuations and Market Studies

Hotels, Motels, and Restaurants

Valuations and Market Studies

Stephen Rushmore, MAI

American Institute of Real Estate Appraisers
430 North Michigan Avenue
Chicago, Illinois

Second Printing: May 1985

ISBN: 0-911780-70-X

Printed in the United States of America

Foreword

In the community where I reside, Washington, D.C., two large, solid, late 1920s, downtown hotels stand on prominent adjacent corner lots. One is better built, better decorated and furnished, and with a much more prestigious reputation and higher rate schedule; that one closed while its neighbor continues to thrive. An appraisal revealed the appropriateness of both business determinations.

In a nearby suburb a large 20-year-old motel, part of a chain, enjoys an annual occupancy rate in excess of 90% despite that it is awkwardly located at the dead end of a maze of highway ramps, lanes, and drives—and is of indifferent and dated architecture. An appraisal analysis revealed why this manifestly bad investment is a winner.

The shortest street in this city is the location of a downtown-fringe, isolated, quarter-acre, industrially zoned lot adjacent to a mainline railroad right-of-way. A small warehouse was built on this lot at the start of World War II. In the mid-1960s, the building was remodeled as an expensive restaurant and was an instant success. Another restaurant is remotely located 12 miles from the city; reservations there must be made days in advance. A third local successful restaurant is accessible only by stair and is 24 feet below the sidewalk in a cellar of a downtown office tower. A fourth, this time seafood, restaurant, two blocks from the city line, in a depressed commercial section, has not been redecorated since its creation as a white-tile eatery in 1923; reservations are not accepted and there is always a wait at meal times. A highly publicized Washington restaurant, frequented by officials of a recent two-term Presidency, permanently closed within weeks of the resignation of its maitre d'.

Perhaps the only thing more risky than investing in hotels and restaurants is appraising them. Whereas this book will certainly not instill infallibility in its readers, it will provide major help to qualified appraisers wanting to engage in the hotel and restaurant specialties by giving them greater confidence. Usually, appraisers know more about both the real estate they are appraising and the process of appraisal than anyone else. That is often not the case when restaurants and/or hotels are involved; in such cases owners and managers frequently know more about the suitability of the real estate for the ongoing or contemplated business than does the impartial appraiser. And, as the appraised subject is generally a going concern, the accountants representing the owners sometimes have significant appraisal knowledge. This book will provide the analytical tools so that the appraiser can exhibit expertness in such company. Knowledge permits impartial opinions to be rendered with confidence by both field appraisers and review appraisers.

The Appraisal Institute is pleased to publish this authoritative work by Stephen Rushmore, MAI, an acknowledged leading appraisal expert regarding the hospitality industry.

Anthony Reynolds, MAI
1983 President
American Institute of Real Estate Appraisers

Preface

Change is always pertinent in the appraisal of real estate, particularly in the area of hotel-motel valuations. Five years have passed since the American Institute of Real Estate Appraisers published the monograph, *The Valuation of Hotels and Motels,* and the techniques for quantifying lodging demand have become more sophisticated and refined. Research has led to the development of an indexing procedure to evaluate the competitiveness of various lodging facilities so that total room-night demand can be allocated among competing hostelries. Hotel investors are now projecting income and expenses using inflated, not constant, dollars. Their expenses are estimated with fixed and variable component analysis, which automatically adjusts for changes in occupancy levels. Capitalization and discounting procedures have advanced considerably and computerization allows for efficient calculation of internal rates of return. All of these changes in the industry are incorporated into this completely revised monograph, *Hotels, Motels, and Restaurants: Valuations and Market Studies.*

As the title indicates, a new chapter dealing specifically with restaurants has been added. The area of food service valuation has never received proper attention in appraisal literature, and I hope that the procedures set forth in this book will provide a starting point for practitioners and researchers.

The purpose of this monograph is to present a logical procedure for gathering and processing data into estimates of market value. A case study, based on a proposed lodging facility with no operating history, is used in Chapters 2, 3, and 6 to demonstrate various market analysis techniques. A second hypothetical property is used in Chapter 7 to illustrate the procedures for valuing a restaurant.

The first chapter presents an overview of the hotel-motel industry. New developments in lodging facilities seem to run in specific cycles, which reflect not only current travel routes and modes of transportation, but also the requirements demanded by individual patrons. The element of change is important because it often causes functional and economic obsolescence and rapid loss in property value.

All appraisals and feasibility studies are based on the principle of supply and demand. In valuing a lodging facility, supply refers to the number and type of competitive transient accommodations located within a defined market area; demand represents the total number of travelers expected to utilize these facilities. The appraiser's initial objective is to evaluate the local supply and demand relationship to determine how a proposed hostelry will fit into the market. By quantifying the total demand into measurable units and allocating these units among the competitive facilities, the property's expected share of the market is established. This information is then converted into an estimated occupancy and average rate, which is used to estimate a projection of revenue.

The appraisal must reflect the investment strategy and rationale of a typical hotel-motel buyer. Because lodging facilities contain unusual elements, such as business value, personal property, and many types of operating risks, a familiarity with hotels and motels as investments is essential.

Appraisers rely on three approaches (cost, sales comparison, and income capitalization) to estimate market value. The income capitalization approach, in which future benefits are discounted at an appropriate rate, is often given the greatest weight for valuing income properties such as hotels and motels. Various rate selection procedures and discounting techniques may be utilized, depending on the assumed investment and income criteria.

Expense projections are developed from comparable properties or published national averages. The data must be adjusted to reflect the individual characteristics of the subject property. When the property's projected revenue is combined with anticipated expenses, the resulting income before interest and depreciation is considered the future benefit; this benefit is capitalized into an estimate of market value.

The restaurant chapter, Chapter 7, follows a similar format, including overviews of the restaurant industry and the factors of supply and demand. Techniques for projecting income and expenses are demonstrated, and a valuation procedure is outlined.

Acknowledgments

Many dedicated people contributed to this monograph. Special recognition goes to Steven Bram, a summer intern at my firm who assisted in preparing the chapter on restaurant valuations. My associate, Suzanne Mellen, developed the simultaneous equation capitalization procedure, and was an invaluable soundingboard for my ideas and theories. Roger Cline and Eric Green were involved in the preparation of my first monograph, *The Valuation of Hotels and Motels,* and undoubtedly influenced the ideas contained in this updated and expanded version.

My colleagues, Daniel Lesser, Karen Rubin, Anne Lloyd-Jones, and Mark Rosinsky of Hospitality Valuation Services, Inc., reviewed this project in its various stages and offered many thought-provoking comments. Appreciation is also extended to my editors Anne Millward, Terri Fisher, John Hazelton, and Denise Adamo.

I would also like to acknowledge the support of my wife, Judy, and our children Cynthia and Stephen, Jr., who curtailed many of their activities while this book was being written.

Stephen Rushmore, MAI

About the Author

Stephen Rushmore, MAI, is president and owner of Hospitality Valuation Services, Inc., a real estate appraisal and consulting firm in Mineola, New York. Operating on a national basis, Rushmore specializes exclusively in assignments involving hotels, motels, and restaurants. Over the past 12 years, he has valued more than 500 lodging facilities, performing appraisals in nearly every state.

Rushmore has a B.S. degree in hotel administration from Cornell University and an M.B.A. from the University of Buffalo. He has held appraisal positions with James E. Gibbons Associates and Helmsley-Spear, Inc. In addition to Institute membership, he is a member of the American Society of Real Estate Counselors, holding its CRE designation.

A frequent lecturer on a variety of hotel topics, Rushmore developed the Institute's seminar on the valuation of hotels and motels. He authored the predecessor to this text and has written many articles that have appeared in various journals. His article "Using Total Project Analysis to Compete for Investment Capital," co-authored with James E. Gibbons, MAI, received the 1975 Robert H. Armstrong Award for the most significant article published in *The Appraisal Journal.*

Contents

1
Growth and Development of the Hotel-Motel Industry

The Origins of the Lodging Industry

The hotels and motels we know today evolved from small, one-room private dwellings that served merchants as early as the sixth century B.C. From this modest beginning, the hotel industry has come to play a vital role in the development of trade, commerce, and travel throughout the world.

The English inn, which came into prominence during the Industrial Revolution (1760), was the forerunner of the modern motel. Located on coach trails, inns provided refuge for weary travelers and protection from lurking robbers and thieves. Accommodations typically consisted of individual, unheated rooms with straw beds for the nobility and common sleeping areas on stone floors for the servants. Hearty food and drink were enjoyed at inns by travelers and local townspeople alike.

The American counterpart of the English inn was the colonial inn and tavern, which grew up in seaport towns and along stagecoach roads. In addition to providing travelers with overnight accommodations, colonial inns were often public gathering places used for courts of law, town meetings, and school classes. Massachusetts recognized the importance of the local inn to statewide commerce and passed a law penalizing any town that did not provide this convenience.

The following description of a colonial inn illustrates how far American hostelries have come in 200 years:

> *Accommodations often meant sleeping on the floor of the "long room," with one's feet turned toward the fireplace and one's head on a rolled-up coat, alongside a dozen or more other persons of both sexes. It meant a quick cold-water wash in an outdoor basin and gingerly use of a communal towel. A warning blast on the landlord's cow horn meant all hands to table, ready to tackle breakfast with fingers and knives.*[1]

The first hotel constructed in the United States was the 73-room City Hotel, located at 115 Broadway in New York City. Completed in 1794, the City Hotel was enormous compared to colonial inns and served as a model for similar establishments in Boston, Philadelphia, and Baltimore.

During the 1800s hotels moved westward and flourished in America's major cities and towns. The Tremont House in Boston began a trend for luxury accommodations by offering unheard of services and amenities: private guest rooms, doors with locks, a washbowl with a water pitcher and free soap, bellboys, French cuisine, and an annunciator system that allowed the front desk to contact guests in their rooms.

As the number of hotels increased, many properties faced the prospect of rapid obsolescence and a consequent loss in value. The City Hotel, for example, became obsolete in 15 years due to competition and was converted into an office building 38 years later. The trend-setting Tremont House was closed for major modernization after 20 years of operation and was considered a second-class property during the last two decades of its 65-year life. Today's hostelries face similar problems because of constant changes in modes of transportation, customer preferences, and competition from newer properties.

The hotels of the mid-1800s followed the railroads westward, and ornate, luxury properties were constructed at major rail centers: the Palmer House in Chicago, Planter's Hotel in St. Louis, and the Palace in San Francisco. The hotel became a status symbol, and cities soon tried to outdo each other by building larger and more expensive facilities. In many cases the hotels developed far exceeded existing or potential markets.

---

[1]Leslie Dorsey and Janice Devine, *Fare Thee Well* (New York: Crown Publishers, Inc. 1964), p. 4.

Travelers who could not afford luxury accommodations usually were forced to stay at rundown roominghouses, which offered minimal services and cleanliness. As rail transportation became more affordable and more middle-class people began to travel, a new type of hostelry was needed to fill the gap between luxury hotels and roominghouses.

E. M. Statler recognized this demand and built the nation's first modern, commercial hotel in Buffalo, New York. When the Buffalo Statler opened in 1908, it offered many revolutionary conveniences: private baths, circulating ice water, full-length mirrors, and free morning newspapers. Statler's slogan, "A room and a bath for a dollar and a half," put clean, comfortable transient accommodations within the reach of millions of Americans and increased the fervor of a newly travel-conscious middle class.

The economic prosperity of the 1920s produced one of the greatest hotel-building booms in the country's history. Encouraged by rising occupancy rates, which exceeded 85% in 1920, hoteliers expanded existing properties and constructed hundreds of new and larger facilities. During this period some cities actually doubled the number of available hotel rooms with the addition of large convention properties. Chicago's 3,000-room Hotel Stevens (now the Conrad Hilton) opened in 1927 and held the title of the "world's largest hotel" for more than 35 years.

The Depression of the 1930s put an end to new construction and sent more than 80% of the nation's hostelries into foreclosure or receivership. Both commercial and pleasure travel came to a virtual standstill, and the average national hotel occupancy fell to just over 50%.

Although the Depression forced many hoteliers out of business, it offered others the opportunity to expand their holdings by purchasing distressed properties from receivers and lenders. During the Depression both Sheraton and Hilton acquired numerous properties; this provided the impetus to establish national chains.

World War II revived the country's hotel industry. The massive movement of defense industry workers and military personnel and their families created an unprecedented demand for transient accommodations, and the national occupancy level soon exceeded 90%. Although most towns and cities needed more lodging facilities during this period, there was little new construction because financing, materials, and labor were unavailable.

The 1950s marked the beginning of a radical change in transportation. The railroad, which had served travelers for over a century, rapidly began to lose customers to the more economical automobile and the faster airplane. The technology that developed during the war produced a more affluent population that enjoyed shorter work weeks, more leisure time, and a new freedom of movement.

The "mobile society" was born, and an increasing number of people welcomed the convenience of highways and airlines.

The once-prime hotel locations, directly across from downtown railway stations, quickly became less desirable and economically obsolete. A more informal lifestyle was developing, and the traveling public seemed willing to sacrifice luxuries such as doormen, bellhops, valet parking, and evening turndown service in exchange for less expensive rooms.

The Birth of the Motel

A new type of lodging facility (highway oriented with inexpensive, "no-frill" accommodations) emerged to meet the needs of travelers. In 1950, the modern motel was born. Although the origins of the motel can be traced to the relatively primitive tourist cabins of the 1930s, the motels of the 1950s offered much better facilities.

Early motels were typically one-story, wood-frame structures built on slabs with approximately 20 to 50 units. The modestly decorated interiors had inexpensive furnishings, particle board walls and ceilings, tile floors, small baths and metal shower stalls, and radios. Few motels at that time provided food and beverage service or meeting rooms.

Although motels were spartan compared to most hotels, they became competitive due to their convenient highway locations, ample free parking, and lower rates. The motel market included vacation travelers—especially young families and senior citizens—salesmen, middle-management businessmen, and per-diem government employees. Operating statistics for the 1950s show steadily declining hotel occupancies, but stable levels for motels. Because the number of motel rooms was increasing at the time, motels obviously were beginning to capture a transient market previously monopolized by hotels.

The first motels were radically different from hotels with respect to size, construction costs, land values, operating ratios, and management requirements. The distinction between hotel and motel has lessened, however, due to a variety of factors:

- Motels began to increase in size with additions to existing properties and more total units constructed for new properties.
- Motels joined referral groups and franchises to obtain national images and greater exposure.
- Motels started offering more amenities: television, air conditioning, shag carpeting, tile baths, telephones, swimming pools, restaurants, lounges, meeting and banquet rooms, and gift shops.

4

- Motels began providing more services: 24-hour telephone switchboard and front desk attendants, nationwide telephone reservation systems, acceptance of credit cards, direct-dial guest room phones, and morning wake-up calls.
- Improved building techniques were introduced, including the use of concrete and steel, preassembled units, and highrise construction.

By the mid-1960s most new motels offered all the facilities and amenities typically available at hotels. At the same time, hotels were modifying their operations to compete with motels. The result has been a gradual merging of the two types of properties into a facility known as the motor hotel. Motor hotels combine the services and facilities of hotels with the convenience of motels.

As the motel evolved into the motor hotel, it began to lose one of its most important competitive advantages—price. By providing more facilities and services, motels were forced to charge higher rates. This resulted in an increasing void at the low end of the room-rate scale and precipitated the creation of the "budget motel."

The Arrival of the Budgets

Budget motels were introduced in the late 1960s and flourished during the building boom of the early 1970s. These hostelries offered accommodations at prices substantially lower than the prevailing rates of the first-class motor hotel chains. To offer this discount, a budget motel incorporates three important factors: lower initial investment costs, operating efficiencies, and high volume.

Lower Initial Investment Costs

Smaller guest rooms, minimal public space, lower land costs, simple no-frill design, and quality construction are responsible for lower initial costs.

Guest rooms in budget motels average 250 square feet; rooms in conventional motor hotels are typically 335 square feet. Smaller rooms reduce construction costs and interior decorating expenditures and less land is required for a budget motel.

Budget motels have eliminated low-revenue public areas such as meeting and banquet rooms, large lobbies, extensive food and beverage facilities, interior corridors, and executive offices.

By reducing the size of the facilities, budget motels require approximately 1.6 aces per 100 rooms, compared to 2.5 acres per 100 rooms for conventional motels. Additional savings are sometimes realized by utilizing secondary locations such as land off an interchange or a short distance from the prime

5

commercial/office area. Most people traveling on a budget are willing to drive a little farther for a better price.

Budget motels are planned for efficient use of materials and space. Guest rooms are double loaded (back-to-back) and constructed on concrete slabs with cinderblock walls between rooms. Modular construction has been successfully utilized in some areas. Landscaping and decorative motifs are kept to a minimum.

Many budget motels maintain construction specifications and standards similar to those of conventional motor hotels. Operators realize that inferior materials and building techniques may produce initial savings, but they make poor investments in the long run when repair and maintenance expenses are considered.

Operating Efficiencies

Compact facilities and fewer guest services contribute to operating efficiencies and resultant lowered expenses.

With smaller guest rooms and reduced public space, budget motels require less time to clean and maintain and can be more efficiently heated and lighted. Some budget chains use maintenance teams that work at several properties, performing routine repairs and preventive maintenance.

The elimination of bellmen, elaborate food and beverage facilities, room service, entertainment, the acceptance of credit cards, and other services reduces payroll and operating expenses. Major savings are realized in the restaurants of budget motels where cafeteria and coffee shop service is typical.

High Volume

Price and location as well as value for the traveler's money are primary reasons for the high volume in budget motels.

The main reason travelers select a budget motel is price. As with any product having an elastic demand curve, a reduction in price increases volume. Operating results substantiate this premise—i.e., budget motels typically operate at higher occupancy levels than surrounding conventional properties. Many budget motels are purposely located next to higher-priced hostelries to attract price-conscious travelers.

Although budget motels have economized in many areas, they tend to provide clean, good-quality guest rooms. The rooms contain comfortable beds; full baths; color television; shag carpeting; standard furnishings and fixtures; and cheerful drapes, bedspreads and wall coverings.

In terms of investment and valuation, budget motels are often more vulnerable to the adverse effects of increased expenses and decreased occupancies. Because of its lower price structure, the breakeven occupancy level for a budget property is generally higher than it is for a standard motel. Appraisers consider this greater risk when projecting income and expenses and establishing the proper capitalization rate.

The 1970 Hotel Boom

While budget motels began to inundate the market, the entire lodging industry experienced the start of a construction boom reminiscent of the 1920s. Many factors contributed to this period of expansion and later led to its demise.

New construction was sparked by the enormous amount of financing made available by all lenders, but particularly by an entity known as the real estate investment trust (REIT). These high-leverage finance companies were created to allow the small investor to participate in real estate mortgages and equities. The concept quickly was accepted by Wall Street, and soon billions of dollars were available to finance real estate projects. Many lenders became so overwhelmed with new money that their underwriting procedures broke down, and some marginal developments were approved.

During the late 1960s and early 1970s, hotel companies were actively expanding their chains through franchising. In a franchise agreement, a motel owner pays an initial franchise fee plus monthly royalty fees to use a hotel chain's name, logo, reservation system, national advertising, and operation manuals. Many lenders and hostelry developers were led to believe that a national franchise would guarantee a successful operation.

The combination of readily available financing and aggressive hotel chains eager to sell franchises resulted in overbuilding and the development of many poorly located, undercapitalized hostelries managed by inexperienced owners. The bubble burst on the lodging industry when inflation caused construction costs and interest rates to escalate; the energy crisis drastically reduced travel; and the recession curtailed business trips, conferences, and conventions.

Operators of marginal properties quickly fell behind in mortgage payments, and lenders were forced to foreclose. As lenders became hostelry owners, they either organized workout departments headed by experienced hoteliers or engaged professional motel management companies to assume operational responsibilities. The lenders' primary objective was to improve profits in order to sell the properties at satisfactory prices. Sales data indicated that lenders were relatively unsuccessful in disposing of distressed motels at prices equal to book value. Most transactions required either substantial all-cash write-downs or purchase-money financing at extraordinarily favorable terms.

The end of the 1970s was a relatively calm period for the lodging industry.

7

Because most lenders were recovering from financial wounds inflicted by the 1975 recession, they had little interest in making hotel/motel mortgages. New construction proceeded on a limited basis, consisting primarily of additions to existing properties and the development of some large, downtown convention-commercial hotels. The rebirth of center city hostelries was a direct result of fuel shortages and the availability of government financing for inner-city redevelopment projects. Highway-oriented properties, on the other hand, were adversely affected by escalating gasoline prices and decreased automobile travel, and lost some of their appeal among investors and hotel companies.

Decreased building activity, combined with the normal retirement of older hostelries from the lodging market and an improving economy, created a favorable supply and demand relationship; this produced record-high occupancy levels in 1978 and 1979. Average room rates increased rapidly as hotel operators took advantage of the excess demand to recoup earlier losses and stay even with inflation.

Just when the environment appeared suitable for a period of renewed hotel expansion, the Federal Reserve tightened the money supply, sending the prime interest rate to record levels. Many new projects are currently in the preliminary planning stages, but the lack of sensible financing has put most hostelry developments on hold. If these constraints are gradually lifted during the early 1980s, the lodging industry should experience another cycle of new construction.

Learning from History

The preceding description of the nation's hotel-motel industry illustrates several important points that could affect the market value of lodging facilities:

1. The typical hostelry experiences a relatively high degree of functional and economic obsolescence. These factors tend to reduce a property's economic life and thereby decrease the period during which an owner can fully recapture invested capital.
2. The growth of the lodging industry is affected by developments in transportation. The first hostelries were located on coach trails until the railroad came and hotels moved closer to passenger terminals. Later, the automobile led to the creation of the motel, and the airplane generated demand for rooms at airport locations. Similarly, a decline in a particular form of transportation can lead to the failure of associated lodging facilities.
3. The budget motel has been a cyclical phenomenon. The rooming house was America's first economy lodging facility. After its popularity declined,

Statler introduced the first full-facility hotel at an affordable price. In the 1950s the highway motel brought rates down for the mass travel market, and 20 years later the "revolutionary" budget motel was introduced.

4. The enormous amounts of financing available during the late 1920s and the early 1970s led to excessive overbuilding and many properties were forced into bankruptcy or foreclosed soon after they opened. Hotel owners soon discovered what usually happens when a property is poorly conceived, under-capitalized, and mismanaged.

2
Demand for Transient Accommodations

When performing hotel-motel valuations and feasibility studies, appraisers are primarily interested in the micro, rather than the macro, aspects of demand. Micro demand for transient accommodations is the demand within a limited geographic area, such as a town, city, or county. By quantifying the micro demand into measurable units such as room nights, half of the supply and demand equation is known. Macro demand is much broader in scope and takes into account national and international travel patterns. Although macro demand receives only limited attention in most appraisal reports, it is an important consideration because it often foreshadows changes in travel trends for micro areas.

Macro Demand

Every five years the U.S. Department of Commerce, Bureau of the Census, studies travel activity across the country and publishes its findings in the "National Travel Survey." The U.S. Travel Data Center issues yearly reports designed to supplement

Table 2.1 Characteristics of an Average Trip

	'67	'72	'75	'76	'80
Person trips (millions)	253	458	660	706	935.10
Person nights	1,275	1,782	2,600	2,865	4,301.46
Persons per trip	1.80	1.94	2.01	2.00	2.09
Nights per trip	5.04	3.88	3.97	4.06	4.60

Source: U.S. Travel Data Center
        Hospitality Valuation Services, Inc.

the five-year government surveys. The information from these two sources provides a good picture of macro travel demand in the United States.

Trip Characteristics

The characteristics of the average trip are shown in Table 2.1.

Between 1967 and 1980, the number of person trips increased 270%. However, it is more significant for the lodging industry that the number of person nights increased just over 237% during this period. Travelers spent fewer nights away from home on the average trip. In fact, the average number of nights per trip has been steadily declining. Faster transportation, including jet planes and interstate highway systems, permits travelers to reach their destinations quicker. Business travelers can now fly halfway across the country, transact their business, and return home the same day. Before jet air travel, this type of trip usually involved one or more nights of lodging.

Vacationers can also travel more miles per day and reach their destinations sooner. Also, vacationers often stay at the homes of friends or relatives, which considerably reduces the need for commercial lodging facilities. The gasoline shortage of 1974 had a significant short-term effect on highway travel patterns. During the height of the oil embargo, travelers drastically reduced both the average number of nights and the miles per trip. Although these travel indicators recovered when fuel became readily available again, the experience demonstrated how dependent the lodging and travel industries are on adequate means of personal transportation.

Other developments, however, have tended to increase the average length of trips, particularly for vacationers. Three-day weekends created by the new "Monday holidays" have increased the number of mini-vacations and weekend "escape packages." Over the past decade, companies have given their employees

**Table 2.2 Distribution of the Overnight Travel
Market by Type of Accommodation**

	1963	1967	1972	1975	1980
Commercial accommodations	24%	31%	34%	33%	37%
Homes of friends or relatives	51%	48%	47%	46%	45%
Other accommodations	25%	21%	19%	21%	18%

Source: U.S. Travel Data Center

more fringe benefits, including longer vacations. Some firms have even implemented the four-day work week. Although these factors do not necessarily mean
increased travel, they do add to the time that families can be away from home.

If the past in any way reflects the future, recent developments in the transportation industry could have a significant effect on the characteristics of the average trip. The supersonic transport may prove to be as revolutionary as the jet
plane, making continental and international trips one-day turnarounds. Higher-
priced gasoline could reduce the mobility of the vacation traveler. Greater use of
mass transportation and the possible rebirth of rail service might prompt travelers to bypass highway facilities. More sophisticated telecommunication systems may someday make in-person business meetings obsolete.

Future travel projections should also reflect positive factors. A growing
number of senior citizens with better retirement incomes and more desire to
travel could increase demand. Increased foreign travel to the United States and a
generally more travel-oriented society could mean more business for the lodging
industry.

The trends and characteristics of the average trip pertain to the entire travel
market. The Bureau of the Census divides the overnight travel market into three
types of accommodations: (1) commercial accommodations—hotels, motels, resorts; (2) homes of friends or relatives; and (3) other accommodations—vacation
homes, boats, trailers, and campers. Since 1963 the percentage distribution has
changed in favor of commercial accommodations (see Table 2.2).

The relative decline in other types of accommodations can be attributed
partly to the fact that vacation homes are unaffordable to most people due to the
high cost of mortgage funds, inflated land values, and costly construction.
Boats, trailers, and recreational vehicles are also beyond the purchasing ability of
many consumers. The introduction of timeshare ownership, however, could

Table 2.3 Distribution of Travel Market by Purpose of Trip

	1963	1967	1972	1975	1980
Visit friends or relatives	40%	41%	39%	40%	35%
Other pleasure	21%	25%	25%	29%	38%
Business and conventions	21%	19%	20%	18%	14%
Other	18%	15%	16%	13%	13%

Source: U.S. Travel Data Center

make other types of accommodations more affordable to the mass market and reverse the decline. This would increase the market share of other accommodations at the expense of commercial accommodations.

Macro travel information is also broken down by the purpose of the trip. Data in this area are divided into four categories: (1) visit friends or relatives; (2) other pleasure trips—sightseeing, recreation; (3) business and conventions; (4) other—personal and other purposes.

Visiting friends or relatives continues to be the primary reason for travel in the United States. Other pleasure trips have captured a greater proportion of the travel market at the expense of business and conventions and other purposes, as shown in Table 2.3.

By combining travel data from the two preceding tables, a profile of the travelers constituting the primary market for commercial accommodations can be drawn (see Tables 2.4 and 2.5).

Based on the data in the preceding tables and the other macro travel statistics presented, some observations about the demand for transient accommodations can be made. The typical commercial lodging facility derives most of its occupancy from business and convention travelers. Although this market segment has always shown a steady increase in person nights, the rate of growth is declining because of faster transportation and more sophisticated communication systems. Both long-term national and local business trends should be carefully evaluated if a hostelry is very dependent on this market. Also, no hotel or motel should anticipate significant demand from the segment of the market visiting friends or relatives. A residential area is generally considered a secondary location for a lodging facility because the surrounding neighborhood generates few room nights.

The proper design for a hostelry depends on the market segments it will attract. For example, a motel catering primarily to business travelers may decrease

Table 2.4   1975 Traveler Profile

	Persons Per Trip	Miles Per Trip	Nights Per trip
Visit friends or relatives	2.25	838	4.19
Other pleasure	2.25	826	4.49
Business and convention	1.39	841	3.01

Source: U.S. Travel Data Service, 1975

Table 2.5   1975 Distribution of Person Nights by Accommodation Type

	Homes of Friends or Relatives	Commercial Accommodations	Other Accommodations
Visit friends or relatives	79%	14%	7%
Other pleasure	12	46	42
Business and convention	18	64	18
Other	60	26	14

Source: U.S. Travel Data Service

the size of its guest rooms slightly and have more rooms with either a studio design or with one double bed. This approach is practical because the double occupancy for the business and convention segment is only 1.4 persons per trip. Resort properties, however, should have larger guest rooms and at least two double beds per unit because the double occupancy for the other pleasure segment is 2.3 persons per trip. Forty-six percent of the individuals in the other pleasure-market segment stay at commercial hostelries. This includes vacationing families, who account for the profitably high double occupancy and more nights per trip. When looking at the micro demand from this segment, the seasonality of the business and the potential competition from campers and second homes should be considered.

Knowledge of long-term macro travel trends is important when valuing a commercial lodging facility. With the economic lives of hostelries averaging 20–40 years, gradual changes in national travel habits could eventually have a major impact on local demand and affect the values of individual properties. Monitoring macro demand enables the appraiser to detect deteriorating or improving trends and make appropriate adjustments in the final valuation.

15

Table 2.6　Typical Traveler Characteristics

	Commercial Travelers	Convention Travelers	Vacation Travelers
Peak travel periods	Fall, winter, spring	Fall, winter spring	North—summer South—winter, spring, summer
Weekly peaks	Mon.-Thurs.	Sun-Thurs.	Variable
Average length of stay	Highway—1-2 nights; Downtown—2-3 nights	3-5 nights	Highway—1 night Downtown—3-5 nights
Double occupancy	1-1.5	High-rate conventions—1.2-1.4 Low-rate conventions—1.3-1.7	1.7-2.5
Use of food facilities:			
Breakfast	50-70%	60-80%*	75-80%
Lunch	10-20%	50-80%*	10-50%*
Dinner	30-50%	40-80%*	50-75%*
Use of beverage facilities	20-60%	30-75%	30-75%
Degree of price consciousness	Low	Medium	Medium-high
Special requirements	Entertainment, quiet rooms, desks with good lighting, convenient parking	Adequate function and exhibit space, active sales organization	Recreational facilities, large guest rooms guest laundry

*Depends on the amount of banquet service
**Depends on the meal plan (American or European)
Source: Hospitality Valuation Services, Inc.

Traveler Characteristics

The characteristics of the various types of travelers are important considerations when quantifying potential demand and designing a lodging facility. Typical characteristics for commercial, convention, and vacation travelers are shown in Table 2.6.

Micro Demand

In preparing a hotel market study and appraisal, accurate quantification of the micro demand is essential. The unit of measurement commonly employed is the room night.

A room night is defined as one transient room occupied by one or more persons for one night. For example, a business traveler who stays at a motel for three nights accounts for three room nights. A family that uses one room for three nights also generates three room nights. If this family had occupied two guest rooms during their stay, the demand would have been six room nights.

The total number of room nights within a defined market area represents the total potential demand, which can be measured on a daily, weekly, monthly, or yearly basis, depending on local travel patterns. The total demand for transient accommodations within a defined micro market area can be quantified using the build-up approach based on an analysis of demand generators or the build-up approach based on an analysis of lodging activity.

The build-up approach based on an analysis of demand generators involves interviews and statistical sampling market research to estimate an area's lodging demand. This is accomplished by totaling the room nights generated from local sources of transient visitation. Drawing from a sample of major transient generators located within a defined market area, interviews and surveys are conducted to determine the amount of demand each source attracts during a specified period of time, such as a week or month. Using various statistical sampling techniques, an area's total room night demand can be quantified.

In the build-up approach based on an analysis of lodging activity, an area's transient room night demand is estimated by totaling the rooms actually occupied in local hotels and motels. Through interviews with hostelry operators, owners, and other knowledgeable individuals, occupancy levels for individual lodging operations and area occupancy trends can be established. The percentage of occupancy for each property times the available number of rooms is multiplied by 365 days to produce the total number of room nights actually occupied each year. After combining these occupancy estimates for each property and adding a factor for the demand that cannot be accommodated during peak periods, the area's total room night lodging demand is quantified.

When properly applied, both approaches produce supportable estimates of lodging demand. In actual practice, a combination of the two procedures is used to save time and unnecessary research effort. For example, an overall area demand is first established by an analysis of lodging activity. Then, selective interviews are conducted at one or more major generators of visitation to verify the transient demand and establish various traveler characteristics. By defining not only the quantity of transient demand, but also its lodging characteristics, the analyst has enough data to develop a micro demand projection.

Because each market area is unique, the analyst's approach often must be adjusted to account for particular demand characteristics. The following section is a general discussion of the market surveying procedures used to measure the demand for commercial lodging facilities in both the analysis of demand generators and the analysis of lodging activity.

Defining the Market Area

The first step in analyzing demand generators or lodging activity is to define the market area. The market area for a lodging facility is the geographical region where the sources of transient visitation (demand) are located. When estimating the boundaries of the market area, four factors must be considered:

1. Travel time between the source of visitation and the subject property.
2. Methods of travel commonly used.
3. Sources of transient visitation.
4. Location of competitive lodging facilities.

Travel time is generally a better measure of distance than miles because highways, road conditions, and travel patterns differ. Most people are willing to travel up to 20 minutes to get from a source of visitation to their lodging accommodations. If the bulk of travel time is spent on high-speed, interstate highways, the market area is larger than if the route follows busy downtown streets.

The means of transportation also affects travel time. For example, a convenient rapid transit system can increase the market area by shortening the length of time needed to reach the subject property. Airport properties that depend on shuttle bus service should consider waiting time. From a travel time point of view, these hostelries should be located no more than 10 minutes away from the airport to allow for a 20-minute round trip.

The analyst should locate the subject property on a detailed road map and draw in 20-minute travel routes as radii from the subject. Connecting the radii creates an irregular circle, which represents the boundaries of the initial market area. To determine the shape of the final market area, certain adjustments must be made to show the influence of competition and other demand characteristics.

Before any modifications are made, however, all potential sources of transient visitation within the initial market area should be identified and located on the map. Any attraction that draws out-of-town travelers who require commercial lodging facilities is a source of transient visitation. A representative list of visitation sources and the methods used to quantify their micro demand are presented later in this section.

After the initial market area has been determined, all competitive hostelries should be located on the map, with their positions in relation to the subject property and sources of visitation noted. Travelers tend to stay at the lodging facility closest to their destination, assuming the property meets certain requirements. If a comparable motel is located between a source of demand and the property being appraised, the competitive facility may attract patrons first, and the subject hostelry will receive the overflow. Care must be taken to evaluate the drawing power of the competition because travelers will generally bypass one facility for another if it better suits their needs and budget. The location of competitive properties between the property being appraised and the attraction generating business can decrease the size of the initial market area and may eliminate some sources from consideration.

In evaluating competition, local travel patterns and popular routings are important factors. Travelers usually prefer to come and go along the same routes and are not likely to venture into unfamiliar areas. If the popular route to a source of demand happens to bypass the property, the potential for capturing that market is greatly reduced. The location of one or more comparable lodging facilities along the route further decreases the drawing power of the subject property. Traffic counts and origination and destination studies prepared by state and local agencies will pinpoint popular routes and identify area travel patterns. By plotting this information on the map showing the initial market area, appropriate adjustments can be made to the perimeter. The resulting enclosure is the final market area and contains the sources of transient visitation available to the property.

Once the market area has been defined, the analyst quantifies the demand by applying the build-up approach based on an analysis of demand generators and/or the build-up approach based on an analysis of lodging activity.

Build-up Approach Based on an Analysis of Demand Generators

This approach is generally performed in three steps: 1) the generators of transient visitation are determined; 2) selective generators of transient visitation are quantified; and 3) proper sampling procedures are analyzed. Each step in the analysis of demand generators will be discussed.

Determining the Generators of Transient Visitation

The generators of transient visitation are determined while defining the final market area. There may be many possible sources of transient visitation and every effort should be made to compile a complete list. The following methods can be used to identify generators of demand.

1.   Interview local hotel-motel managers to determine where they derive their

occupancy. Ask for a percentage breakdown on the types of customers (e.g., commercial, convention, vacation) and try to learn the names of specific firms or groups that use the facility on a regular basis.

2. Obtain a directory of local businesses and identify those with regional or national operations that are likely to attract out-of-town customers, suppliers, vendors, or company representatives.

3. A convention and visitors bureau often maintains statistics pertaining to area visitation. Request a list of recent conventions and meetings that utilized local hostelries. Determine if the initial market area has any popular tourist or vacation attractions. Visitor counts and projections can be helpful if their reliability can be verified.

4. Visit car rental agencies, especially those at local airports, to determine which firms regularly rent cars. This information will indicate which area businesses attract out-of-town visitation. These agencies also can supply information about which motels are popular among their clients.

5. Drive around the area. Look for concentrations of out-of-state cars in industrial parks, office complexes, government centers, regional hospitals, and so forth. The parking lots of local hostelries also contain many market indicators. Do the cars belong to out-of-state or in-state residents? Do they belong to businessmen traveling alone (clean and neat) or families on vacation (luggage, games, roadmaps)? A late night parking lot count can indicate a highway motel's occupancy, assuming one vehicle per room. Even more important, a parking lot count shows the relative competitiveness of area hostelries if all are surveyed on a particular night. One night's count is not necessarily indicative of annual occupancy, so additional factors should also be surveyed.

6. Interviews with Chamber of Commerce officials, visitor information center employees, taxi drivers, gas station operators, and restaurant managers are often helpful in identifying potential sources of transient visitation. In addition, the local building department can provide information on proposed projects and changes in highway patterns.

Identifying the prime generators of demand within a given market area is relatively simple. When the process is completed, the list will probably contain one or more of the following: Businesses—office buildings, industrial parks, research facilities, manufacturing plants; government centers; airports; convention centers and conference facilities; colleges and universities; tourist attractions; vacation and recreation areas; parks and scenic areas; hospitals; sport attractions; casinos; military bases; trade and professional associations; convenient highway stopping points; regional shopping centers; and special events—

state fairs, parades. For market areas with many demand generators, the list should rank the sources in order of their estimated potential. The items with the greatest possibility of attracting out-of-town visitors should be researched first so that the appraiser can conduct a thorough analysis of the prime sources.

Quantifying Selective Generators of Transient Visitation
The final and most important step in the market survey sequence is the quantification of the total demand into measurable units, i.e., room nights. By estimating the number of room nights for each generator of visitation located within the subject's final market area, the total micro demand can be determined.

In addition to quantifying total demand, the survey should outline the general characteristics of the travelers who make up the potential market. The following factors help define the demand and may also be useful in designing a proposed hostelry:

- Demand Factors
  Number of nights per stay
  Number of people per room
  Periods of use during the year
      Definition of seasonality
      Fluctuations in use during the year
      Fluctuations in use during the month
      Fluctuations in use during the week
  Price willing to pay
  Food, beverage, entertainment, and telephone usage

- Design Factors
  Number of people per guest room
      Space requirements
      Bed requirements
      Bathroom requirements
      Closet and storage requirements
  Use of guest rooms for purposes other than sleeping (e.g., meetings, entertainment, interviewing, or displays.)
      Space requirements
      Furniture and layout
      Lighting and decor
  Restaurant and lounge facilities
      Space requirements
      Decor, menu and price

Kitchen equipment
    Staffing
Meeting and banquet facilities
    Space requirements
    Types of configuration
    Special equipment
Recreational facilities
Methods of travel
    Parking requirements
    Entrance loading and baggage requirements

The market surveying techniques that are most effective for quantifying potential demand and defining specific traveler characteristics are determined using the list of demand generators. Research techniques may include personal and telephone interviews, letter questionnaires, and use of available data and surveys.

Regardless of which techniques are chosen, it is most important to locate and question the persons with the most knowledge about the subject. For a hotel demand study, these persons are typically those who make hotel reservations, including secretaries, executive transfer departments, travel departments, personnel and recruitment departments, convention and visitor bureau placement departments, tour operators and travel agents, airline flight service and customer relations departments, and college alumni and athletic offices. Purchasing agents and buyers, executives, receptionists, college admissions officers, and park rangers who meet out-of-town visitors might be questioned. Security departments, convention and visitor bureau registration and research departments, and hospital admissions departments who control visitation data are also good sources.

Personal interviews produce the most reliable data, but they are usually very time-consuming. In areas with numerous sources of visitation, personal interviews can be limited to those with the greatest potential for generating room nights. A checklist of essential items to cover should be devised and interview time should be limited to five or 10 minutes. Use appointments only if an initial "drop-in" visit produces no results.

Some of the key questions typically asked during an interview include: How many out-of-town visitors do you average each week, month, or year? What is the purpose of the visitation? How long do the visitors stay? Are the visitors visiting any other demand sources in the area? Where are the visitors staying now? What rates are they willing to pay?

Once these questions are answered, more detailed questions should be asked to determine some of the characteristics of the market. The preceding demand

and design factors can be used as a guide. The interviewer should always inquire if there are any other people in the organization who might have contact with visitors. The purpose of the interview should be specified by the interviewer because the more information the interviewer is willing to provide, the more information he or she will receive.

Telephone interviews are less time-consuming, but they rarely produce the same quality of data. Less important demand sources can be interviewed over the phone and later seen personally if greater potential is discovered.

Letter questionnaires are useful for mass surveys where there are hundreds of identifiable demand sources. A short, simple form that can be completed in less than five minutes usually yields the best results. When using this type of survey, correct identification of the person best suited to answer the questions is critical. A brief letter explaining the purpose of the survey should accompany each questionnaire. A greater response will be obtained if the letter is signed by someone who is known locally. A self-addressed, stamped envelope for returning replies must be enclosed.

Occasionally, data pertaining to local transient demand are available from surveys conducted by various groups and municipal agencies. These data are normally part of larger studies for urban renewal or redevelopment projects, proposed convention centers, master development plans, and so forth. Some organizations that may perform market surveys include Chambers of Commerce, convention bureaus, municipal planning departments, redevelopment agencies, financial institutions, and utility companies. Data obtained from these sources should be verified. If usable, they can provide excellent information and a good starting point for defining the local transient market.

Applying Proper Sampling Procedures
All major generators of transient visitation should be surveyed with a personal or telephone interview or a mailed questionnaire. However, in market areas with many secondary generators of visitation, these techniques may not be practical. Time restraints and the inability to identify the names or addresses of smaller generators often necessitate some form of sampling.

Sampling is a market research procedure whereby conclusions about a large number of demand generators are drawn from a thorough analysis of a representative portion. Properly applied, sampling generally yields more accurate results than complete surveys because more time can be devoted to correct interviewing and data-collecting techniques.

The key to good sampling is selecting the unit of comparison that best reflects the total market. For example, a frequently used measure of potential commercial traveler demand is "room nights per square foot of office space." By interviewing a representative sample of office space users and estimating how many out-of-town visitors are received over a given period of time, a unit of comparison can be developed. The number of visitor room nights is divided by the total square footage of office space within the sample. Multiplying this factor by the amount of office space within the final market area produces an indication of the potential commercial demand. If necessary, adjustments can be made for possible double counting of travelers visiting more than one firm.

Other units of comparison that may reflect transient visitation are population, employment, university enrollment, hospital beds, traffic counts, retail sales, and convention attendance. Many books have been written on correct sampling and market research procedures. Although every market area requires a somewhat specialized approach, three basic concepts should be followed:

1. The sample must be representative of the total market.
2. Data and information from the sample must be factual and without bias.
3. Units of comparison should reflect market behavior.

Analyzing demand generators provides an estimate of the total number of room nights available in the market area and specific information about the characteristics of the demand. The total potential demand must then be divided among all the competitive lodging facilities before an estimate of the market capture rate for the subject property can be made. The procedures for allocating the demand will be described in later chapters.

An example of the build-up approach on an analysis of demand generators is demonstrated in the case study that follows this chapter.

Build-up Approach Based on an Analysis of Lodging Activity

The build-up approach based on an analysis of lodging activity is generally performed in five steps:

1. Identify all competitive lodging facilities in the market area and determine their individual room counts.
2. Estimate the percentage of occupancy for each competitive hotel or motel on an annual basis.
3. Determine the accommodated room night demand by multiplying each property's room count by its annual occupancy and then by the 365 days in a year.
4. Allocate each property's total accommodated room night demand among the primary market segments (i.e., commercial, convention, vacationer) within the market area.

5. Estimate the amount of unaccommodated demand for each market segment.

Identify All Competitive Lodging Facilities

To identify all competitive lodging facilities within the market area, select only those lodging facilities that attract the same type of clientele. For example, if the subject is a luxury hotel, the demand shown by budget motels would not be appropriate. The room count for each property can be obtained either from the general manager or from lodging facility directories. A hotel room has various definitions, but basically it is the smallest rentable unit providing a bathroom and an individual door with a key.

Estimate the Occupancy of Each Competitive Facility

Obtaining accurate occupancy data from all the competitive lodging facilities is important. Because these statistics usually involve proprietary information, the analyst may have to employ special tactics in collecting reliable operating figures.

The investigation starts with verified sources of occupancy data, such as actual income and expense statements obtained during other appraisal assignments or from local appraisers. Hotel accounting firms and area hotel associations often compile occupancy rates for specific geographic areas. These data may identify individual properties, or they may group hotels with similar characteristics. Occasionally, municipalities will provide room tax data on a property-by-property basis, which can be converted into occupancy estimates.

Once all the hard occupancy data are accumulated, the analyst should conduct interviews with hotel operators. If the subject property is an existing lodging facility, the general manager, sales manager, auditor, or front desk manager may exchange occupancy information with nearby properties. Even if this practice is not followed, these individuals generally will have a fairly accurate notion of their competition's occupancy levels. When interviewing management from either the subject property or its competition, the interviewer must take note of any bias on the part of the person being interviewed. Collecting occupancy statistics by interviewing the owners and managers of competitive lodging facilities is time-consuming and usually produces very unreliable data. If it is necessary to use this approach, certain rules should be followed to elicit the best information.

1. Have the manager of the subject property make the introductions and set up the interviews.
2. Hold face-to-face interviews, don't use the telephone.
3. Explain the purpose of the assignment fully. If the analysis will benefit other hotels (i.e., with property tax reductions), say so at the outset.

4. Discuss area occupancy trends in general before zeroing in on specific properties. Ask each source the occupancy rates for all competitive lodging facilities. By cross-checking this information against verified occupancy levels, any upward or downward bias can be identified.
5. Try to get written documentation of occupancy levels from daily reports or financial statements.

When all the occupancy statistics have been accumulated, select the most supportable data and assign occupancy levels to each of the competitive lodging facilities in the market area.

Determine Accommodated Room Night Demand
The accommodated room night demand is the number of hotel and motel rooms within a market area that are actually occupied during a 12-month period. The calculation is made by multiplying each competitive property's room count by its annual occupancy and then by 365. Adding the accommodated room night demand for each individual property produces the area's accommodated room night demand.

Example

Competitive Hotels	Room Count		Annual Occupancy		Days per Year		Accommodated Demand (Room Nights)
A	300	×	80%	×	365	=	87,600
B	250	×	78	×	365	=	71,175
C	200	×	82	×	365	=	59,860
D	175	×	75	×	365	=	47,906
Total area accommodated demand							266,541

Allocate Demand Among the Market Segments
Because the characteristics of demand, such as future growth trends and seasonality, vary from one segment to another, the total area demand is allocated among the market segments. While interviewing for occupancy data, the analyst should ask which market segments constitute the propertys' total accommodated demand. Try to get percentages, and make sure the sum equals 100%. When these data are compiled for each competitive property, the total area demand can be segmentized. The following tables break down the data from the preceding example.

26

Competitive Hotels	Percentage Allocation of Room Night Demand		
	Commercial	Convention & Groups	Vacationers
A	30%	60%	10%
B	40	40	20
C	40	30	30
D	30	10	60

Competitive Hotels	Total Accommodated Demand	Allocation of Room Night Demand		
		Commercial	Convention & Groups	Vacationers
A	87,600	26,280	52,560	8,760
B	71,175	28,470	28,470	14,235
C	59,860	23,944	17,958	17,958
D	47,906	14,372	4,791	28,743
Total	266,541	93,066	103,779	69,696

Estimate Unaccommodated Demand

The previously calculated room night demand is based on achieved occupancy levels; it represents the demand actually accommodated in the area's lodging facilities. Because hotels and motels cannot sell more rooms than they have, some excess, unaccommodated, demand exists during peak travel periods. Depending on the local supply and demand relationship, excess demand may result from strong weekday commercial demand, special events in the area, large conventions, or peak seasonal attractions and holiday periods. The amount of unaccommodated room night demand increases as an area's occupancy rises. For example, the unaccommodated demand is generally greater in markets where the area occupancy level is 80% than in markets where it is 65%.

To quantify the unaccommodated demand, it might be advisable to ask hostelry owners or managers how many times a year the hotel sells out, i.e., operates at 100% occupancy. Some hotel reservation systems provide monthly reports outlining the number of unaccommodated reservation requests. This number would represent unaccommodated demand.

An estimate of the unaccommodated demand should be made for each market segment; it may be expressed either as a percentage of the accommodated demand or as a number of room nights. Using figures from the previous example, the unaccommodated demand could be expressed as follows.

Market Segment	Total Accommodated Room Night Demand	Percent Unaccommodated	Total Room Night Demand
Commercial	93,066	8%	100,512
Convention & groups	103,779	7	111,043
Vacationers	69,696	3	71,787
Total			283,342

An example of the build-up approach based on an analysis of lodging activity is demonstrated in the case study that follows this chapter. In theory, the total room night demand estimated by analyzing both demand generators and lodging activity should be the same. In actual practice, the analysis of lodging activity is most often selected because it yields more reliable data with less research. Sometimes analysts will employ a combination of the approaches with excellent results.

Projecting Room Night Demand

The total room night demand established by an analysis of lodging activity represents the actual room nights accommodated (plus any added unaccommodated demand) in the market area over the past 12 months, or Year 0. To develop an estimate of the future lodging demand, the analyst must project the Year 0 demand for one or more future years at an appropriate rate of growth, decline, or stability. This projection should be based on expected area economic trends—particularly those trends that will have a direct impact on transient demand. Some economic indicators that reflect lodging activity include: construction activity (particularly office and commercial construction), office space rental activity, employment growth, new industrial development, traffic counts, convention center usage and advance bookings, transient visitor growth, population, retail sales and buying power, housing starts, building permits, and industrial production. The analyst should also be aware of any new generators of visitation that may emerge in the market area. Returning to the example, future demand is projected as follows.

Market Segment	Room Night Demand Year 0	Projected Annual Growth Rate	Projected Room Night Demand		
			Year 1	Year 2	Year 3
Commercial	100,512	3%	103,527	106,633	109,832
Convention & groups	111,043	2	113,263	115,529	117,839
Vacationers	71,787	1	72,504	73,229	73,962
Total	283,342		289,294	295,391	301,633

As with the build-up approach based on the analysis of demand generators, the total potential area demand must be allocated among all the competitive lodging facilities before the subject property's capture can be determined. The procedures for allocating demand will be described in subsequent chapters.

Food, Beverage, and Banquet Demand

In addition to surveying the transient lodging demand, the local potential for food, beverage, and banquet business also must be quantified. This is accomplished with surveying procedures like those previously described, with special emphasis on area groups and businesses that are likely to use meeting and banquet facilities. Competition for this market includes not only other area hostelries, but also restaurants, catering halls, and clubs. The unit of demand for food and beverage is known as a cover, which is one diner for one meal. (The concept is similar to the room night concept.) The total number of covers within a given market area represents the potential food, beverage, and banquet demand.

Recognizing trends in macro demand and accurately measuring micro demand are essential requirements for a well-documented hotel appraisal. Most sources of demand for a successful, existing property with an established operating history have already been defined. Proposed and distressed hostelries will require more market research. The estimated demand is one of the key ingredients for establishing a lodging facility's potential revenue.

Case Study

The following case study is presented to illustrate the market analysis and valuation procedures described in this monograph. The example will be developed further in Chapters 3 and 6, demonstrating the collection and development of data that leads to a final opinion of value. The property being appraised is a proposed 200-room Sheraton Inn located in a suburban area, but the techniques employed to quantify demand and project income and expenses are applicable to all types of lodging facilities. The location and data are realistic, but hypothetical.

Because every appraisal assignment is unique, the techniques used to collect and process data into an estimate of value must be tailored to meet each particular situation. Few assignments require the detailed analysis set forth in this case study. Some factors that influence the utilization of the various approaches are: the availability of data, the nature of the market, the nature of the subject, and time and economic considerations. An experienced hostelry consultant can generally arrive at a credible estimate of value using a more abbreviated set of approaches.

Background Information

A proposed 200-room Sheraton Inn is under consideration for a seven-acre parcel located within a major metropolitan area. This highly visible location is adjacent to two major highways; I-495 is a heavily traveled, east-west artery connecting various suburban communities with a nearby urban center, and Route 110 is a four-lane, north-south feeder road that provides access to several large industrial and office parks.

The surrounding neighborhood has experienced tremendous growth over the past 10 years as the nearby urban center has extended its area of influence. What was once rich farmland now supports residential developments, regional shopping malls, office complexes, and industrial districts. Several large aerospace and communications manufacturers also have established plants in the area; these manufacturers are supported by many smaller subcontracting production firms. The high technology of local businesses is reflected in an affluent population with large disposable incomes, attractive homes, and a leisure-oriented lifestyle.

Although the aerospace industry tends to be highly cyclical, most of the larger plants have long-term government contracts. County planners expect moderate growth to continue. Over 40% of the land remains undeveloped and the area has been attracting many firms from the nearby urban center.

The property being appraised will be developed by a local contractor who owns several similar motels outside the state. He plans to operate under a Sheraton franchise and employ a manager trained at one of his other properties. The motel will have 200 guest rooms, a 180-seat restaurant, a 150-seat lounge, a 40-seat lobby bar, and a health club. Banquet facilities will include a 400-seat room, a 100-seat room, and three 50-seat rooms. The decor and construction specifications indicate a top-quality property capable of attracting high-rate patrons.

Micro Demand

The micro demand is based on the available room nights located within a defined market area. For illustrative purposes, both the build-up approach based on an analysis of demand generators and the build-up approach based on analysis of lodging activity will be utilized. The following outline lists the steps required to quantify the micro demand.

1. Define the market area
2. Analyze demand generators
   Determine the generators of transient visitation
   Survey and quantify selective generators
   Extrapolate unaccountable demand from sample
3. Analyze lodging activity
   Identify all competitive lodging facilities
   Estimate the occupancy of each competitive facility
   Determine accommodated room night demand
   Allocate demand among market segments
   Estimate unaccommodated demand
   Project room night demand

Defining the Market Area

The initial market area is the geographic region located within 20 minutes travel time of the property. The area is not served by any form of public transportation, so travel time applies to automobile driving only.

On a detailed highway map, the property is located at the junction of I-495 and Route 110. A route is then traced along each major highway starting at this intersection and ending at a point 20 driving minutes away based on average highway speeds and road conditions. The accompanying map illustrates that the radiating routes are the longest for I-495 and Route 110. Secondary roads intersecting these two highways should also be measured for travel time. The end points of all possible routes on the map are joined by a continuous line; the resulting shape resembles a circle that has been pushed in on four sides (see Figure 2.1, page 32).

Analysis of Demand Generators

Determining Generators of Transient Visitation

Local Chamber of Commerce officials, county planners, and real estate brokers were interviewed to determine generators of transient visitation located in the market area. Most of the area's major businesses and attractions that attract overnight visitors are described in the following list. The attractions can be located by number on the map in Figure 2.1.

1. *Office park.* This fully developed and leased, 2,000,000-sq. ft. office park located directly across I-495 from the proposed Sheraton. The office park houses many regional sales and service departments and national firms.

2. *Aerospace firm.* This major aircraft component manufacturer has

31

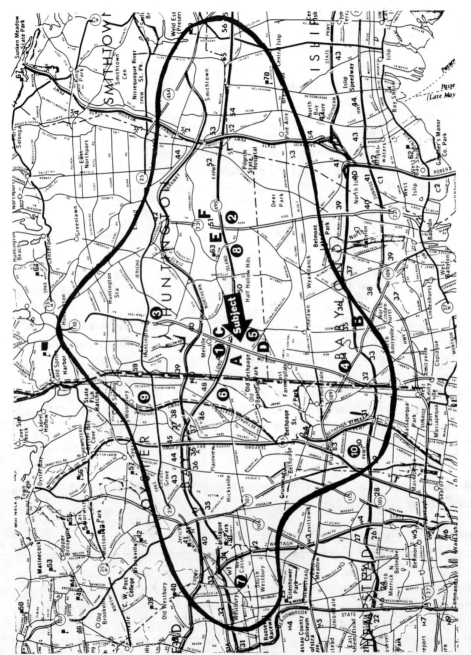

Figure 2.1

3,500,000 square feet of building space and employs more than 15,000 people. It is situated one exit east of the subject, adjacent to I-495.

3. *Communications firm.* The research-oriented division of a national communications firm employs 10,000 people in a facility of more than 3,000,000 square feet. This major office complex is located two miles north of the subject on Route 110.

4. *Aircraft engineer producer.* The jet engine manufacturer currently employs 5,000 people and occupies more than 2,000,000 square feet of building space. This firm is situated on Route 110, approximately three miles south of the proposed Sheraton.

5. *High technology research park.* This office-research park consists of 25 communication-oriented research facilities owned by major manufacturers, located adjacent to the subject property directly south. The park is fully developed and contains approximately 1,000,000 square feet of laboratory and office space.

6. *Industrial park.* The established park houses 100 small and medium-size manufacturing firms that perform subcontracting work for the aircraft engine producer (4). Located one mile east of the proposed Sheraton on the service road next to I-495, the industrial park has some excess land for future expansion. The current total building area of the firms located in the park is approximately 2,000,000 square feet.

7. *Office district.* A downtown-type office district with an inventory of 2,520,000 square feet of high-rent office space is located nine miles west of the subject property next to an I-495 interchange. The firms occupying space in this office district are primarily engaged in financial, legal, and insurance services.

8. *New industrial park.* This new, 700-acre industrial park with approximately 200 acres currently developed is situated five miles east of the subject property at an I-495 exit. The park has 1,350,000 square feet of space still under lease, and favorable future growth trends are indicated.

9. *Regional mall.* Located on a secondary highway approximately five miles northeast of the proposed Sheraton, this 75-acre regional shopping mall has 135 stores occupying 1,500,000 square feet of leaseable area.

10. *State hospital.* A 1,000-bed state mental hospital located eight miles southwest of the subject on a secondary highway attracts some commercial visitation.

11. *Convention center.* The three-year-old convention center with 50,000 square feet of floor area is located on Route 110 as is the subject property, just south of a nearby Hilton Hotel. This facility, used primarily for trade shows and local events, can accommodate up to 7,000 people.

12. *Vacation destination.* A beach resort area that attracts vacationers

during the summer months and weekend travelers during the rest of the year is 4-5 hours east of the subject by car.

Surveying and Quantifying Selective Generators

These twelve potential generators of demand indicate that the transient market is composed primarily of commercial, meeting and convention, and vacation travelers.

The commercial demand in the area includes five nights per week. All travel is by automobile, so many commercial visitors arrive Sunday night to begin work early Monday morning. The commercial demand is low Sunday night, then increases and remains fairly level Monday, Tuesday, Wednesday, and Thursday nights; demand drops off significantly on Friday and Saturday.

The meeting and convention demand is generated primarily by the new convention center and by several research-oriented firms that hold conferences and training sessions in the area. The bulk of this demand originates during the fall, winter, and spring months, with Sunday through Thursday representing the peak convention days. While commercial travelers hardly ever use lodging facilities on Friday or Saturday night, certain types of conventions prefer weekends and holiday periods when rates are typically lower.

The market area surrounding the proposed Sheraton has no tourist attractions to draw vacation travelers. Some demand is generated by I-495, which leads to a resort area approximately 4½ hours away. A limited demand is generated by vacationers visiting friends and relatives in the area. Vacationer travel is strongest during the summer months, weekends, and holiday periods. This negative correlation in respect to commercial demand greatly benefits facilities that cater to both market segments.

A series of personal interviews, telephone surveys, and letter questionnaires were used to determine the number of room nights produced by each generator of transient visitation. The following summary shows how the different generators were surveyed and how the demand was quantified into an estimate of room nights. The commercial segment was surveyed first, followed by meetings and conventions, and then by vacation travelers.

Commercial Demand. *Office park.* (#1 on map) Because this office park is very near to the subject property and a high percentage of capture is anticipated, a thorough survey was performed to quantify the park's potential demand. Personal interviews with 20 of the park's tenants were conducted. Large and small space users, including local and regional firms, were interviewed. The total space utilized by these 20 companies was approximately 200,000 square feet, or 10% of the total occupied space in the park. The results of the interviews were converted

34

to a unit of comparison based on the square footage of office space.

It was determined from the interviews that every 10,000 square feet of rented office space in the park generated approximately one visitor per week, who stayed an average of three nights, i.e., three room nights per 10,000 square feet. Extrapolation from is finding indicates that the 2,000,000-sq. ft. office park will attract an average of 200 transient visitors per week, who will generate approximately 600 room nights. Because the office park is fully developed, the commercial demand generated by this source is expected to remain stable in the foreseeable future.

The projected demand for the office park is:

Year	Rented Office Space	Visitation Factor	Visitors Per Week	Commercial Room Nights Per Week
0	2,000,000 sq.ft.	10,000	200	600
1	2,000,000 sq.ft.	10,000	200	600
2	2,000,000 sq.ft.	10,000	200	600
3	2,000,000 sq.ft.	10,000	200	600
4	2,000,000 sq.ft.	10,000	200	600
5	2,000,000 sq.ft.	10,000	200	600

Aerospace firm (#2). The security department of this huge manufacturing complex provided the best information on transient visitation. Security requires all visitors to register before entering the premises. The information requested on the registration log includes home address, nature of visit, local address (motel), business affiliation, and length of stay in the area. Based on an analysis of the log over a 24-month period, it was estimated that the aerospace firm attracted approximately 110 outside visitors per week; these visitors stay at local motels for an average of two nights per visit. Over the past several years, this type of visitation has remained fairly stable. The projected demand for the aerospace firm is:

Year	Visitors Per Week	Commercial Room Nights Per Week
0	110	220
1	110	220
2	110	220
3	110	220
4	110	220
5	110	220

Communications firm (#3). The bulk of the outside visitation to the communications firm will be quantified later under the meeting and convention market segment. The demand is generated by weekly training programs for equipment installers.

Discussions with management indicated that most of the transient, commercial visitors are out-of-town suppliers, sales people, and manufacturers' representatives. Many of these visitors pass through the firm's purchasing department. A surveyor was permitted to interview all out-of-town visitors to this area for a one-week period. Because the visitation to the purchasing department is uniform throughout the year, a one-week survey was deemed sufficient.

These interviews indicated that approximately 200 out-of-town, commercial visitors came to the communications firm each week and that the average length of stay was one day. Because the size of the communications firm is expected to remain constant, no increase in room night demand is projected. The demand for the communications firm is estimated as follows:

Year	Visitors Per Week	Commercial Room Nights Per Week
0	200	200
1	200	200
2	200	200
3	200	200
4	200	200
5	200	200

Aircraft engine producer (#4). This firm recently moved into the area and maintains few records pertaining to outside visitation. However, before constructing the plant, the company was required to submit to the county an economic impact study outlining the firm's potential benefits to the area. One of the benefits cited was motel patronage from visitors to the plant. A footnote stated that their estimate was based on visitation histories from the firm's other plants throughout the United States. According to this study, approximately 12,850 room nights would be generated during the first year, or an average of 247 room nights per week. This figure was expected to increase approximately 5% each succeeding year. The projected demand for the aircraft engine producer is shown on the following page.

High technology research park (#5). Eight of the 25 firms located in the research park were interviewed by telephone. Each firm attracted 10 outside visi-

Year	Estimated Yearly Room Nights	Weeks Per Year	Commercial Room Nights Per Week
0	12,850	52	247
1	13,470	52	259
2	14,145	52	272
3	14,870	52	286
4	15,600	52	300
5	16,380	52	315

tors per week and each visitor stayed an average of three nights. There is no land available to expand the park, so the transient demand is expected to remain level. The projected demand for the research park is as follows:

Year	Firms	Visitors Per Week Per Firm	Average Length of Stay	Commercial Room Nights Per Week
0	25	10	3	750
1	25	10	3	750
2	25	10	3	750
3	25	10	3	750
4	25	10	3	750
5	25	10	3	750

Industrial park (#6). A letter survey was mailed to the tenants of this industrial park, and a fair number responded. Based on the replies received, it was estimated that every 30,000 square feet of building area generated approximately three room nights per week. The projected demand for the industrial park is shown at the top of page 38.

Office district (#7). A list of tenants in the office district was compared to the list of tenants occupying the office park (#1). The office district had more local firms (e.g., accounting and legal firms) that probably would not generate as much visitation as the regional and national firms with offices in the park. Therefore, the office park's visitation factor of one visitor staying three nights for every 10,000 square feet was decreased to one visitor staying three nights for every 20,000 square feet in the office district. Local developers saw definite potential for growth in the amount of occupied office space in this district. Most

Year	Total Area of All Buildings	Visitation Factor	Room Nights Per Week	Commercial Room Nights Per Week
0	2,000,000 sq.ft.	30,000	3	200
1	2,000,000 sq.ft.	30,000	3	200
2	2,000,000 sq.ft.	30,000	3	200
3	2,000,000 sq.ft.	30,000	3	200
4	2,000,000 sq.ft.	30,000	3	200
5	2,000,000 sq.ft.	30,000	3	200

experts agreed that a 5% yearly growth rate could be expected, and this would cause the commercial demand to increase accordingly. The projected demand for the office district is:

Year	Rented Office Space	Visitation Factor	Visitors Per Week	Commercial Room Nights Per Week
0	2,520,000 sq.ft.	20,000	126	378
1	2,660,000 sq.ft.	20,000	133	399
2	2,800,000 sq.ft.	20,000	140	420
3	2,940,000 sq.ft.	20,000	147	441
4	3,080,000 sq.ft.	20,000	154	463
5	3,240,000 sq.ft.	20,000	162	486

New industrial park (#8). The type of tenants occupying the new industrial park were more national in scope than those at the established industrial park (#6). The survey of the established industrial park indicated a visitation factor of one visitor per 30,000 square feet of space staying an average of three nights, or one room night per 10,000 square feet of space. This visitation factor was adjusted to one visitor per 15,000 square feet staying two nights, or a ratio of one room night per 7,500 square feet of space; this reflects the higher level of visitation for the nationally oriented companies within the park. The new industrial park has 1,350,000 square feet of space currently under lease. Its expected growth rate for next year is 27%, which will decline approximately four percentage points over the foreseeable future. The projected demand for this park is as follows.

38

Year	Total Area of All Buildings	Visitation Factor	Visitors Per Week	Commercial Room Nights Per Week
0	1,350,000 sq.ft.	15,000	90	180
1	1,725,000 sq.ft.	15,000	115	230
2	2,130,000 sq.ft.	15,000	142	285
3	2,535,000 sq.ft.	15,000	169	338
4	2,955,000 sq.ft.	15,000	197	395
5	3,390,000 sq.ft.	15,000	226	452

Regional mall (#9). Many tenants of the regional mall are national retailers. Each store is visited on a regular basis by home office personnel who take inventories and prepare audits. Based on studies of similar malls in other parts of the country, the projected demand is estimated as follows:

Year	Commercial Room Nights Per Week
0	100
1	105
2	110
3	115
4	120
5	125

State hospital (#10). State officials visit this property weekly to perform various administrative functions. The hospital director estimates the weekly demand generated by this facility to be:

Year	Commercial Room Nights Per Week
0	95
1	95
2	95
3	95
4	95
5	95

Totaling the commercial room night demand from these ten identifiable sources of commercial visitation results in the following total, accountable commercial demand.

Potential Commercial Demand Within Market Area

	Projected Room Nights Per Week					
Source	Year 0	Year 1	Year 2	Year 3	Year 4	Year 5
1. Office park	600	600	600	600	600	600
2. Aerospace firm	220	220	220	220	220	220
3. Communications firm	200	200	200	200	200	200
4. Aircraft engine firm	247	259	272	286	300	315
5. Research park	750	750	750	750	750	750
6. Industrial park	200	200	200	200	200	200
7. Office district	378	399	420	441	463	486
8. New industrial park	180	230	285	338	395	452
9. Regional mall	100	105	110	115	120	125
10. State hospital	95	95	95	95	95	95
Total accountable demand	2,970	3,058	3,152	3,245	3,343	3,443

In addition to the accountable demand, a certain amount of unaccountable commercial demand must be recognized from sources inadvertently overlooked, those not included in the survey, and others outside the market area (passing-through demand). Overflow from adjacent market areas also must be considered. Depending on the size of the market area and the surveying procedures utilized, the unaccountable demand generally is 10%—40% of the total demand.

Because the commercial demand survey appeared to be thorough and the researchers were confident that all major sources of commercial visitation had been evaluated, an unaccountable commercial demand factor of 20% was deemed appropriate. This additional demand results in the following total commercial room night demand shown on page 41.

The commercial demand growth expectations quantified in the survey indicated an overall yearly commercial demand increase of approximately 3%. This rate of growth appears reasonable for an economically active market area.

Meetings and Convention Demand. The primary source of information concerning the meeting and convention segment is generally the local convention and visitors bureau, which is responsible for booking and tracking this type of visitation. Discussions with the director of the local convention bureau revealed that the area has three main generators of meetings and conventions: the conven-

Potential Commercial Demand Within Market Area

	Year 0	Year 1	Projected Room Nights Year 2	Year 3	Year 4	Year 5
Total accountable demand	2,970	3,058	3,152	3,245	3,343	3,443
Unaccountable demand (20%)	594	613	630	650	669	689
Total commercial demand (week)	3,564	3,671	3,782	3,895	4,012	4,132
	×52	×52	×52	×52	×52	×52
Total commercial demand (year)	185,328	190,892	196,664	202,540	208,624	214,864

tion center (#11), the communications firm (#3)—training sessions, and the research park (#5)—seminars.

Convention center (#11). The three-year old convention center is experiencing the growth of usage typical for a facility of this type. Past efforts to attract large conventions were generally unsuccessful because the area has had an insufficient supply of hotel accommodations. The addition of the subject Sheraton and a new Best Western Hotel (currently under construction) should alleviate the undersupply somewhat. Nevertheless, the center is expected to serve regionally oriented, small and medium-size groups.

Discussions with the convention center manager showed a current usage of 110 days per year. The typical event attracts approximately 600 out-of-towners, and the double occupancy factor averages 1.5. Multiplying the days of usage per year by 600 people per event, and dividing the product by the double occupancy factor of 1.5 yields in the present year meetings and convention demand from the convention center.

The numbers of days of usage per year is expected to increase in the foreseeable future by four days per year. The following table shows the meetings and convention demand generated by the convention center.

Year	Days of Usage Per Year	People Per Event	Double Occupancy	Meeting & Convention Room Nights Per Year
0	110	600	1.5	44,000
1	114	600	1.5	45,500
2	118	600	1.5	47,000
3	121	600	1.5	48,500
4	125	600	1.5	50,100
5	129	600	1.5	51,700

Communications firm (#3). The communications firm holds weekly training programs for equipment installers. Each session begins Sunday evening and ends Friday at noon, representing four nights of demand. Students attend classes at a specially designed, company-owned conference center during the day, and are housed (double occupancy) at nearby hotels. Class size averages 200 students, and 50 classes are scheduled per year. The following table shows the meetings and convention demand generated by the communications firm.

Year	Rooms Per Class	Classes Per Year	Days Per Class	Meeting & Convention Room Nights Per Year
0	100	50	4	20,000
1	100	50	4	20,000
2	100	50	4	20,000
3	100	50	4	20,000
4	100	50	4	20,000
5	100	50	4	20,000

Research park (#5). While surveying the commercial demand within the research park, the researchers also found that a strong meeting and seminar demand was generated by this concentration of research-oriented businesses. Through interviews and statistical samplings, it was determined that every four room nights of commercial demand produced one room night of meeting and convention demand. Using this ratio of commercial to meeting visitation, the estimate of meetings and convention demand for the research park is:

Year	Commercial Room Nights Per Week	Ratio of Commercial to Meeting Visitation	Weeks Per Year	Meeting & Convention Room Nights Per Year
0	750	.25	52	9,750
1	750	.25	52	9,750
2	750	.25	52	9,750
3	750	.25	52	9,750
4	750	.25	52	9,750
5	750	.25	52	9,750

The .25 ratio used was specifically developed for this particular research park, which appears to generate a sizable number of seminars. It is unlikely that this ratio could be applied to other sources of commercial visitation that are not as meeting-oriented.

As with the commercial segment, a certain amount of meetings and convention demand is unaccountable because of the surveying techniques used in the build-up approach based on the analysis of demand generators. Drawing upon the researchers' knowledge of the local market, an unaccountable meetings and convention demand factor of 15% was considered appropriate. The chart on page 44 shows potential meetings and convention demand within the market area.

Potential Meeting and Convention Demand Within Market Area

Source	Map Number	Projected Room Nights Per Year					
		Year 0	Year 1	Year 2	Year 3	Year 4	Year 5
Convention Center	11	44,000	45,500	47,000	48,500	50,100	51,700
Communications firm	3	20,000	20,000	20,000	20,000	20,000	20,000
Research park	5	9,750	9,750	9,750	9,750	9,750	9,750
Total accountable demand		73,750	75,250	76,750	78,250	79,850	81,450
Unaccountable demand (15%)		11,061	11,287	11,512	11,737	11,977	12,217
Total meeting and convention demand		84,812	86,537	88,262	89,987	91,827	93,667

Vacationer Demand. Although the subject's market area holds no real attraction for vacationers, it does lie on a main route to a resort area. Research determined that some of the travelers going to and from the resort area would use the motels along the interstate as intermediate stopping points. An origination and destination study performed by the state highway authority provided an interesting bench mark for measuring this demand. They estimated that 2% of the weekend traffic volume passing through the subject's market required overnight accommodations.

When the 2% factor, along with a 15% unaccommodated demand factor, was applied to the traffic count surveys and projections, the following estimate of the potential vacationer demand was produced.

Potential Vacationer Demand Within Market Area

Year	Traffic Volume (Vehicles Per Day)		Vehicles Per Year	2% Requiring Area Lodging	Unaccountable Demand (15%)	Total Vacationer Demand Per Year
	Saturdays	Sundays				
0	21,500	18,000	2,055,000	41,100	6,165	47,265
1	21,700	18,200	2,074,000	41,500	6,220	47,720
2	21,900	18,400	2,096,000	41,900	6,308	48,208
3	22,100	18,600	2,116,000	42,330	6,349	48,679
4	22,300	18,800	2,137,000	42,744	6,411	49,155
5	22,500	19,000	2,158,000	43,160	6,474	49,634

Total Demand. The total room night demand for the subject's market area is the sum of the demands projected for each of the three market segments. (See table on page 46.)

It is apparent that the build-up approach based on the analysis of demand generators has definite drawbacks as a market quantification technique. Considerable time and manpower can be required to properly survey all major demand generators. The reliability of the data obtained from this type of survey is often highly variable, depending on the expertise of the surveyor. In large cities or extended metropolitan areas, the number of demand generators to be surveyed can make this market quantification technique impractical. Unless the percent of unaccountable demand is kept within reasonable limits, this technique is unreliable.

In conclusion, the build-up approach based on the analysis of demand generators works well in market areas with limited sources of visitation. This technique may be used in conjunction with the build-up approach based on lodging

Projected Yearly Area Demand (Room Nights)

	Year 0	Year 1	Year 2	Year 3	Year 4	Year 5	Year 6	Year 7
Commercial	185,328	190,892	196,664	202,540	208,624	214,864	221,346	227,986
Meeting & convention	84,812	86,537	88,262	89,987	91,827	93,667	95,538	97,449
Vacationers	47,265	47,720	48,208	48,679	49,155	49,634	50,165	50,667
Total	317,405	325,149	333,134	341,206	349,606	358,165	367,049	376,102

activity where certain large generators of visitation have an important impact on the local market demand. As with any surveying procedure, the analyst must justify the cost of the survey with its benefits and accuracy.

Analysis of Lodging Activity

Identifying Competitive Lodging Facilities

A survey of the market area was performed to determine which lodging facilities would compete directly with the proposed Sheraton Inn. This identification process included not only existing hotels and motels, but also those proposed and under construction.

Because the subject property is to be a first-class, nationally franchised facility, nonaffiliated motels with less than 100 rooms were considered noncompetitive and excluded from the sample. The following competitive motels were identified, and their room counts were determined from various travel directories. The motels are identified by letter in Figure 2.1.

Existing Facilities		**Facilities Under Construction**	
A. Days Inn	150 rooms	F. Best Western	170 rooms
B. Suncrest Motel	135 rooms		
C. Holiday Inn	220 rooms		
D. Hilton Hotel	300 rooms		
E. Ramada Inn	185 rooms		

Although the Days Inn is a budget property, its national franchise and good-quality rooms make it competitve with the Sheraton. The Suncrest is an established, independent property with a loyal following.

Estimating the Occupancy of Each Competing Facility

Interviews were conducted with the general manager of each competitive property. Information was obtained on current occupancy levels, average rates, and the percentage relationship between each market segment and the total number of room nights captured by each property.

Although several of the managers were reluctant to reveal their operating ratios, the interviewers checked their findings against in-house statistics and data from other sources. They concluded that the following chart reflects last year's probable occupancy percentages for the five existing lodging facilities.

Facility	Estimated Percentage of Occupancy for Previous 12 Months
Days Inn	90%
Suncrest Motel	75
Holiday Inn	85
Hilton Inn	80
Ramada Inn	80

Determining Accommodated Room Night Demand

The total accommodated room night demand within the market area is calculated by multiplying each competitive property's room count by its annual occupancy and then by 365.

	Number of Rooms		Estimated Annual Occupancy		Days Per Year		Accommodated Demand (Room Nights)
Days Inn	150	×	.90	×	365	=	49,275
Suncrest Motel	135	×	.75	×	365	=	36,956
Holiday Inn	220	×	.85	×	365	=	68,255
Hilton Inn	300	×	.80	×	365	=	87,600
Ramada Inn	185	×	.80	×	365	=	54,020
Total area accommodated demand							296,106

With 990 existing rooms in the market area, the number of total available room nights is: $990 \times 365 = 361,350$. Dividing the total accommodated demand of 296,106 by 361,350 total available room nights shows the current area occupancy to be 82%.

Allocating Demand Among the Market Segments

In the interviews, the general managers of the competitive properties were asked to determine the percentage relationship between each market segment and the total demand. The results of these interviews are shown in the first chart on page 49.

Estimating Unaccommodated Demand

It was determined that several times each year, the area's lodging facilities were filled to capacity and travelers had to settle for smaller, less desirable motels or seek accommodations outside the market area. Most of the unaccommodated

48

Percentage Relationship

	Commercial	Meetings and Conventions	Vacationers
Days Inn	75%	—	25%
Suncrest	60	20%	20
Holiday Inn	55	30	15
Hilton Inn	45	45	10
Ramada Inn	60	25	15

Room Nights

	Total Accommodated Demand	Commercial	Meetings and Conventions	Vacationers
Days Inn	49,275	36,956	—	12,319
Suncrest	36,956	22,174	7,391	7,391
Holiday Inn	68,255	37,540	20,477	10,238
Hilton Inn	87,600	39,420	39,420	8,760
Ramada Inn	54,020	32,412	13,505	8,103
Totals	296,106	168,502	80,793	46,811

Projected Yearly Area Demand (Room Nights)

	Year 0	Year 1	Year 2	Year 3	Year 4	Year 5	Year 6	Year 7
Commercial	185,352	190,913	196,640	202,540	208,616	214,874	221,321	227,960
Meeting and convention	84,832	86,529	88,260	90,025	91,825	93,662	95,535	97,446
Vacationers	47,279	47,752	48,230	48,712	49,199	49,691	50,188	50,690
Total	317,463	325,194	333,130	341,277	349,640	358,227	367,044	376,096

demand took place Monday through Thursday nights during periods of heavy commercial occupancy. Some meeting and convention travelers were turned away and occasionally vacationers had to find rooms elsewhere. The percentage of unaccommodated demand for each market segment is commercial—10%; meetings and convention—5%; and vacationers—1%. Multiplying the percent unaccommodated by the number of room nights actually accommodated yields the total unaccommodated room night demand. Combining the accommodated and unaccommodated demand results in the estimate of the area's total transient demand.

Accommodated and Unaccommodated Transient Demand

Segment	Accommodated Demand R.N. Per Year	Percent Unaccommodated	Unaccommodated Demand R.N. Per Year	Total Transient Demand
Commercial	168,502	10%	16,850	185,352
Meeting and convention	80,793	5	4,039	84,832
Vacationers	46,811	1	468	47,279
	296,106		21,357	317,463

Dividing the total transient demand of 317,463 by 361,350 available room nights shows the current potential area occupancy to be 88%.

Projecting Room Night Demand

The total transient demand of 317,463 room nights represents the demand in the market area at a point in time that will be termed Year 0. An investigation of area economic indicators showed a healthy business climate. Some projected trends made by the local Chamber of Commerce, an economic development agency, and the state university are summarized below:

	Projected Annual Growth Rate
New office space	3%
New industrial space	4
Population	2
Housing	1
Retail sales	5
Traffic counts	2
Employment	3
Convention attendance	2

Given these projected growth rates and their impact on the three market segments, the following transient demand growth appears reasonable.

Market Segment	Projected Yearly Growth Rates
Commercial	3%
Meetings and convention	2
Vacationers	1

Using these annual growth rates, the second chart on page 49 shows the projected yearly area demand for each market segment over the next seven years.

The build-up approach based on the analysis of lodging activity generally requires less field work and produces a more supportable demand estimate than the build-up approach based on the analysis of demand generators. All competitive lodging facilities must be identified and accurate estimates of occupancy must be obtained.

3
Supply of Transient Accommodations

An appraiser should be familiar with macro and micro supply factors. Long-term macro supply trends often have a significant effect on local hostelries, particularly with respect to size, layout, design, chain affiliation, financial structure, and type of management. Knowledge of the micro supply is needed to predict the relative competitiveness of area properties and to estimate the subject property's probable market share.

Macro Supply

It is difficult to determine the macro supply for transient lodging accommodations because there is no uniform, long-term census that quantifies the number of hostelry units on a yearly basis. The problem is one of definition. What constitutes a lodging facility? Should properties such as rooming houses, residential hotels, dormitories, camps, seasonal resorts, and motels of fewer than 10 units be included? The U.S. Bureau of the Census has information dating back to 1939, but the definition of a lodging facility used at that time included many properties that bear little resemblance to what would be considered competitive lodgings today.

Pannell Kerr Forster and Company and Hospitality Valuation Services, Inc. compile annual statistics on the number of hotels and motels in the United States using census data. The national trends since 1948 are shown in Table 3.1.

The percentage increases in the combined totals for the 1948–1980 period indicate supply-demand trends in the lodging industry:

Growth in rooms occupied	45%
Growth in number of establishments	66%
Growth in number of available rooms	86%

The growth in rooms occupied represents the demand for transient accommodations; the growth in the number of available rooms represents the supply. Because the number of occupied rooms rose at a slower rate than the number of available rooms, the average percentage of occupancy has declined steadily. Between 1948 and 1980, the percentage of occupancy dropped from 89% to 70%; this drop was felt equally by hotels and motels.

The statistics also reveal a 400% increase in the number of motel and motor hotel rooms and a 16% decrease in the number of hotel rooms. Although roadside motels have replaced many older downtown hotel properties, much of the growth can be attributed to changing definitions. The lodging industry has always tried to distinguish between hotels and motels (motor hotels); during the 1940s and 1950s, the differences between the two properties were apparent. Since then, however, motels have become more like hotels—multi-story facilities with extensive food, beverage, and banquet facilities; at the same time, hotels have acquired many characteristics of motels—convenient parking, efficient design, and smaller public areas. The lodging industry has reached the point where the words "hotel" and "motel" can be used almost interchangeably, and classifying statistics on the basis of terminology has become meaningless.

The average number of rooms per property has steadily increased. Higher fixed expenses, particularly higher salaries and energy costs, have made many smaller hostelries uneconomical. Except for budget motels and properties with extraordinarily high occupancies or average rates, facilities with fewer than 100 units are not economical in today's market.

The slow growth in the number of occupied rooms (demand) and the rapid increase in the number of available rooms (supply) may call the feasibility of all new hostelries into question. This is definitely a problem in areas that have become overbuilt during periods of prosperity. However, from a macro point of

Table 3.1 Hotel and Motel Trends in the United States

	1948	1960	1965	1970	1975	1980
Hotels (25 or more guest rooms)						
Number of establishments	10,425	9,300	7,750	7,435	7,325	7,340
Number of rooms available per day	861,000	789,000	707,950	702,800	708,750	719,300
Average number of rooms per establishment	83	85	91	94	97	98
Average number of rooms occupied per day	779,350	546,100	467,375	434,250	428,800	503,500
Percentage of occupancy	91%	69%	66%	62%	60%	70%
Average rate per occupied room	N/A	$14.34	$14.79	$20.53	$27.27	$46.26
Motels and motor hotels (all sizes)						
Number of establishments	12,410	27,440	29,800	30,000	30,500	30,500
Number of rooms available per day	266,400	742,525	1,030,550	1,178,950	1,317,100	1,372,500
Average number of rooms per establishment	21	27	35	39	43	45
Average number of rooms occupied per day	227,850	508,050	673,850	750,600	786,300	960,700
Percentage of occupancy	86%	68%	65%	64%	60%	70%
Average rate per occupied room	N/A	$11.00	$11.84	$15.93	$20.29	$32.41
Combined totals						
Number of establishments	22,835	36,740	37,550	37,435	37,825	37,840
Number of rooms available per day	1,127,400	1,531,525	1,738,500	1,881,750	2,025,850	2,091,800
Average number of rooms per establishment	49	42	46	50	54	55
Average number of rooms occupied per day	1,007,200	1,054,550	1,141,225	1,184,850	1,215,100	1,464,200
Percentage of occupancy	89%	69%	66%	63%	60%	70%
Average rate per occupied room	N/A	$13.65	$14.65	$19.50	$20.55	$37.17

Source: U.S. Census Data, Pannell Kerr Forster & Company and Hospitality Valuation Services, Inc. estimates for hotels and motels with payrolls.

view, a certain number of new facilities is required to replace older rooms that are periodically withdrawn from the market. Also, although the average occupancy in 1980 was estimated at 70%, newer properties typically attract patrons at the expense of older hostelries; the average does not necessarily represent the operating results of a modern facility.

Hotel-Motel Chains

Every year the American Hotel and Motel Association compiles a directory of hotel-motel chains and publishes a chain lodging analysis that describes the growth of various hostelry chains. A chain is defined as any group of three or more hotels, motels, or resorts operated under a common name or by one owner or operator.

Table 3.2 shows the recent impact of hostelry chains on the supply of lodging facilities in the United States.

In 1979 chain properties accounted for two-thirds of the hostelry rooms in the United States. These figures show a large increase from 1970, when chains represented approximately one-third of all available lodging units. Although chain properties have consistently out-performed independents in average occupancy, they tend to operate at slightly lower average rates. Table 3.3 lists the 25 largest hotel chains in the United States.

The rapid growth of hostelry chains between 1970 and 1975 can be attributed to three factors: franchising, management contracts, and internal expansion.

Table 3.2   United States Chain Analysis

	1971	1975	1979
Chain properties	4,700	8,667	10,875
Chain rooms	706,249	1,123,212	1,326,612
Total rooms	1,890,000	2,025,000	2,080,000
Chain rooms as a percent of total	37%	55%	64%
Occupancy—chain	70%	67%	69%
Occupancy—independent	69%	65%	63%
Rate—chain	$14.41	$19.37	$41.67
Rate—independent	$17.41	$22.09	$44.09

Sources: American Hotel & Motel Association and Laventhol & Horwath

Table 3.3   25 Largest U.S. Chains, 1980

	Total Properties	Total Rooms
Holiday Inns, Inc.	1,544	256,186
Best Western International, Inc.	1,814	152,503
Ramada Inns, Inc.	606	87,012
Sheraton Hotels	319	74,584
Hilton Hotels	200	70,845
Friendship Inns International	932	68,300
Howard Johnson	513	58,801
Days Inns of America	312	41,988
Trusthouse Forte	505	37,830
Quality Inns International	324	37,453
Best Value Inns	547	31,300
Motel 6	291	30,639
Hyatt Hotels	53	27,100
Marriott Hotels	64	26,785
Rodeway Inns International	143	17,294
Western International Hotels	23	15,300
LaQuinta Motor Inns	92	10,847
Red Carpet/Master Host Inns	89	10,749
AMFAC Hotels and Resorts	24	10,500
Hotel Systems of America	63	8,545
Pick Americana Hotels	28	8,299
Econo–Travel Motor Hotels	135	8,007
Dunfey Hotels	20	7,780
Radisson Hotels	22	7,192
Stouffer Hotels	20	7,018

Source: *Lodging Hospitality* published in *Travel Market Yearbook*

Because most lodging facilities constructed since 1970 have some type of chain affiliation, the appraiser should have a basic understanding of the costs and benefits of belonging to a chain.

Franchising

A franchise is an agreement between a hotel-motel company (usually a national or regional chain) and an independent hostelry owner whereby the owner pays a fee to use the name, trademarks, and various services offered by the chain. This situation creates certain benefits and costs for both the owner and the chain.

Benefits to the Owner (Franchisee)

Instant identity, recognition, and image. Every chain has its own image, which indicates its price (economy, standard, or luxury) and market (family/vacation, commercial, or convention). To have a positive effect, the franchise image must conform to the facilities offered and the available market.

Reservation or referral service. Most franchises have some type of centralized reservation system that enables guests to reserve a room by calling a toll-free number. Some of the larger chains offer computerized services; others have teletype and phone connections with individual properties. A good reservation system generates approximately 15%–30% of a property's occupancy.

Chain advertising and sales. All major franchises publish a directory in which each property is briefly described and location and rate information are provided. The extent of media advertising and actual sales solicitation varies from chain to chain. In most cases the business generated through the reservation system and national or regional promotions cannot support an individual hostelry. Sales efforts on a local level are also necessary.

Procedure manual. Chains urge all their properties to follow standardized systems and procedures. Operating manuals are provided, and periodic inspections of each franchisee ensure that policies and standards are being maintained. Some chains conduct training schools to instruct management on basic operational techniques.

Management assistance. Most chains can provide specialized assistance in the various aspects of hotel-motel development and management, such as planning, operations, and marketing. These services generally are not covered by the normal franchise fee and are contracted for separately.

Group purchasing. Chains require that their properties use certain identity items such as ashtrays, monogrammed towels, silver and china, and uniforms. They offer group purchasing programs that reduce the cost of these items to owners.

Costs to Owner

Every year *Hospitality Magazine,* a leading lodging industry trade journal, publishes a franchise/membership directory. This directory lists the basic membership requirements and fees for hostelry chains. Table 3.4 is taken from the 1982 directory. (See page 60.)

Required facilities. Most chains require that an affiliated property have a minimum number of rooms and a food outlet on the premises or next door. Approximately three-quarters of the nation's chains also require a swimming pool.

Membership fees. Franchise chains require an initial fee that is generally determined by the size of the property. A continuing royalty fee, based on a percentage of room sales, is then paid each year. There are additional charges for chain advertising and reservation services. Depending on the individual franchise fee structure and the number of rooms booked through the reservation system, the actual cost of a franchise varies from 2%–8% of gross room sales. Most franchises are for terms of 10–25 years.

Required standards. Franchises must adhere to certain construction, design, operational, and maintenance standards. Standards are set for building materials, heating and air conditioning requirements, the size of guest rooms, the type of decor, the hours of operation, minimum staffing, pricing, advertising approval, and cleaning and maintenance specifications. Failure to follow required standards can jeopardize the franchise.

Liability to Owner

In granting a franchise, the chain makes no guarantee or financial commitment to the success of the property. Should a property fail, the chain can immediately withdraw its franchise and demand removal of all forms of identity. The owner assumes all financial liabilities.

Benefits to Chain (Franchisor)

Inexpensive, low-risk expansion. Franchising allows hostelry chains to expand their operations with minimal capital and personnel investments. Increased representation improves the chain's recognition, which tends to increase occupancies. The cash flow from franchise fees and royalties is attractive to publicly held companies.

Allied expansion. Several chains have developed allied businesses to support their franchises and company-owned operations. These businesses include interior designers, building contractors, furniture equipment and supply dealers, travel agencies, and tour packagers.

Costs to Chain

Franchise services. Chains must provide the services described in the franchise agreement. The reservation system and chain advertising comprise the bulk of their responsibility.

Quality control. Inspection, supervision, and enforcement of franchise procedures and standards are essential. One neglected property can harm the reputation of the entire chain. The need for strict quality control has led some chains to abandon their franchise programs because enforcing operational standards proved impossible.

From a valuation point of view, a franchise is neither a requirement nor a guarantee of success. A franchise well-suited to local market demand can pro-

Table 3.4 What It Takes to Join a Chain

| | Franchise/membership requirements | | | | | Franchise/membership fees | | | | |
Name of chain	Min. no. rooms	Food facilities	Meeting space	Swimming pool	Laundry	Initial fee	Royalty	Advertising fee	Reservations fee	Other fees
Best Value Inns/Superior Motels	25					$1,950/for first 25 rooms; $5 each additional room	none	$3.75/room/year	$2.85/room/month	sign purchase
Best Western International	none			•		$8,248 (for 100-room property)	none	$20,421 (for 100 rooms)	$3,650 (for 100 rooms)	none
Budget Host Inns	none					none	annual dues: $300 for first 30 units + $5 each additional unit	none	none	sign purchase
Comfort Inns	none			•		conversion: $7,500; new property: $15,000	3% gross rooms income	1% gross rooms income	1% gross rooms income + 25¢/booked reservations	none
Days Inns of America	100	•		•	•	$15,000 first 100 rooms; $100/room over 100 rooms; restaurant: $5000	5% gross lodging; 3% gross restaurant & other on-premise business	6¢/room/day or 1% gross lodging volume; whichever is greater	$2.25/room/month +.7% gross room sales + $1.15/reservation	training fee

	Rooms				Initial Fee	Royalty	Marketing/Advertising	Reservation	Other
Downtowner/-Passport Motor Inns	50	•	•	•	D-$2,500 conversion; $5,000 new construction; P-$1,000-$3,250 based on number of rooms	D-2% gross rooms revenues; P-$150-$300/month based on number of rooms	D-1% gross rooms revenues; P-$125-$275/month based on number of rooms	$2.45/confirmed reservation + $1/room/night	none
Econo-Travel Motor Hotels	40				conversion: $3,750; new construction: $7,500	2% gross rooms revenues	1½% gross rooms revenues	combined with adv. fee	none
Friendship Inns International	none			•	$2,000	$30/room/year	none	$2.45/reservation after guest arrives	none
Granada Royale Hometels	160 (all suites)		•		$50,000	4% gross suites revenues	1% gross suites revenues	1% gross suites revenues	none
Hilton Inns	100	•	•	•	$150/room to 100 rooms; then $100/room	5% room sales	none	$3.90/reservation	none
Holiday Inns	100		•	•	$300/room; $30,000 minimum	4% gross rooms revenue	1% gross rooms revenue	1% gross rooms revenue	$3.30/room Holidex fee

Table 3.4 What It Takes to Join a Chain (cont.)

| Name of chain | Franchise/membership requirements | | | | | | Franchise/membership fees | | | | |
	Min. no. rooms	Food facilities	Meeting space	Swim-ming pool	Laundry	Initial fee	Royalty	Advertising fee	Reservations fee	Other fees
Howard Johnson	120	•	•	•		$20,000	$8.50/room/ month or 5% gross sales	4¢/room/ day + .35% gross room sales; maximum 11¢/room/day	$2/room/ month; 1% gross room sales; $150 equipment charge + $100/ month	sign fee
Knights Inns	100		•	•	•	$100/room	3%	none	none	4-6% mgt. fee
Magic Key Inns	none					$500	$16.20/room/ year	none	5% earned income	
Quality Inns	none	•	•	•		conversion: $7,500; new: $15,000	3% gross rooms income	1% gross rooms income	1% gross rooms income + 25¢/ booked reservation	none
Quality Royale	none	•	•	•		conversion: $7,500; new: $15,000	3% gross rooms income	1% gross rooms income	1% gross rooms income + 25¢/ booked reservation	none
Ramada Inns	100	•				$20,000	$5.17/room/ month or 3% gross rooms revenue	1.2% gross rooms revenues	$450/ month + 1% gross rooms revenues + 25¢/ transaction	none

Red Carpet Inns Master Hosts	50	•	new: $10,000; conversion: $5,000	2% gross rooms revenue	10¢/room/day	$4/reservation	none
Rodeway Inns International	100	• •	new: $15,000; conversion: $7,500	3% gross rooms revenue	1% gross rooms revenue	$3.75/room/month + .4% gross room sales	sign fee
Scottish Inns	25	•	$30/room; minimum $1,500	1% room revenues	1% room revenues	$150./room/month	none
Sheraton	100	• •	new: $15,000 + $100/room over 150 rooms maximum of $40,000; conversion: $15,000	5%	none	1.6 gross room sales with minimum of $6/room/month and maximum of $11.50/room/month	none
Summit Hotels	300	• •	$50,000	2% gross rooms revenue	2.5% gross rooms revenue	combined with adv. fee	none
Super 8 Motels	20		$15,000	4% gross rooms revenue	1% gross rooms revenue	none	none
TraveLodge International	none		$100/room; $10,000 minimum	2½% gross rooms revenue	3½% gross rooms revenue	combined with adv. fee	none

vide a competitive advantage over both independent properties and those with ineffective affiliations. Naturally, any competitive advantage enhances the business value of the property.

Remember that franchises are not permanent and are usually terminated when the property is sold. The new owners must apply for and be granted a new franchise, which could entail bringing an outdated hostelry up to current chain standards. It may cost several hundred thousand dollars to maintain a franchise affiliation; the appraiser must be sure to consider this factor in determining the property's present value.

Management Contracts

A management contract is an agreement between a management company (operator) and a property owner (investor) whereby the operator assumes complete managerial responsibility for the hostelry. For this service, the operator is paid a fee based on a prescribed formula. The owner has no voice in operational policies, procedures, and day-to-day management. Nevertheless, the owner is financially responsible for the property and must replenish operating capital if necessary. The difference between a management contract and a lease is that under a management contract the residual income (and loss) after payment of all expenses, including the management fee, goes to the owner; a lease requires the residual income (and loss) after payment of rent to go to the tenant, or operator.

Benefits to Investor

Professional management. Management contracts allow the inexperienced investor to participate in the benefits of hostelry ownership without becoming involved in day-to-day management problems. Management companies offer professional talent, proven methods of operation, and relief from most of the operational burden. An owner who contracts with a hostelry chain benefits from the chain's image, reservation system, and advertising programs.

Profitable affiliation. Some chains do not franchise, so the only way an owner can obtain the benefits of a potentially profitable affiliation is through a management contract.

Borrowing power and possible operator investment. Many lenders are more willing to make loans on hostelries that are managed by reputable management companies, rather than by individual operators. Occasionally a management company will pay to obtain a particularly desirable contract. They may invest initial working capital, inventories, or furniture, fixtures, and equipment.

Costs to Investor

Management fees. Unlike franchise fees, management fees are typically negotiated by the investor and the operator. Projected operating results, the expected ratio of food and beverage volume to rooms revenue, services offered by the operator, financial investment of the operator, and the property's desirability may influence the amount of the fee. The fee structure for management contracts is generally determined by: a percentage of a defined gross revenue (usually 3%–8%); a percentage of a defined gross revenue as a basic fee, plus a percentage of a defined operating income as an incentive fee (usually 3%–5% of the gross and 5%–10% of the net); or a percentage of a defined operating income (usually 15%–25%).

From the investor's point of view, a fee structure based on a percentage of the operating profit is more desirable than one based on a percentage of gross revenue. Because the investor receives only the residual income after all expenses have been paid, a fee structure that provides an incentive to maximize revenue and minimize costs would be the logical choice.

Required facilities and standards. Management companies require that the properties they operate meet certain physical specifications pertaining to size, layout, design, and decor. Operators actively participate in the planning of new hostelries and the renovation of existing ones. The investor must provide sufficient funds to maintain the property properly and to replace short-lived items periodically.

Benefits to Operator

Inexpensive expansion with quality control. Like franchises, hotel chains can expand with a low capital investment and still keep the quality control of in-house management.

Good profit potential. Management contracts offer good potential for profit, especially with high-volume operations. Because the owner is responsible for all expenses, the financial risk to the operator is minimal.

Costs to Operator

Management services. In addition to providing the standard franchise services of a reservation system and chain advertising, the operator employs a staff of regional managers, supervisors, and specialists in areas such as food and beverage service, accounting, marketing, and engineering.

The quality of the management provided by a professional hotel company varies depending on the chain and on the individual property. The appraiser should thoroughly evaluate management's effectiveness to determine whether current operating results indicate competent supervision. The assumption of competent management is discussed in a subsequent section.

Internal Expansion

Some of the growth in hostelry chains between 1970 and 1980 can be attributed to internal expansion. The availability of capital allowed chains to construct new facilities and purchase existing properties. In many instances, chains were buying their own franchises.

Future of Chains

Hotel-motel chains should continue to dominate the supply of transient accommodations; in fact, their market share will probably increase. The 1980 recession curtailed new development, and recent chain expansion is largely the result of reshuffling franchises on existing properties and increasing the number of management contracts. In the future, there should be more management contracts, less franchising, and a further reduction in the number of chain-owned properties.

Independent Hotels and Motels

The number of nonaffiliated hotels and motels has been rapidly declining. Most of the properties in this group are small "mom and pop" motels constructed during the 1950s and 1960s. Most of these hostelries are now on the brink of external obsolescence due to the proliferation of larger, more modern chain operations. New budget chains have hurt independent lodging facilities deeply.

The major disadvantage facing most independent hostelries is the lack of identity. Travelers usually prefer a known product that offers services, accommodations, and rates within an expected range. An independent can create its own identity with massive advertising campaigns, a highly visible and convenient location, a large number of repeat customers, or facilities and services of superior quality.

When valuing an independent hotel or motel, the appraiser should be aware of the additional risk factors involved. Unless circumstances clearly indicate that the independent can overcome the competitive disadvantages, the market will usually reflect either a lower stabilized net income or a higher capitalization rate for this property.

Types of Lodging Facilities

Hotels and motels are designed and located to attract one or more specific markets. The five basic types of lodging facilities are: commercial, convention, resort, highway, and airport lodgings. Although the transient market overlaps all five types of facilities in varying degrees, commercial, convention and resort hostelries tend to be market-oriented, while highway and airport properties are location-oriented.

Commercial hostelry. This facility caters primarily to business people and is generally near concentrations of industrial and office buildings, restaurants, and entertainment outlets. Facilities typically include small meeting and conference rooms, a medium-sized restaurant, a lounge, and a small swimming pool. Because occupancy at commercial hostelries usually declines on weekends, many new properties have installed elaborate recreational amenities (e.g., year-round swimming pools, tennis courts, and health clubs) in an attempt to capture weekend family business. Commercial hostelries rarely attract convention or resort patronage.

Convention hostelry. Specifically designed to handle large groups and functions, facilities in a convention hostelry include one or more large ballrooms and additional break-out rooms for meetings and conferences. Exhibit space and special sample rooms are also popular. Convention properties typically require extensive restaurant and lounge facilities and efficient room service. A convention hostelry may attract commercial travelers, but rarely resort patronage unless it is located at a destination resort area.

Resort hostelry. Usually located in a resort area, the amenities typically found in a resort property include meeting and conference rooms; a medium-to-large restaurant (depending on the dining plan—American or European—and the availability of outside restaurants); lounge and entertainment rooms; and recreational facilities such as a swimming pool, golf, tennis, skiing, ice skating, and boating. A resort hotel is either group-oriented, with convention-type meeting space, or individual-oriented, with minimal meeting room facilities. Resorts rarely attract commercial patronage.

Highway hostelry. This facility offers a convenient location, usually adjacent to a major interstate, and normally attracts commercial patronage during the week. Depending on traffic patterns, it may also serve as an intermediate stopover for weekend travelers and vacationers. Facilities are similar to those offered at a commercial hostelry, but meeting space is less important. Good visibility and convenient access are vital. Highway properties rarely attract convention patronage.

Airport hostelry. Situated near a commercial airport, an airport hostelry caters to both commercial travelers and small groups. Occupancy is also derived from airline crews and passengers whose flights have been delayed. Several small meeting rooms, attractive suites, sample rooms, a restaurant, and a lounge are typical facilities. The airport hostelry rarely attracts large conventions or resort travelers.

Classes of Lodging Facilities

Each type of lodging facility can be classified according to its rate structure and the quality of its facilities. The designations are luxury, standard, and economy.

To determine the class of a lodging facility, consider the relative rate structure as compared to other hotels and motels in the area. Geographic area greatly affects class. For example, a luxury property in Austin, Texas might be considered a standard-rate hotel in New York City. Of equal importance are the type of facilities, the physical condition, and the quality of service. Again, class is relative and should not be determined on a nationwide basis. Some of the factors to be considered when determining the class of a lodging facility are: the quality of the architecture, construction, and decor; the allocation of space; the size of public areas and guest rooms; the quality of mechanical equipment; the quality and type of amenities; the operator or franchise image; the caliber of service; and the quality of food and beverages offered.

After all the properties within a given market area have been studied with respect to rates, facilities, and service, classes can be assigned. Hostelries with the highest rates and best service and facilities are designated as luxury class. Medium-rate properties with good facilities and service are considered standard. Lower-rate hostelries with fair to poor facilities and service comprise the economy class.

To understand the degree of competitiveness between the various types and classes of hostelries, the analyst must be familiar with the macro supply of transient accommodations. This information is used to analyze the accommodations within a defined market area—that is, the micro supply.

Micro Supply

Another term for the micro supply of hotels and motels is competition. The previous section has described how to identify the type of lodging (commercial, convention, resort, highway, or airport) and how to classify properties according to their relative rate structure and the quality of their facilities and service (luxury, standard, or economy). Compiling this information for all the hostelries within the appraised property's market area allows the analyst to weigh the relative competitiveness of each property and to estimate how much of the market demand it is likely to attract. The market share is expressed as a percentage, so the total of all competing properties, including the subject, should equal 100% for each source of visitation.

The actual procedure for allocating the area's total market demand to each of the lodging facilities can be accomplished by an analysis of customer preference items or an analysis of competitive indexes. Just as the two build-up approaches quantify an area's demand by determining the actual generators of transient visitation, and the demand indicated by all lodging activity, the two approaches for allocating total demand to individual properties concentrate on the nature of the visitation and the characteristics of the lodging activity. Due to these similarities, the demand allocation based on an analysis of customer preference items is generally used in conjunction with the build-up approach based on an analysis of demand generators; demand allocation based on an analysis of competitive indexes is usually applied in conjunction with the build-up approach based on an analysis of lodging activity. Each of the demand approaches will be described in detail and demonstrated in the case study that follows this chapter.

Demand Allocation Based on an Analysis of Customer Preference Items

The demand allocation based on an analysis of customer preference items generally begins after the build-up approach based on an analysis of demand generators has been completed. Once the final market area is defined and the sources of transient visitation are identified, surveyed, and quantified, this approach can be applied. The first step is to identify the area's competing lodging facilities by type and class. As described previously, hotels and motels can be categorized as commercial, convention, resort, highway, and airport. Each type is further divided into three classes—luxury, standard, and economy. Interviews with area hotel managers and a review of published room rate information can facilitate this categorizing procedure.

The second step is to allocate the demand from each source of visitation among the subject property and the other area hostelries based on the characteristics of the demand and the relative competitiveness of the supply. This allocation is based on customer preference items.

Choosing a hotel or motel is actually a complex procedure. Several customer preference items influence the selection of a particular lodging facility.

Hotel and motel patrons can be grouped into three basic categories, according to the primary purpose of these trips.

1. Commercial—business travel, either alone or in groups of fewer than five.
2. Convention—gathering for groups, meetings, lectures, seminars, or visiting trade shows.
3. Vacation—recreation, sightseeing, or visiting friends and relatives.

A further breakdown of each group reveals customer reaction to room rates;

economy accommodations will appeal to highly rate-conscious travelers, standard rates draw moderately rate-conscious customers, and individuals who regard rates of little importance will choose luxury lodgings.

Combining the three customer categories with the three rate reactions produces nine types of guests (e.g., commercial-economy rate, convention-standard rate, vacation-luxury rate). Each customer preference item represents a specific characteristic guests consider in choosing one hostelry over another. Six of the most prominent customer preference items are:

Item	Consideration
Price	Economic
Travel distance	Time, convenience
Quality of facilities	Comfort, status, atmosphere
Amenities	Comfort, status, recreation, convenience, atmosphere
Management	Comfort, atmosphere
Image	Status

Ranking the six customer preference items in order of importance establishes a basis for predicting how guests will choose among several lodging facilities in a particular market area. Table 3.5 ranks the preference items listed above.

For example, an economy-minded commercial traveler will drive further (more travel time) to stay at a hostelry offering favorable prices. This same traveler will probably select a property with quality facilities over a lower-quality hostelry with more amenities. Similarly, a standard-rate vacation traveler places primary emphasis on a hotel's amenities and price, regarding travel time as a secondary consideration.

A market share distribution can be made by carefully analyzing the preferences and characteristics of the typical transient traveler visiting the market area and matching these selection criteria with the competitive hotel-motel supply. Each competitive property should receive a portion of the overall market share; the size of the portion will depend on the property's relative competitiveness and its ability to attract a particular type of traveler. The sum of all the allocated market shares for each generator of demand should equal 100%.

The number of room nights captured by an individual property can be calculated by multiplying each generator's percentage market share allocated to the hostelry by the total number of room nights quantified in the build-up approach based on an analysis of demand generators. The total of all allocated room nights from all generators of demand is divided by the property's room count

Table 3.5. Customer Preference Items

	Economy	Standard	Luxury
Commercial			
Most important	1 Price	Travel time	Image
	2 Travel time	Quality	Quality
	3 Quality	Price	Management
	4 Management	Image	Travel
	5 Amenities	Management	Amenities
Least important	6 Image	Amenities	Price
Convention			
Most important	1 Price	Amenities	Image
	2 Amenities	Quality	Amenities
	3 Quality	Price	Quality
	4 Management	Image	Management
	5 Travel time	Management	Travel time
Least important	6 Image	Travel time	Price
Vacation			
Most important	1 Price	Amenities	Image
	2 Amenities	Quality	Amenities
	3 Quality	Price	Quality
	4 Management	Image	Management
	5 Travel time	Management	Travel time
Least important	6 Image	Travel time	Price

Source: Hospitality Valuation Services, Inc.

multiplied by 365 to produce the estimate of occupancy. The following example illustrates how customer preference information can be used to allocate the room nights generated by a source of visitation among the subject property and all competing lodging facilities.

Example

The subject property is a proposed commercial, nationally franchised motor hotel offering typical amenities at standard rates. There are three competing lodging facilities within the market area. Competition A is a luxury rate, commercial-type, nationally franchised hotel with high-quality facilities and a good image. Competition B is a standard rate, commercial-type, nationally franchised motel with good-quality facilities. Competition C is an economy rate, commercial-type, independent motel with fair facilities.

The home office of a prominent national manufacturing company is one

Table 3.6.   Estimate of Out-of-Town Visitation

Type of Visitor	Typical Rate Preference	Estimated Total Yearly Room Nights	Facilities Currently Used
Corporate executives	Luxury	3,700	Competition A
Middle management	Standard	5,000	Competition B
Visiting salespeople	Standard and economy	7,500	Competition B and C

generator of transient visitation within the market area. Based on a survey of various department heads, an estimate of the firm's out-of-town visitation is developed as shown in Table 3.6.

The property being appraised will be constructed approximately eight minutes by car from this source of visitation. The other properties also have good locations. Competition A is 15 minutes from the source of visitation, Competition B is 12 minutes away, and Competition C is 10 minutes away.

The allocation of room nights generated by this source of visitation is based on the assumption that most corporate executives will continue to travel the extra seven minutes to stay at Competition A because it offers the best image and quality. Some may use the new facility if Competition A is full or inclement weather or some other factor makes a closer location more desirable. The allocation of room nights based on customer preference items for this market segment is shown in Table 3.7.

Middle-management visitors will choose either the new property or Competition B. Because the property being appraised will be newer and four driving

Table 3.7   Allocation Of Room Nights for Corporate Executives

Lodging Facility	Estimated Market Share	Room Nights
New property	5%	185
Competition A	94%	3,478
Competition B	1%	37
Competition C	0%	0

minutes closer, it may capture a sizable portion of this market. Competition B may respond by upgrading its facilities and/or lowering its rates. If there are minimal differences in travel time, the quality of facilities, and price, image and management could be deciding factors. The allocation of room nights for this market segment is shown in Table 3.8.

Economy-minded visiting salespeople will probably drive the extra two minutes to take advantage of the low rate offered by Competition C. Standard-rate salespeople, like the middle-management visitors, must choose between the new property and Competition B. The allocation of room nights for this market segment is shown in Table 3.9.

The total demand from this particular source of visitation allocated to the appraised property is 5,685 room nights. This represents 185 room nights for corporate executives, 3,250 for middle management, and 2,250 for visiting salespeople. If the subject contains 150 guest units, the 5,685 room nights would equate to approximately 10% of occupancy.

Quantifying the total demand generated by all sources of visitation and allo-

**Table 3.8   Allocation of Room Nights
for Middle Management**

Lodging Facility	Estimated Market Share	Room Nights
New Property	65%	3,250
Competition A	1%	50
Competition B	29%	1,450
Competition C	5%	250

**Table 3.9   Allocation of Room Nights
for Visiting Salespeople**

Lodging Facility	Estimated Market Share	Room Nights
New property	30%	2,250
Competition A	1%	75
Competition B	24%	1,800
Competition C	45%	3,375

cating the room nights among the subject and competing properties is accomplished as described above. The result is an estimate of occupancy—the total number of all room nights allocated to the appraised property divided by the property's total available rooms per year:

$$\frac{\text{Total number of room nights}}{\text{Number of rooms} \times 365} = \text{Estimated occupancy}$$

Demand Allocation Based on an Analysis of Competitive Indexes

The demand allocation based on an analysis of competitive indexes is usually employed in conjunction with the build-up approach based on an analysis of lodging activity. The approach assumes that the accommodated room night demand for each competitive hostelry has been determined and allocated among the appropriate market segments. To calculate new market shares for area hostelries when another lodging facility has been added to the market, a rating factor known as the competitive index is used.

The competitive index shows how well each property in the market area competes for a particular market segment. The index represents the number of times each year one room is occupied by one type of traveler (i.e., commercial, convention, vacationer); stated somewhat differently, it is the number of room nights actually accommodated per year, per room, per market segment. The competitive index is calculated by dividing one competitive property's annual, accommodated room night demand for an identified market segment by the property's room count.

Example

Assume that the local market consists of three competitive lodging facilities. Hotel A has 300 rooms and market research indicates that, over the last 12 months, it has operated at 80% occupancy with 50% of its total accommodated demand coming from the commercial segment. The number of accommodated room nights per year for Hotel A is calculated:

300 rooms $\times$ 365 days $\times$ .80 $\times$ .50 = 43,800 commercial room nights

Hotel A's commercial segment competitive index is:

$$\frac{43,800}{300} = 146 \text{ competitive index}$$

The data and competitive indexes for Hotels B and C are presented in the following chart:

Hotel	Number of Rooms	Yearly Occupancy	Percent Commercial Demand	Commercial Room Nights Per Year	Commercial Competitive Index	Fair Share	Commercial Market Share	Penetration Factor
A	300	80%	50%	43,800	146	44.5%	52.2%	117%
B	250	75	30	20,531	82	37.0	24.5	66
C	125	95	45	19,505	156	18.5	23.3	125
Total	675			83,836		100.0%	100.0%	

The competitive indexes show that Hotel C is somewhat more competitive than Hotel A in the commercial segment, and that both Hotels A and C are significantly more competitive than Hotel B. The average market share or fair share is calculated by dividing each hotel's room count by the total number of rooms within the market ($300 \div 675 = 44.5\%$ fair share for Hotel A). Thus, if Hotel A were to capture its average or fair share of the commercial market, it would receive 44.5% of the demand. In fact, Hotel A is capturing 52.2% of the commercial market ($43,800 \div 83,836 = 52.2\%$), and is thereby penetrating 117% of its fair share ($52.2 \div 44.5 = 117\%$). Hotel C is the most competitive property for commercial demand, with a competitive index of 156 and a penetration factor of 125%. However, it has only 125 rooms, so it captures 23.3% of the commercial market, which is the smallest share.

Now, assume that Hotel D enters the market, adding 200 rooms to the total supply. Market research and analysis of its location, amenities, management, and other competitive characteristics indicate that Hotel D will be more competitive than Hotel B for commercial demand, but somewhat less competitive than Hotel A. The competitive index for Hotel D should fall somewhere between 82 and 146, but probably closer to the 146. It was also anticipated that Hotel D will become more competitive during its first two years of operation. Therefore, based on market research and judgmental considerations, the competitive index for Hotel D in Year 1 is estimated as 120, and the index for Year 2 is 130.

Because this new property has entered the market, the commercial demand must be reallocated among four hotels and the market shares and commercial room nights captured must be recalculated. The charts on the following page illustrate this procedure.

The room count of each property is multiplied by its respective commercial competitive index to yield the "market share adjustor." This number is a hypothetical allocation of the area's room nights, assuming that Hotel D creates a new demand equal to its room count times its competitive index. The purpose of this intermediate step is to calculate each property's new market share by dividing the market share adjustor for one property by the total market share adjustor for all four properties:

Hotel A Market Share—Year 1

$$\frac{43,800}{107,836} = 40.6\%$$

When Hotel D opens, the commercial market share of Hotel A drops from 52.2% to 40.6%, due to market dilution from the additional 200 rooms. Because the opening of Hotel D is not expected to increase the actual number of commer-

Year 1

Hotel	Number of Rooms	Commercial Competitive Index	Market Share Adjustor	Commercial Market Share	Commercial Room Nights Captured	Fair Share	Penetration Factor
A	300	146	43,800	40.6%	34,052	34.3%	118%
B	250	82	20,531	19.0	15,962	28.6	67
C	125	156	19,505	18.1	15,164	14.3	127
D	200	120	24,000	22.3	18,658	22.8	97
Total	875		107,836	100.0%	83,836	100.0%	

Year 2

Hotel	Number of Rooms	Commercial Competitive Index	Market Share Adjustor	Commercial Market Share	Commercial Room Nights Captured	Fair Share	Penetration Factor
A	300	146	43,800	39.9%	33,432	34.3%	116%
B	250	82	20,531	18.7	15,671	28.6	65
C	125	156	19,505	17.8	14,888	14.3	124
D	200	130	26,000	23.6	19,845	22.8	104
Total	875		109,836	100.0%	83,836	100.0%	

cial room nights accommodated within the market area, the current demand of 83,836 must be reallocated among the four hotels. This is done by multiplying the recalculated market share by the room night demand:

Hotel A Commercial Room Night Captured—Year 1

40.6% × 83,836 = 34,052 room nights

The additional 200 rooms also lowers the fair share of Hotel A from 44.5% to 34.3%. The penetration of Hotel A, however, increases from 117% to 118% of its fair share; this happens because the new rooms of Hotel D that are diluting the market are less competitive in Year 1. All three of the existing hotels show gains in their penetration factors in Year 1. When Hotel D reaches a stabilized level of operation in Year 2, its market share will exceed its fair share and its penetration factor will increase; at this time, the other three competitive hotels will begin to feel the added competitiveness of Hotel D. The penetration factors for all three existing hotels will decline to levels below those of the initial year.

The key to this example is the use of the competitive index in the calculation of a property's market share. This unique factor enables the analyst to compare many competitive aspects of a lodging establishment on an index basis, regardless of the property's room count or changes in the overall supply of accommodations. The example assumes that the relative competitiveness of the existing three hotels remains constant, while the new hotel becomes more competitive. This is generally the situation experienced by established lodging facilities operating at stabilized occupancies. However, if market research indicates that any of these properties is becoming more or less competitive, its index can be modified upward or downward.

The example illustrates demand allocation based on an analysis of competitive indexes for the commercial market segment. The same procedure could be used to allocate group and meeting demand, vacationer demand, or any other quantifiable source of visitation within the market area. The ultimate result is a total room night estimate for the subject property that can be converted into a projection of occupancy by dividing the total projected room nights by the number of available room nights. This result is shown in the following table.

In actual practice, analysts generally use a combination of customer preference items and competitive indexes to allocate room night demand among competitive lodging facilities. Both approaches call for judgments on a wide variety of competitive factors. Experience in hostelry operations and analysis can prove invaluable in determining the most probable sequence of events.

Applying the four approaches for quantifying and allocating room night demand produces an estimate of future occupancy levels for the subject prop-

Hotel D—Projected Room Nights

	Year 1	Year 2
Commercial	18,658	19,845
Group and meeting	26,270	27,560
Vacationer	9,420	10,185
Total	54,348	57,590
Available room nights:		
200 × 365	73,000	73,000
Projected Occupancy	74.4%	78.9%

erty. These levels may indicate one stablized occupancy or a series of occupancies in the future.

Average Rate

The estimate of occupancy is based on an assumed rate structure that reflects the market or economic rent for comparable facilities in the area. The average rate per occupied room describes an overall rate structure in a single number; it is the weighted average of rooms sold at the single rate, double rate, commercial rate, and so forth. The average rate per occupied room for an existing facility is calculated by dividing the property's gross rooms revenue by the number of rooms occupied for a given period of time:

$$\frac{\text{Gross rooms revenue}}{\text{Number of rooms occupied}} = \text{Average rate per occupied room}$$

The primary objective in examining both macro and micro demand relationships is to determine how a new lodging facility will fit into the local market. The resulting projected occupancy and average rate measure market acceptance in numerical terms and forms the basis for estimating the property's gross room revenue. The formula is:

Percentage occupancy × average rate × number of rooms × 365 = gross room revenue

The gross room revenue represents a major profit center for hostelries and provides a basis for comparing many important operating ratios. Its use in valuing lodging facilities is demonstrated in subsequent chapters.

The following case study concerns the Sheraton Inn property that was described in Chapter 2.

Case Study

Micro Supply

The micro supply, or competition, affects the allocation of potential demand (room nights) among the subject Sheraton Inn and other area lodging facilities. There are three steps in allocating the area demand and projecting the subject's market share:

1. Identify competing lodging facilities by type and class.
2. Allocate the projected area room night demand to the subject property based on an analysis of customer preference items or competitive indexes.
3. Convert the number of room nights allocated to the subject into an estimate of occupancy.

Identifying Competing Lodging Facilities

Five existing motels and one under construction are located within the market area of the property being appraised or close enough to one or more local sources of visitation to be considered competitive. The following descriptions of the competitive lodging facilities were obtained by personal inspection and interviews with management.

Facility	Number of Units	Type and Class	Average Rate	Occupancy
A. Days Inn	150	commercial economy	$29.00	90%
B. Suncrest Motel	135	commercial economy	33.00	75
C. Holiday Inn	220	commercial standard	40.00	85
D. Hilton Hotel	300	commercial group luxury	48.00	80
E. Ramada Inn	185	commercial standard	38.00	80
F. Best Western (under construction)	170	commercial standard	40.00	—

Days Inn is an economy-class facility situated on the southwestern corner of I-495 and Route 110, directly across the street from the Sheraton. Constructed approximately four years ago, the property has an 80-seat coffee shop, but no cocktail lounge or meeting space. It enjoys the highest occupancy in the area, attracting strong weekday commercial patronage and a large portion of the weekend vacationer trade. The $29.00 average rate is the lowest of all the competitive properties. The Days Inn franchise is one of the strongest budget affiliations available, as its excellent occupancy level demonstrates.

Suncrest Motel is located approximately four miles southeast of the Sheraton on the Southern State Parkway, one exit east of Route 110. This 135-room property was constructed 15 years ago and currently suffers from extensive physical deterioration and functional obsolescence. It offers a 100-seat restaurant, a 125-seat lounge, and two meeting rooms seating 150 and 50. Although the Suncrest has no national franchise, it was one of the first motels in the area; a loyal following of commercial customers allows it to maintain a 75% occupancy with an economy-level average rate of $33.00.

Holiday Inn is situated directly across I-495 from the subject property. This locally popular lodging facility has a good mix of commercial and meeting patronage and enjoys an occupancy of 85%. Its average rate is $40.00. Constructed eight years ago, the standard-class Holiday Inn has a 150-seat restaurant, a 130-seat lounge, and three meeting rooms seating 30, 30, and 250. The property is well-maintained and the chain's national reservation system is one of the best in the industry.

Hilton Hotel is adjacent to the convention center, approximately ¼ mile south of the Sheraton on Route 110. This 300-room, meeting- and convention-oriented hotel derives a substantial portion of its occupancy from visitors to the convention center. Built six years ago, the Hilton offers a 150-seat rooftop gourmet restaurant, a 200-seat, all-purpose restaurant, a 150-seat disco, and a 40-seat lobby lounge. Its extensive meeting and banquet facilities include five rooms seating 50 each, two rooms seating 100 each, and a ballroom with a capacity 600. The Hilton identification is world-renowned for commercial and convention travelers; its luxury-class image is consistent with a $48.00 average rate and an 80% occupancy level.

Ramada Inn is located one exit east of the Sheraton on the north side of I-495. This ten-year-old motel has a 130-seat restaurant, a 150-seat lounge, two 50-seat meeting rooms, and a banquet room with a capacity of 150. The property is in good condition for its age because very little maintenance has been deferred. Its national franchise with Ramada Inns, Inc. helps maintain a strong 80% occupancy with a standard-class average rate of $38.00. The Ramada is popular with commercial travelers and attracts some meeting patronage.

Best Western Motel, currently under construction, is expected to be fully operational within one year. Located immediately north of the Ramada Inn, it will have 170 rooms, a 130-seat restaurant, a lounge seating 60, and meeting rooms with capacities of 30, 30, and 200. The developers are planning to make this a standard-class property and they project that the average rate will approach $40.00 in today's dollars. The Best Western chain is the largest in the U.S. and is highly recognized by travelers.

Allocating Demand to the Competing Lodging Facilities

In this case study, the area demand will be allocated using both the demand allocation based on an analysis of customer preference items and demand allocation based on an analysis of competitive indexes. Although the projected annual area room night demand quantified by the build-up approach based on an analysis of demand generators and the build-up approach based on an analysis of lodging activity produce almost identical results, this case study will pair the results of the demand generator approach with the customer preference allocation and the lodging activity approach with the competitive index allocation. In normal fieldwork, these four approaches are typically matched in this manner.

Demand Allocation Based on an Analysis of Customer Preference Items

The proposed 200-room Sheraton Inn will be a commercial-type motor inn classified as upper-standard to luxury. Its facilities will compare to those offered by the Holiday Inn, Ramada Inn, and Best Western; they will be somewhat more extensive than the Days Inn and Suncrest Motel. The Hilton Hotel has more meeting and banquet space, but the Sheraton will offer the same class of service and facilities. The three primary market segments ranked customer preference items for standard-to-luxury class lodging facilities as follows:

Priority	Commercial	Meeting & Convention	Vacationer
1	Image	Image	Image
2	Quality	Amenities	Amenities
3	Management	Quality	Quality
4	Travel time	Management	Management
5	Amenities	Travel time	Travel time
6	Price	Price	Price

Based on these customer preference items and the preceding description of competing hostelries, the following procedure would be used to allocate the room night demand from the sources of visitation, which have been quantified using the build-up approach based on demand generators. The allocation will be made separately for each of the three market segments—commercial, meeting and convention, and vacationers.

Commercial Demand. *Office park (#1).* This high-quality office park has many highly successful tenants and attracts first-class travelers who now patronize the better-quality hotels such as the Hilton, Holiday Inn, and Ramada Inn. Because the office park is very near the subject site, it is expected to be a major contributor of transient visitation.

Based on the quality orientation of the typical visitor to this park and the convenient location of the subject property, the Sheraton should capture 25% of this demand in its first year of operation, i.e., Year 3 of the room night projection. As the Sheraton becomes established in the marketplace, its share of this demand source should grow; research indicates that market shares of 28% in development Year 4 (the second year of operation) and 30% in development Year 5 (the third year of operation) are reasonable. The following chart illustrates the weekly room night demand that the Sheraton is expected to capture from the office park during its first three years of operation.

Operational Year	Commercial Room Nights Per Week	Percent Capture	Room Nights Allocated to Sheraton
1	600	25%	150
2	600	28	168
3	600	30	180

Aerospace firm (#2). Many visitors to this source are government employees on limited expense per diems. Although a few stay at the nearby Ramada Inn, most prefer the lower-priced Days Inn. Very few stay at the Holiday Inn or Hilton Hotel. With Best Western opening next year adjacent to the aerospace firm and the limited budgets of most of the transient visitors, the Sheraton will probably not capture many room nights from this source. The subject will be the upper-standard-to-luxury property closest to the aerospace firm, so it should attract some of the higher echelon management visitors. The projected commercial capture of 5% represents 11 room nights per week.

Operational Year	Commercial Room Nights Per Week	Percent Capture	Room Nights Allocated to Sheraton
1	220	5%	11
2	220	5	11
3	220	5	11

Communications firm (#3). The typical visitor to this demand generator is a high-level salesperson whose expense account allows him or her to stay at better-quality lodging facilities such as the Hilton Hotel, Holiday Inn, or Ramada Inn. The Sheraton will be nearby, and its quality accommodations and amenities should be quite competitive. Given the Holiday Inn's proximity to this source and the competition from the Hilton Hotel, the Sheraton Inn is expected to capture 15% of the communications firm's transient commercial demand.

Operational Year	Commercial Room Nights Per Week	Percent Capture	Room Nights Allocated to Sheraton
1	200	15%	30
2	200	15	30
3	200	15	30

Aircraft engine firm (#4). Interviews with local hotel managers indicate that most visitors to this firm tend to be somewhat price-conscious; they generally use the area's economy-type lodging facilities such as Days Inn and Suncrest Motel. However, travelers to the aircraft engine firm typically arrive via I-495 and pass the Sheraton on Route 110, so a 10% capture appears possible.

Operational Year	Commercial Room Nights Per Week	Percent Capture	Room Nights Allocated to Sheraton
1	286	10%	28
2	300	10	30
3	315	10	32

High technology research park (#5). The typical visitor to these research

84

firms is a well-educated, science-oriented person traveling on an expense account who has little price sensitivity for quality accommodations. Most of the transient visitation generated by this park are currently captured by the Hilton Hotel, with the overflow going to the Holiday Inn and Ramada Inn. Because the Sheraton Inn will be immediately adjacent to this demand generator and its facilities will be comparable to the Hilton's, it should attract 26% of this demand in the first year of operation, 28% in Year 2, and 30% in Year 3.

Operational Year	Commercial Room Nights Per Week	Percent Capture	Room Nights Allocated to Sheraton
1	750	26%	195
2	750	28	210
3	750	30	225

Industrial park (#6). A written survey used to quantify the demand from this source indicates that most of its transient visitation are somewhat price-sensitive and use the nearby Days Inn and the Suncrest Motel. The Sheraton Inn will probably attract only 5% of this demand.

Operational Year	Commercial Room Nights Per Week	Percent Capture	Room Nights Allocated to Sheraton
1	200	5%	10
2	200	5	10
3	200	5	10

Office district (#7). The type of traveler visiting this office district is similar to the quality-conscious individual identified in the office park (#1) section. The office district, however, is located on the fringe of the market area, almost 10 miles west of the Sheraton. A deluxe Hyatt Hotel, which is five miles west of the office district and outside the subject's market area, appears to be the first choice of travelers visiting these offices. Although the Sheraton's facilities will be as good as those of the Hyatt, the subject could not reasonably expect to draw more than 5% of this demand because of the driving distance involved.

Operational Year	Commercial Room Nights Per Week	Percent Capture	Room Nights Allocated to Sheraton
1	441	5%	22
2	463	5	23
3	486	5	24

New industrial park (#8). Like the visitors to the industrial park (#6), most of the visitors to this part are expected to be price-sensitive salespersons preferring economy properties such as Days Inn and Suncrest Motel. A 5% capture of this demand generator is a reasonable projection.

Operational Year	Commercial Room Nights Per Week	Percent Capture	Room Nights Allocated to Sheraton
1	338	5%	16
2	395	5	20
3	452	5	23

Regional mall (#9). Although commercial visitors to a shopping mall tend to be somewhat price-sensitive, the Sheraton and Holiday Inns are the closest lodging facilities and should equally share 20% of this demand, i.e., each will receive 10%.

Operational Year	Commercial Room Nights Per Week	Percent Capture	Room Nights Allocated to Sheraton
1	115	10%	11
2	120	10	12
3	125	10	13

State hospital (#10). The market survey of hospital visitors shows an extremely price-sensitive demand. The Sheraton will probably not draw more than 1% of this market.

86

Operational Year	Commercial Room Nights Per Week	Percent Capture	Room Nights Allocated to Sheraton
1	95	1%	1
2	95	1	1
3	95	1	1

Unaccountable Demand. After the 10 demand generators were quantified using the build-up approach based on demand generators, a 20% factor was included as unaccountable demand. The Sheraton will have approximately 15% of the rooms within the market area, so its fair share of the unaccountable demand would be 15%. A 10% unaccountable demand capture was considered more appropriate, however, because of the price sensitivity within the market.

Operational Year	Commercial Room Nights Per Week	Percent Capture	Room Nights Allocated to Sheraton
1	650	10%	65
2	669	10	67
3	689	10	69

The accompanying table (see page 88) summarizes the potential commercial demand captured by the Sheraton Inn. Because the room night demand was estimated on a weekly basis, the total must be multiplied by 52 to obtain the yearly commercial room nights for the Sheraton.

Meeting and Convention Demand. *Convention center (#12).* Approximately two-thirds of the convention demand is currently staying at the nearby Hilton Hotel and the Holiday Inn. The Sheraton Inn should be equally competitive and pick up 25% of this market. A 20% capture is estimated in Year 1, increasing to 25% in Years 2 and 3.

Operational Year	Meeting & Convention Room Nights Per Year	Percent Capture	Room Nights Allocated to Sheraton
1	48,500	20%	9,700
2	50,100	25	12,525
3	51,700	25	12,925

Potential Commercial Demand Captured By Sheraton

Source	Year 1			Year 2			Year 3		
	Room Nights Demand Per Week	Percent Capture	Room Nights Captured	Room Nights Demand Per Week	Percent Capture	Room Nights Captured	Room Nights Demand Per Week	Percent Capture	Room Nights Captured
Office park	600	25%	150	600	28%	168	600	30%	180
Aerospace firm	220	5	11	220	5	11	220	5	11
Communications firm	200	15	30	200	15	30	200	15	30
Aircraft engine firm	286	10	28	300	10	30	315	10	32
Research park	750	26	197	750	28	211	750	30	223
Industrial park	200	5	10	200	5	10	200	5	10
Office district	441	5	22	463	5	23	486	5	24
New industrial park	338	5	16	395	5	20	452	5	23
Regional mall	115	10	11	120	10	12	125	10	13
State hospital	95	1	1	95	1	1	95	1	1
Unaccountable demand	650	10	65	669	10	67	689	10	69
Total commercial room nights per week			541			583			616
Weeks per year			× 52			× 52			× 52
Total commercial room nights per year			28,132			30,316			32,032

Communications firm (#3). Housing for students attending classes at the communications firm is provided on a contractual basis, with room rate as the determining factor. The Suncrest Motel and Ramada Inn are currently receiving most of this business; it is unlikely that the Sheraton Inn would reduce rates sufficiently to attract the students. Therefore, no capture is anticipated.

Research park (#5). Most meeting and seminar visitors from this source use the Ramada Inn and the Suncrest Motel. Due to price sensitivity, a percent capture for the Sheraton Inn was estimated at 10% in Year 1, 12% in Year 2, and 14% in Year 3.

Operational Year	Meeting & Convention Room Nights Per Year	Percent Capture	Room Nights Allocated to Sheraton
1	9,750	10%	975
2	9,750	12	1,170
3	9,750	14	1,365

Unaccountable demand. The Sheraton is expected to attract its fair share, or 15%, of the unaccountable meeting and convention demand in Year 1, 18% in Year 2, and 22% in Year 3.

Operational Year	Meeting & Convention Room Nights Per Year	Percent Capture	Room Nights Allocated to Sheraton
1	11,737	15%	1,760
2	11,977	18	2,155
3	12,217	21	2,565

The table on page 90 summarizes the potential meeting and convention demand captured by the Sheraton Inn on an annual basis.

Vacationer Demand.   Although the Sheraton Inn will have an excellent location adjacent to I-495, which is the primary vacationer highway, the subject's high-rise structure, luxury rates, and commercial image are generally not attractive to typical vacationers. A somewhat low capture, perhaps 6.75%, is expected in Year

Potential Meeting and Convention Demand Captured by Sheraton

Source	Room Nights Demand Per Year	Year 1 Percent Capture	Room Nights Captured	Room Nights Demand Per Year	Year 2 Percent Capture	Room Nights Captured	Room Nights Demand Per Year	Year 3 Percent Capture	Room Nights Captured
Convention center	48,500	20%	9,700	50,100	25%	12,525	51,700	25%	12,925
Communications firm	20,000	0	0	20,000	0	0	20,000	0	0
Research park	9,750	10	975	9,750	12	1,170	9,750	14	1,365
Unaccountable demand	11,737	15	1,760	11,977	18	2,155	12,217	21	2,565
Total meeting and convention demand per year			12,435			15,850			16,855

1; an increase to 10% is anticipated in Year 2; and 12.3% capture is estimated for Year 3.

Operational Year	Vacationer Room Nights Per Year	Percent Capture	Room Nights Allocated to Sheraton
1	48,679	6.75%	3,285
2	49,155	10.0	4,915
3	49,634	12.3	6,104

The following chart summarizes the number of room nights the Sheraton Inn is expected to capture from the three area market segments during the first three years of operation.

Summary of Room Nights Captured by Sheraton Inn

	Year 1	Year 2	Year 3
Commercial	28,132	30,316	32,032
Meetings and conventions	12,435	15,850	16,855
Vacationers	3,285	4,915	6,104
Total room nights captured	43,852	51,081	54,991

The Sheraton Inn will have 73,000 room nights available each year (200 rooms × 365 days). Based on the summary of room nights captured, the anticipated occupancies for the subject are as follows:

Operational Year	Room Nights Captured	Room Nights Available	Percentage Occupancy
1	43,852	73,000	60%
2	51,081	73,000	70
3	54,991	73,000	75

Demand Allocation Based on Analysis of Competitive Indexes

In the case study in Chapter 2, the room night demand was quantified by the build-up approach based on lodging activity. Using the occupancy rate of each competitive hostelry and the percentage relationship between each market segment and the total demand, the accommodated room night demand for all five competitive properties can be calculated by market segment. The competitive index is derived by dividing the annual accommodated room night demand by each property's room count. The first chart on page 93 shows the competitive indexes for the existing lodging facilities.

Using the location, facilities, management, image, and amenity attributes of the Sheraton Inn, the proper competitive indexes for each market segment can be estimated; the hotel can then be ranked within the overall market and its market share can be calculated. Because the Best Western has no operating history or established level of competitiveness, its competitive indexes must also be estimated.

In general, the various attributes of the Sheraton Inn indicate that it should be highly competitive for meeting and convention demand, moderately competitive in the commercial market, and not very competitive in the vacationer market.

Looking first at the commercial segment, where the competitive indexes of the existing facilities range from 131 to 246, the Sheraton's facilities appear similar to those of the Holiday Inn and Ramada Inn. The subject's locational features are almost identical to the Holiday Inn's, and its rate structure will be comparable to the Hilton.

Based on these factors, the Sheraton's commercial competitive index should increase over the first three years of operation and approach the levels attained by the Holiday Inn and Ramada Inn. The estimated commercial competitive index for the Sheraton Inn is 155 for Year 1, 165 for Year 2, and 170 for Year 3.

The Best Western is expected to attract fewer commercial travelers because it is somewhat removed from the concentration of commercial activity. Its competitive indexes are projected at 130, 140, and 150 for the first three years of its operation.

Figure 3.1 shows the projected commercial competitive indexes for each of the lodging facilities in the local market.

The excellent meeting facilities of the Sheraton and its good image in the meeting and convention market should give the subject a competitive index higher than those of the Holiday Inn and Ramada Inn. Because the Hilton Hotel has the key convention location adjacent to the convention center, the Sheraton's meeting and convention competitive index should be somewhat lower than the Hilton's. The estimated meeting and convention competitive index for the Sheraton Inn is 70 for Year 1, 95 for Year 2, and 100 for Year 3.

Rapid index growth is normal in the meeting and convention market be-

Competitive Indexes—Existing Lodging Facilities

Hotel	Room Count	Accommodated Room Nights			Competitive Index		
		Commercial	Meetings & Conventions	Vacationers	Commercial	Meetings & Conventions	Vacationers
Days Inn	150	36,956	—	12,319	246	—	82
Suncrest Motel	135	22,174	7,391	7,391	164	55	55
Holiday Inn	220	37,540	20,477	10,238	171	93	47
Hilton Inn	300	39,420	39,420	8,760	131	131	29
Ramada Inn	185	32,412	13,505	8,103	175	73	44

Market Share Calculations—Commercial Segment

	Operational Year 1 Development Year 3				Operational Year 2 Development Year 4			
	Index	# of Rooms	Market Share Adjustor	Percent Market Share	Index	# of Rooms	Market Share Adjustor	Percent Market Share
Days Inn	246	150	36,900	16.55%	246	150	36,900	16.28
Suncrest Motel	164	135	22,140	9.93	164	135	22,140	9.76
Holiday Inn	171	220	37,620	16.82	171	220	37,620	16.54
Hilton Hotel	131	300	39,300	17.65	131	300	39,300	17.37
Ramada Inn	175	185	32,375	14.51	175	185	32,375	14.28
Best Western	140	170	23,800	10.66	150	170	25,500	11.23
Sheraton Inn (subject)	155	200	31,000	13.88	165	200	33,000	14.54
Total			223,135	100.00			226,835	100.00

Figure 3.1   Competitive Index—Commercial Segment

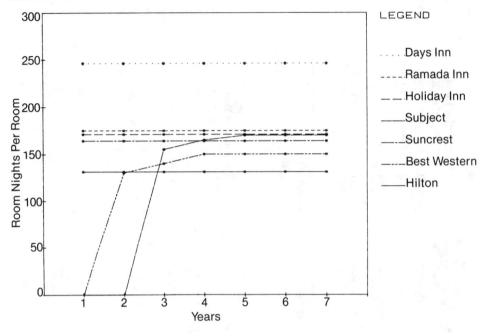

Source: Hospitality Valuation Services, Inc.

cause groups tend to reserve their hotels several years in advance, and it generally takes a newer property some time before it can enter the cycle.

The Best Western is expected to be moderately competitive in this market with indexes of 30, 40, and 60 for its first three years.

Figure 3.2 shows the projected meeting and convention competitive indexes for each of the lodging facilities within the local market.

The Sheraton Inn is not expected to attract a strong vacationer demand because of its price, facilities, and commercial image. It is expected to be somewhat more competitive than the Hilton Hotel, which is not visible from the interstate, but less competitive than the Ramada Inn and the Holiday Inn, which have lower prices and more vacationer-oriented images. The estimated vacationer competitive index for the Sheraton Inn is 20 for Year 1, 32 for Year 2, and 40 for Year 3.

The Best Western has a strong family image and should be highly competitive in the vacationer market. It will probably come in just below the Days Inn, with indexes of 40, 50 and 60.

Figure 3.3 shows the vacationer competitive indexes for each of the lodging facilities within the local market.

94

Using the competitive indexes for all the lodging facilities within the market area, the individual market shares for each property can be calculated. Each property's room count is multiplied by its competitive index, to yield the market share adjustor. To determine the market share for a particular hotel, the property's market share adjustor is divided by the sum of the market share adjustors for all the properties. The bottom chart on page 93 illustrates these calculations.

The same procedure is performed for each market segment and operational

Commercial Segment Market Share (Percentage)

Operational Developmental	Year 1	Year 2	Year 1 Year 3	Year 2 Year 4	Year 3 Year 5	Year 4 Year 6	Year 5 Year 7
Days Inn	21.93	19.39	16.55	16.28	16.21	16.21	16.21
Suncrest Motel	13.16	11.63	9.93	9.76	9.73	9.73	9.73
Holiday Inn	22.28	19.70	16.82	16.54	16.46	16.46	16.46
Hilton Hotel	23.39	20.68	17.65	17.37	17.29	17.29	17.29
Ramada Inn	19.24	17.01	14.51	14.28	14.22	14.22	14.22
Best Western	—	11.59	10.66	11.23	11.18	11.18	11.18
Sheraton Inn (subject)	—	—	13.88	14.54	14.91	14.91	14.91
Total	100.00	100.00	100.00	100.00	100.00	100.00	100.00

Meeting and Convention Segment Market Share (Percentage)

Operational Developmental	Year 1	Year 2	Year 1 Year 3	Year 2 Year 4	Year 3 Year 5	Year 4 Year 6	Year 5 Year 7
Days Inn	0.00	0.00	0.00	0.00	0.00	0.00	0.00
Suncrest Motel	9.15	8.61	7.28	6.72	6.65	6.65	6.65
Holiday Inn	25.34	23.84	20.16	18.62	18.45	18.45	18.45
Hilton Hotel	48.79	45.89	38.80	35.84	35.52	35.52	35.52
Ramada Inn	16.72	15.72	13.29	12.28	12.17	12.17	12.17
Best Western	—	5.94	6.69	9.27	9.19	9.19	9.19
Sheraton Inn (subject)	—	—	13.78	17.27	18.02	18.02	18.02
Total	100.00	100.00	100.00	100.00	100.00	100.00	100.00

Vacationer's Segment Market Share (Percentage)

Operational Developmental	Year 1	Year 2	Year 1 Year 3	Year 2 Year 4	Year 3 Year 5	Year 4 Year 6	Year 5 Year 7
Days Inn	26.32	22.98	20.78	19.42	18.95	18.95	18.95
Suncrest Motel	15.79	13.79	12.46	11.66	11.37	11.37	11.37
Holiday Inn	21.87	19.10	17.26	16.15	15.75	15.75	15.75
Hilton Hotel	18.71	16.34	14.77	13.81	13.47	13.47	13.47
Ramada Inn	17.31	15.11	13.66	12.78	12.46	12.46	12.46
Best Western	—	12.68	14.33	16.09	15.69	15.69	15.69
Sheraton Inn (subject)	—	—	6.74	10.09	12.31	12.31	12.31
Total	100.00	100.00	100.00	100.00	100.00	100.00	100.00

year. The charts on pages 95 and 96 show the calculated market shares by seg-ment, by year, and by property.

Multiplying the percentage of market share for the Sheraton Inn by the total projected room nights for a particular segment within the market produces the estimated number of room nights captured for the subject property.

Commercial Segment Projected Room Nights Captured, Sheraton Inn—Subject

Operational Year	Market Share	Projected Commercial Segment Demand	Projected Commercial Segment Room Nights Captured
1	13.88	202,540	28,113
2	14.54	208,616	30,332
3	14.91	214,874	32,038
4	14.91	221,321	32,999
5	14.91	227,960	33,998

Meeting and Convention Segment Projected Room Nights Captured, Sheraton Inn—Subject

Operational Year	Market Share	Projected Meeting and Convention Segment Demand	Projected Meeting and Convention Segment Room Nights Captured
1	13.78	90,025	12,405
2	17.27	91,825	15,858
3	18.02	93,662	16,877
4	18.02	95,535	17,215
5	18.02	97,446	17,559

Vacationers Segment Projected Room Nights Captured, Sheraton Inn—Subject

Operational Year	Market Share	Projected Vacationers Segment Demand	Projected Vacationers Segment Room Nights Captured
1	6.74	48,712	3,283
2	10.09	49,199	4,964
3	12.31	49,691	6,117
4	12.31	50,188	6,178
5	12.31	50,690	6,240

Adding the results for each segment produces the total projected room night capture for the Sheraton Inn.

Summary of Projected Room Nights Captured, Sheraton Inn—Subject

	Year 1	Year 2	Year 3	Year 4	Year 5
Commercial	28,113	30,332	32,038	32,999	33,998
Meetings & conventions	12,405	15,858	16,877	17,215	17,559
Vacationers	3,283	4,964	6,117	6,178	6,240
Total	43,801	51,154	55,032	56,392	57,797

Figure 3.2   Competitive Index—Meetings and Convention Segment

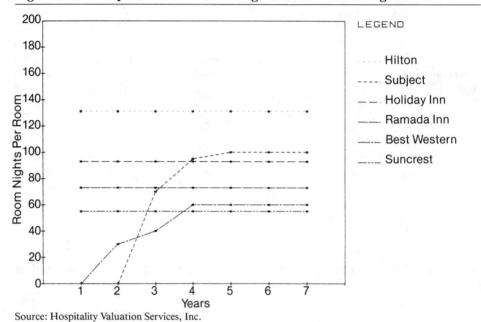

Source: Hospitality Valuation Services, Inc.

Figure 3.3   Competitive Index—Vacationers Segment

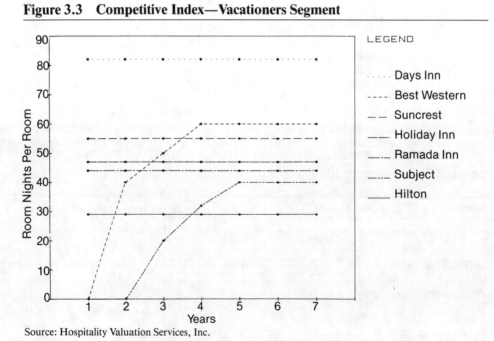

Source: Hospitality Valuation Services, Inc.

98

Estimating Occupancy

The Sheraton Inn's occupancy is calculated by dividing the projected room nights captured by its 73,000 available room nights. The market share is the demand captured divided by the area's total demand. The fair share is the subject's room count divided by the total number of competitive rooms in the market area. The accompanying chart illustrates these calculations.

Occupancy and Market Share Calculations, Sheraton Inn—Subject

	Year 1	Year 2	Year 3	Year 4	Year 5
Room nights captured	43,801	51,154	55,032	56,392	57,797
Room nights available	73,000	73,000	73,000	73,000	73,000
Projected occupancy	60%	70%	75%	77%	79%
Demand captured	43,801	51,154	55,032	56,392	57,797
Total demand	341,277	349,640	358,227	367,044	376,096
Market share	12.8%	14.6%	15.4%	15.4%	15.4%
Subject's rooms	200	200	200	200	200
Total rooms	1,360	1,360	1,360	1,360	1,360
Fair share	14.7%	14.7%	14.7%	14.7%	14.7%

The chart shows the Sheraton's occupancy increasing from 60% in Year 1 to 79% in Year 5. Any occupancy increase after Year 3 is attributed to a growth in the room night demand, not an increase in the subject's competitiveness. This would indicate a natural break, and reflects a stabilized occupancy level of 75%.

The chart also illustrates that the Sheraton's market share will be less than its fair share for Years 1 and 2 as business builds. From Year 3 on, its market share will exceed its fair share. These relationships are typical for new lodging facilities and indicate a realistic projection of occupancy.

4
Hotels and Motels As Investments

Like most real estate investments, hotels and motels consist of *land* and *improvements* (buildings, permanent equipment, parking area, swimming pool, etc.) Commercial land generally represents no more than 20% of the total property value. Hotels and motels are unique real estate investments because they contain many elements not typically found in income-producing properties. These characteristics affect both the risks and the benefits associated with hostelry investments; they demonstrate the highly specialized nature of this type of real estate.

Unique Investment Elements

A hostelry derives value from certain, unique characteristics:

1. *Furniture, fixtures, and equipment.* This includes guest room, dining room, and lounge furnishings; kitchen equipment; front office and administrative equipment; and items of decor. These items can account for up to 25% of the total property value.

2. *Retail-type business.* Hostelries require specialized and highly trained management. They are also labor-intensive; employee wages and benefits may represent as much as 40% of gross revenues.

3. *Inventories and working capital.* Lodging facilities use many expendable items such as linen, paper supplies, cleaning materials, food and beverages. Working capital is used for house banks and a petty cash fund and to finance accounts receivable.

When valuing a hotel or motel, the appraiser must accurately define the elements to be included in the final value. For example, if the purpose of the appraisal is to estimate the value of the real estate alone, appropriate adjustments must be made to separate out the value of the furniture, fixtures and equipment; the business value; and the cost of the inventories and working capital. The following is a general discussion of these elements and how they influence the risks, benefits, and value of a hostelry investment.

Furniture, Fixtures and Equipment

Furniture, fixtures, and equipment, or F, F & E, as they are known in the trade, are essential to the operation of a lodging facility, and their quality often influences the class of a property. Included in this category are all nonreal estate items that are normally capitalized, not treated as expenses.

Table 4.1   Typical Useful Lives for Various Items of F, F, & E

Item	Number of Years
Furnishings	
Lobby	5–12
Restaurant	5–12
Guest rooms	
Casepieces	8–15
Mattresses	5–8
Carpet	
Lobby	3–6
Corridor	2–4
Guest rooms	4–8
Drapes	4–8
Bedspreads	3–6
Kitchen equipment	8–25

Source: Hospitality Valuation Services, Inc.

102

Furniture, fixtures, and equipment are exposed to heavy use and must be replaced regularly. The useful lives of these items are determined by their quality, durability, and the amount of use.

Periodic replacement of furniture, fixtures, and equipment is essential to maintain the quality, image, and income of a lodging facility. Capitalized expenditures are not included in the operating statement, but they do affect an owner's cash flow, so an appraisal should reflect these expenses in an appropriate reserve for replacement.

A reserve for replacement allowance can be estimated straight line or as a percent of the gross. To estimate a reserve with the straight-line method, divide the estimated future replacement cost of the item by the weighted-average useful life (usually 8-10 years). Using the percent of the gross, a replacement reserve of 2%-3% of the gross revenue reflect both the quality of the facilities (average rate) and the use they receive (occupancy).

In some appraisals, the value of the F, F, & E must be separated from the value of the real estate. This separation is required in property tax assessments or when a lender is unable to use chattel as mortgage security. The procedure is to deduct the income attributed to the personal property from the hotel's overall net income by multiplying either the current value or the replacement cost of the F, F, & E by factors representing returns on and of the F, F, & E. A return on F, F, & E reflects the owner's cost of capital and is used with the current market value of the F, F, & E in place. A return of F, F, & E is the same as a reserve or replacement and is based on the replacement cost of the chattels and their estimated useful lives.

Example

This example illustrates two methods for separating the F, F, & E from the real estate, assuming a new hotel where the current value of the F, F, & E is the same as the replacement cost. Consider a hostelry investment with the following characteristics:

Market value of furniture, fixtures, and equipment	$1,475,000
Total revenue	7,345,000
Net income before management fee	2,035,000
Management fee	367,000
Net income after management fee	1,668,000
Overall capitalization rate	13.8%
Percent of gross replacement reserve	2.5%
Average useful life of F, F, & E	8 years

103

Return of F, F, & E based on percent of gross:

Net income		$1,668,000
Less: return on F, F, & E $1,475,000 × .138	=	− 204,000
Less: return of F, F, & E $7,345,000 × .025	=	− 184,000
Income attributed to real estate		$1,280,000

Value of real estate:

$$\frac{\$1,280,000}{.138} = \$9,275,000$$

Return of F, F, & E based on straight line:

Net income		$1,668,000
Less: Return on F, F, & E $1,475,000 × .138	=	− 204,000
Less: Return of F, F, & E $1,475,000 ÷ 8	=	− 184,000
Income attributed to real estate		$1,280,000

Value of real estate:

$$\frac{\$1,280,000}{.138} = \$9,275,000$$

Because furniture, fixtures, and equipment have relatively short lives, and different methods of accelerated depreciation and investment tax credits are allowed, investors receive numerous tax shelter benefits.

Although first mortgage lenders do not always finance F, F, & E, they often require that any chattel mortgages or furniture leases be subordinate to their positions. Therefore, conservative investors will generally finance F, F, & E with equity capital. Some of the new lodging facilities that became distressed in the early 1970s were overleveraged with large first mortgages and high constant furniture leases. Using a great amount of financing naturally increases the risk and contributes to default.

Retail-Type Business: Business Value

A lodging facility is a labor-intensive, retail-type business that depends on customer acceptance and highly specialized management skills. In an apartment or office building tenants sign leases for one or more years, but a hostelry experiences a complete turnover of patronage every two to four days. A bad reputation spreads rapidly and can have an immediate effect on occupancy.

Separating the value of a hotel's business from the value of its real estate is a controversial topic. It is difficult to determine exactly where income attributed to the business stops and income from the real estate begins. In an appraisal assignment in which the market value encompasses the entire property, the business is part of the "going-concern" value and is not separated from the real estate. However, some insurance laws, condemnation proceedings, and property tax assessments require a "pure" real estate value, which necessitates treating business value as a separate entity.

One way to quantify a hostelry's business value is to consider a hypothetical rental based on comparable market lease terms and provisions. Valuing the leased fee position using comparable market rent yields the value of the real estate encumbered by the lease. When this value is subtracted from the overall property value, the value of the business remains.

Example
Consider a property with the following characteristics:

Total revenue	$ 7,345,000
Net income before F, F, & E deduction	2,035,000
F, F, & E deduction	388,000
Net income after F, F, & E deduction	1,647,000
Market rent	16% of gross revenue
Leased fee discount rate	.1267
Overall capitalization rate	.1380

Value of property:

$$\frac{\$1,647,000}{.138} = \$11,935,000$$

Value of leased fee (real estate):

$$\$7,345,000 \times .16 = \$1,175,200 \text{ (market rent)}$$

$$\frac{\$1,175,200}{.1267} = \$ 9,275,000$$

Value of business:

Value of property	$11,935,000
Less: value of real estate	− 9,275,000
Value of business	$ 2,660,000

A second method for separating a hostelry's business value from its property value is to assume the owner enters into a management contract with a hotel company to take over all operating responsibilities of the property. The cost of professional management, the management fee, would then represent a fair estimate of the income attributed to the business.

Example

Total revenue	$ 7,345,000
Net income before F, F, & E deduction	2,035,000
F, F, & E deduction	338,000
Net income after F, F, & E deduction	1,647,000
Management fee	5% of total revenue
Overall capitalization rate	.138

Income attributed to business (management fee):

$7,345,000 × .05	=	$ 367,000

Income attributed to real estate:

Net income after F, F, & E deduction	$ 1,647,000
Less: income attributed to business	− 367,000
Income attributed to real estate	$ 1,280,000

Value of the property:

$$\frac{\$1,647,000}{.138} \qquad = \qquad \$11,935,000$$

Value of the real estate:

$$\frac{\$1,280,000}{.138} \qquad = \qquad \$ 9,275,000$$

Value of the business:

Value of the property	$11,935,000
Less: value of the real estate	− 9,275,000
Value of the business	$ 2,660,000

The two methods produce identical estimates of real estate and business values. The first method is a common valuation procedure for separating the two values, but obtaining economic rents is becoming increasingly more difficult because few hostelries are leased today. The second method estimates business value based on a management fee, which is more compatible with current operating practices.

Inventories and Working Capital

In most instances inventories and working capital are not included in an estimate of a lodging facility's market value. At the time of closing, any inventory on hand is normally "purchased" by the buyer on a dollar-for-dollar basis, just as fuel oil, taxes, and insurance are adjusted. Working capital is withdrawn by the seller and replaced by the buyer. This process is repeated when the property changes hands again, and the result is full recovery of all monies invested in working capital.

If an appraiser wishes to include inventories and working capital in the property value, an appropriate amount must be added to the capitalized net income.

General Risks and Benefits

So far this chapter has described three unique hostelry characteristics and their potential effects on value. To develop an appropriate equity return rate, the appraiser must also consider several general factors related to hotel investments.

Long start-up periods. Lodging facilities usually experience a one- to four-year start-up period before reaching a level of income that can support normal financing and equity requirements. Operators of some convention properties try to alleviate part of the cash drain by pre-selling during construction. In most instances, however, hostelry investors are advised to budget an adequate cash reserve to carry the property until its occupancy and rate achieve profitability.

Food and beverage risks. The food and beverage department involves high risk, yields low profits, and is a source of constant aggravation for most operators. Opening for breakfast, providing room service, and extending coffee shop hours are essential for competitive reasons, but these practices erode profits for many hostelries. The industry generally sees the food and beverage department not as a profit center, but as a necessary service provided strictly for the guests' convenience. Except for a few high-volume banquet operations, most hotels and motels lose money on food and beverages when all expenses (administrative and general, marketing, energy costs, property operations, and maintenance) are properly allocated. This potential loss of income constitutes a major risk factor and can adversely affect market value.

Rapid functional obsolescence. The layout, design, construction materials and amenities of lodging facilities are constantly changing. Over the past 15 years, the industry has gone from exterior corridors to interior hallways, black-and-white televisions to color televisions (often with in-room movies), outdoor pools to enclosed health spas, live entertainment to discotheques, large ballrooms to conference centers, and hand accounting to computerized systems. Each innovation means that existing properties must either alter their facilities or suffer functional obsolescence. Often the correction of functional deficiencies is not economically justified, and the property gradually becomes less competitive. The proliferation of new lodging facilities within the market area tends to amplify the functional obsolescence of older properties. The resulting decline in competitive standing constitutes a definite risk factor for hostelry investors.

Susceptibility to external obsolescence. The events of the early 1970s demonstrated how external factors can adversely affect the lodging industry. The energy crisis drastically reduced automobile travel, especially in the vacation market. The major recession that followed forced businesses to curtail commercial travel. The greater use of air transportation, more sophisticated communication systems, and competition from new forms of accommodations (such as campers) are all examples of macro factors that lead to economic obsolescence.

On a micro level, many motels constructed during the 1950s were forced out of business by the changeover from U.S. highways to modern interstates. The deterioration of downtown areas caused restaurants, lounges, and other places of entertainment to move to the suburbs. These uncontrollable factors create constant risks for lodging facilities. In most cases, external obsolescence cannot be cured, and the property experiences an immediate drop in value.

Nonliquidity. Selling a lodging facility is a highly specialized transaction. Because the market is limited to a comparatively few potential buyers, generating interest sometimes takes three months or longer. Once a prospective purchaser is found, many time-consuming details must be worked out (e.g., arranging financing, transfer of licenses, leases, service contracts and franchise agreements; structuring equity and tax shelter programs; and performing appraisals and surveys). In many instances the seller is forced to maintain an interest in the property by taking back purchase money financing.

There are, however, some aspects of hostelry investing that help offset the negative features.

Favorable tax treatment. Lodging facilities qualify for subchapter S tax treatment; this enables investors to limit their liability through corporate ownership, but be taxed as if they were a partnership. Much of the personal property can be depreciated over a short period of time, and new purchases often qualify for investment tax credits. Hotels and motels generate good tax shelter benefits and are well-suited for investment by syndications.

Potential for large profits. Once the income from a lodging facility exceeds its breakeven point, profits tend to increase rapidly. As shown in later chapters, a large portion of hostelry expenses are fixed and do not vary significantly with occupancy.

Financial returns from a hotel investment are derived from the annual cash flow after debt service (equity dividend), mortgage amortization, and the potential value appreciation realized when the property is sold. Over the past 10 years, the perceived equity returns demanded by hostelry investors have ranged from a high of 20%-25% to a low of 8%-12%. Equity dividends are influenced by a variety of circumstances, such as the condition of the market, general real estate and hotel-motel risk factors, individual property risk factors, supply and demand ratios, the availability and cost of financing, and tax benefits.

Equity build-up through mortgage amortization and value appreciation is another investment consideration. These two factors form the basis of the Ellwood method of valuation, which uses the concept of "equity yield." Today, most hostelry investors are still thinking in terms of "cash on cash" or equity dividend. They find the concepts of equity yield and reversionary value somewhat difficult to understand; they generally use the band of investment technique to derive overall capitalization rates. However, investors are rapidly becoming more sophisticated, and discounted cash flow analysis, before- and after-tax equity yield calculations, and other computer techniques will become accepted appraisal procedures in the near future.

5
Market Value and the Valuation Process

Hotels and motels are income-producing, investment properties that are periodically bought, sold, financed, refinanced, condemned, assessed, and bequeathed. Each of these activities usually requires a professional appraisal to provide an estimate of the property's market value.

Market value is defined:

> *The most probable price in cash, terms equivalent to cash, or in other precisely revealed terms, for which the appraised property will sell in a competitive market under all conditions requisite to fair sale, with the buyer and seller each acting prudently, knowledgeably, and for self-interest, and assuming that neither is under undue duress.*[1]

Fundamental assumptions and conditions presumed in this definition are

---

[1] *The Appraisal of Real Estate,* 8th ed. (Chicago: American Institute of Real Estate Appraisers, 1983), p. 33.

1. Buyer and seller are motivated by self-interest.
2. Buyer and seller are well informed and are acting prudently
3. The property is exposed for a reasonable time on the open market.
4. Payment is made in cash, its equivalent, or in specified financing terms.
5. Specified financing, if any, may be the financing actually in place or on terms generally available for the property type in its locale on the effective appraisal date.
6. The effect, if any, on the amount of market value of atypical financing services, or fees shall be clearly and precisely revealed in the appraisal report.

There are other definitions of market value:

The highest price in terms of money which a property will bring if exposed for sale in the open market, allowing a reasonable time to find a purchaser who buys with knowledge of all the uses to which it is adapted and for which it is capable of being used.

The price at which a willing seller would sell and a willing buyer would buy, neither being under abnormal pressure.[2]

The market value of a lodging facility may include the value of the going concern, which includes the business value; furniture, fixtures and equipment; and sometimes inventories and working capital. Market value is estimated by applying the valuation process, and the opinion of market value is usually communicated in a written appraisal report.

In appraising real estate for market value, the appraiser considers three approaches:

1. Cost approach, which is sometimes referred to as the summation approach.
2. Sales comparison approach, which is sometimes referred to as the direct sales or market data approach.
3. Income capitalization approach, which is sometimes referred to as the income approach.

[2]*Appraisal Terminology and Handbook,* 5th ed. (Chicago: The American Institute of Real Estate Appraisers, 1967), p. 102.

Cost Approach

The cost approach is based on the assumption that an informed purchaser will pay no more for a property than the cost of producing a substitute property with the same utility. In the cost approach, market value is estimated by computing the current cost of replacing the subject's improvements and subtracting any depreciation.

The cost of replacing a property is generally estimated on a square-foot basis, using figures from a construction cost manual published by a recognized cost reporting service. The value of the land is then added to the replacement cost estimate.

Depreciation is defined as a loss in value caused by one or more of the following factors:

1. Physical deterioration—the physical wearing out of the property.
2. Functional obsolescence—the property's lack of desirability in layout, style, and design, as compared to a new property serving the same function.
3. External obsolescence—the loss in value from causes outside the property itself.

Appraisal literature recommends using the cost approach for new properties, which are not yet affected by the various forms of depreciation, and for unique or specialized improvements such as churches and libraries that have no comparable market or income potential.

Lodging facilities are particularly vulnerable to functional changes, physical deterioration, and uncontrollable external factors. In some instances a hostelry can suffer from functional and external obsolescence before its construction is completed. As the building and other improvements begin to age and depreciate, the resultant loss in value becomes more difficult to quantify. Estimating the impact of even minor forms of obsolescence involves unsupportable judgments that weaken the credibility of the cost approach.

A more significant reason why the cost approach is seldom used to value existing hotels and motels is that the underlying assumptions do not reflect the investment rationale of typical hostelry buyers. Lodging facilities are income-producing properties that are purchased to realize future profits. Replacement (or reproduction) cost has little bearing on an investment decision when the buyer's primary concern is the potential return on equity.

The cost approach can be a meaningful standard of measurement, however, in determining the feasibility of a proposed hostelry. When used in conjunction with the income capitalization approach, the cost approach will verify a project's economic feasibility. For example, if the value obtained by the income capitalization approach is equal to or greater than the replacement cost plus the land value, the project is considered economically feasible. If, however, the value estimated by the income capitalization approach is less than that determined by the cost approach, the investors should either scrap the project, reduce capital costs, or lower their desired return. If this is the case, an additional equity investment may be needed to secure sufficient financing.

The data used to estimate the replacement cost should come from a qualified source such as an experienced contractor, architect, engineer, or a construction cost manual. The land value is established either by the purchase price (if appropriate) from sales of comparable parcels, or the capitalization of ground rental.

Table 5.1 shows ranges of typical replacement costs, land values, and soft costs for luxury, standard, and economy accommodations.

Sales Comparison Approach

The sales comparison approach is based on the assumption that an informed purchaser will pay no more for a property than the cost of acquiring an existing property with the same utility. Using this approach, market value is estimated by comparing the sale prices of recent transactions involving properties similar to the property being appraised. Any dissimilarities are resolved with appropriate adjustments. These differences may pertain to time, age, location, construction, condition, layout, equipment, size, or external economic factors.

The reliability of the sales comparison approach depends on three factors:

1. Availability of comparable sales data.
2. Verification of sales data.
3. Degree of comparability, i.e., the extent of adjustment necessary to equalize the differences between the subject and the comparable property.

The sales comparison approach often provides a highly supportable estimate of value for homogeneous properties, such as vacant land and single-family homes, where the adjustments are few and relatively simple to compute. For larger and more complex properties, such as office buildings, shopping centers and hotels, the required adjustments often are numerous and more difficult to estimate.

For example, consider the following possible differences between a property being appraised and a similar motel located directly across the street, which was sold last year.

114

Table 5.1 Typical Hotel/Motel Development Costs

	Improvements	Furniture & Equipment	Land	Pre-Opening	Operating Capital	Total
1976						
Luxury	32,000– 55,000	5,000–10,000	4,000–12,000	1,000–2,000	1,000–1,500	43,000– 80,500
Standard	20,000– 32,000	3,000– 6,000	2,500– 7,000	750–1,500	750–1,000	27,000– 47,500
Economy	8,000– 15,000	2,000– 4,000	1,000– 3,500	500–1,000	500– 750	12,000– 24,250
1979						
Luxury	36,000– 65,000	8,000–15,000	5,000–20,000	1,500–3,000	1,500–2,000	52,000–105,000
Standard	25,000– 36,000	5,000–10,000	3,000–11,000	1,000–2,000	1,000–1,500	35,000– 60,500
Economy	10,000– 20,000	3,000– 5,000	1,500– 6,000	500–1,000	750–1,000	15,750– 33,000
1981						
Luxury	45,000– 80,000	10,000–20,000	8,000–22,000	2,000–3,500	2,000–2,500	67,000–128,000
Standard	25,000– 40,000	7,000–13,000	4,000–12,000	1,200–2,500	1,200–2,000	38,400– 70,000
Economy	13,000– 25,000	4,000– 7,000	2,000– 7,000	700–1,200	900–1,200	20,600– 41,400
1983						
Luxury	55,000–100,000	12,500–20,000	10,000–24,000	2,300–4,000	2,000–2,800	81,800–150,800
Standard	35,000– 50,000	9,000–15,000	5,000–13,000	1,400–3,000	1,300–2,200	51,700– 83,200
Economy	18,000– 32,000	5,000– 8,000	3,000– 8,000	800–1,500	900–1,300	27,700– 50,800

Source: Hospitality Valuation Services, Inc.

- Seller takes back purchase-money financing
- Different franchise affiliation
- Better visibility
- More parking facilities
- Larger restaurant and smaller lounge
- Enclosed swimming pool
- Higher-grade furnishings
- Two vanity sinks per guest room

These are just a few of the many potential adjustments needed to make the indicated sale price of the comparable property reflect the market value of the property being appraised. The task is often difficult and generally unsupported by market data.

Although the sales comparison approach is seldom given substantial weight in a hotel appraisal, it can assist in bracketing a value to check the value derived by the income capitalization approach.

Example

While appraising a standard-rate commercial hotel, the appraiser researched the market and discovered two recent sales. One sale involved a luxury motel with a value of $90,000 per room. The other sale was a standard-rate motel that was obviously less attractive than the property being appraised; it had a value of $45,000 per room.

Although an exact estimate of value for the appraised property based on this data would be difficult to support, a range within which the final estimate should fall has been established. If the income capitalization approach results in a value indication that is outside this range, the appraiser knows that the data must be reevaluated. Occasionally, appraisers may utilize a gross income multiplier in the sales comparison approach. If this tends to reflect the actions of the market, it can be considered in the appraisal.

As in all appraisals, the market must be researched to locate comparable sales with which to support an estimate of market value.

Income Capitalization Approach

The income capitalization approach converts anticipated future benefits of property ownership (dollar income) into an estimate of present value. In hotel/motel valuation, this approach typically employs a discounting procedure.

116

The income capitalization approach is generally the preferred technique for appraising income-producing properties because it most closely reflects the investment rationale and strategies of typical buyers. This is particularly true of hotel and motel properties, where relatively high risks make this type of deal suitable for investment purposes only. The cost and sales comparison approaches are generally inappropriate for appraising lodging facilities because they require many unsubstantiated judgmental adjustments. Most of the data used in the income capitalization approach has already been adjusted by market factors, which reduces the unsupportable, subjective content.

To use the income capitalization approach, the appraiser must:

1. Project net income for a specified number of years.
2. Select an appropriate discount factor or capitalization rate.
3. Apply the proper discounting and/or capitalization procedure.

Each of these steps is discussed in detail to illustrate how it is incorporated into the income capitalization approach.

Projecting Net Income

Many terms are used to describe net income that is ready to be capitalized into an estimate of value—net income before recapture, net income before depreciation, or net operating income. All of these terms are defined as the annual net income before financial charges such as the recapture of debt service are deducted. In conformance with the *Uniform System of Accounts for Hotels,* this concept is referred to as "income before interest and depreciation."

According to the income capitalization approach, the projection of income before interest and depreciation is based on two assumptions: projected income and expenses are expressed in inflated dollars and management is competent.

In the first edition of this book, the use of constant dollars for all hotel projections was recommended. As inflation became a more important consideration to both hotel lenders and investors, however, it became apparent that interest, discount, and capitalization rates were being adjusted upward for inflation. Most hotel investors now base their purchases on expected future benefits with inflation built in.

Projected income and expenses are usually based on competent management because the quality of management plays an important role in the profit potential of a lodging facility. The appraiser must equalize the effects of varying managerial expertise by assuming that the property being appraised will be competently managed. Management quality can be "poor," "competent," or "superior." If the property is currently under poor management, the appraiser is justified in projecting improved operating results based on competent management. On the other hand, if the subject has superior management, the projected income and expenses used to estimate market value should reflect less managerial skill, i.e., lower revenue and/or higher expenses. This rule does not apply if management is under a long-term contract and would not change in the event of a sale, or if the appraiser is estimating investment value rather than market value. Investment value is the value to a particular investor based on individual financial and managerial requirements. It differs from market value in that market value must represent the actions of typical buyers and, therefore, reflect average, competent management.

The groundwork for projecting income before interest and depreciation has already been described. The appraiser defines the market area, locates and quantifies the demand, and allocates the room nights among the competitive facilities. This procedure provides the necessary information to formulate an estimate of occupancy and average rate. Based on these data, room revenue and other sources of income, such as food and beverage sales and telephone income, can be computed. Expense data are available from actual operating statements, if the subject is an existing property, or from comparable properties and national averages, if the subject is a proposed facility. The process of projecting income and expenses is described later.

The Hotel-Motel Life Cycle

The expected flow of income before interest and depreciation is important when selecting the appropriate discounting procedure. All real estate investments have individual life cycles that show the rise and fall of net income over the property's economic life. Most income-producing properties attain full economic potential relatively quickly. This level is then maintained for a number of years, until it gradually declines as various forms of depreciation erode the income.

Lodging facilities generally take some time to achieve their maximum level of income. A typical hostelry will experience a slowly rising occupancy in the first two to four years of operation; in many instances the income before interest and depreciation will not cover normal debt service during this period. A stabilized level of income normally is reached sometime between the second and fifth year of operation; this represents the property's discounted average net income. The income before interest and depreciation will usually rise above the stabilized level for a few years, and then gradually start to decline between the seventh and tenth year because of physical deterioration and/or functional and external obsolescence. The decline continues over the remaining economic life of the prop-

Table 5.2 Typical Life Cycle for a 200-Room Motel

	Income Before Interest and Depreciation	
Year	Inflated Dollars	Constant Dollars (Year I)
1	$ 200,000	$ 200,000
2	680,400	630,000
3	1,096,416	940,000
4	1,360,489	1,080,000
5	1,632,587	1,200,000
6	1,895,433	1,290,000
7	2,094,674	1,320,000
8	2,330,801	1,360,000
9	2,443,228	1,320,000
10	2,558,726	1,280,000
11	2,633,888	1,220,000
12	2,704,701	1,160,000
13	2,769,987	1,100,000
14	2,828,409	1,040,000
15	2,878,450	980,000
16	2,918,396	920,000
17	2,946,311	860,000
18	2,960,014	800,000
19	2,957,054	740,000
20	2,934,677	680,000
21	2,889,793	620,000
22	2,818,947	560,000
23	2,718,270	500,000
24	2,583,444	440,000
25	2,409,649	380,000
26	2,191,512	320,000
27	1,923,052	260,000
28	1,677,493	210,000
29	1,294,066	150,000
30	7,276,792*	781,000*

*Reversionary land value

erty. The life cycle of a lodging facility is not predetermined, however; it can be lengthened or shortened, depending on how much maintenance and periodic upgrading the owner is willing to do. Table 5.2 and Figure 5.1 show a typical life cycle for a 200-room motel.

Figure 5.1   Typical Life Cycle—200-Room Motel

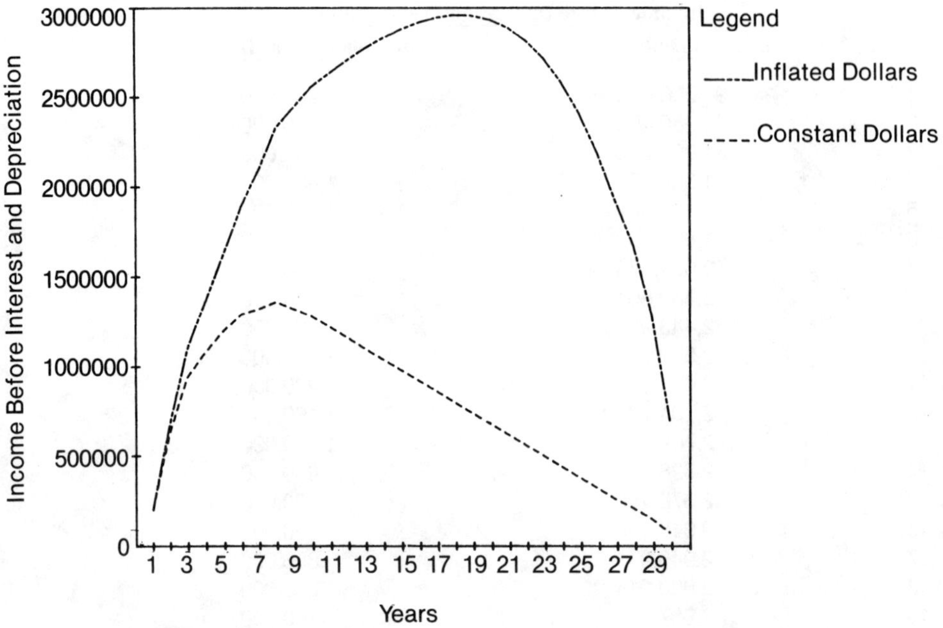

Source: Hospitality Valuation Services, Inc.

Proposed hotels and motels are appraised as of the beginning of their life cycles, but existing lodging facilities may be appraised at any point in the cycle. By estimating a property's position in the life cycle, the appraiser can project future income before interest and depreciation and select the proper discounting procedure.

Selecting Appropriate Capitalization Rates and Discount Factors

Capitalization rates and discount factors are used to convert expected future income into an indication of value. These rates and factors have an interest component, which reflects the return *on* capital, and a recapture component, which provides for a return *of* capital.

Theoretically, the interest component can be derived through risk and investment analysis. Starting with a base rate representing a safe investment, such as a federally insured savings account, the analyst makes a series of upward adjustments to reflect different elements of risk and investment burden. For example:

120

	%
Safe rate (minimum risk)	X
Add for general hostelry risk	I_1
Add for management burden	I_2
Add for food and beverage risk	I_3
Add for rapid functional obsolescence	I_4
Add for nonliquidity	I_5
Add for other elements	I_6
	Total

In practice, estimating the magnitude of each upward adjustment is too subjective to provide a supportable interest rate. It is more reliable to utilize the analytical expertise of the hundreds of money managers who comprise the nation's lending institutions.

Basically, a hostelry investment is made up of a large amount of mortgage money (60%–75% of the total investment) and a smaller amount of equity capital (25%–40%). The interest rate on a hostelry mortgage is established by the lender, who takes into consideration all possible risks. Obviously, the mortgagee is in a more secure position than the equity investor but, in the event of a foreclosure, the lender may be forced to assume the equity position.

One of the best sources of information on actual hotel-motel mortgage interest rates is the data compiled quarterly by the American Council of Life Insurance, which represents 20 life insurance companies.

Table 5.3 shows the typical interest rates and other lending terms obtained for permanent hotel and motels loans over the past 10 years.

Table 5.3 Typical Hotel and Motel Mortgages

	1972	1973	1974	1975	1976	1977	1978	1979	1980	1981	1982
Average interest rate	8.92	9.10	9.65	10.34	10.06	9.79	9.94	10.83	12.86	14.53	15.16
Average percent constant	10.5	10.6	11.0	11.4	11.2	11.12	11.02	11.9	13.2	15.1	16.8
Average term (Years/months)	21/4	22/2	20/8	21/6	22/9	20/0	20/3	18/0	16/11	13/6	12/11
AA utility bonds	7.60	7.80	9.04	9.43	8.92	8.43	9.10	10.22	12.99	15.29	14.79

Sources: American Council of Life Insurance, Washington, D.C.
Moody's Bond Record

121

One flaw in the data supplied by the American Council of Life Insurance is that they are three to six months old; it takes that much time to collect and distribute this financial information. This is a major difficulty because, in today's rapidly changing money market, mortgage rates can vary one or more points within a few weeks.

To obtain up-to-date hotel mortgage information, Hospitality Valuation Services, Inc. used linear regression to research the relationship between hotel mortgage interest rates and the rates and yields on other types of money market instruments. An extremely close association was found between the interest rates on hotel mortgages and the yields on the AA, long-term utility bonds reported in "Moody's Bond Survey." Because Moody's publishes bond data on a daily basis, the regression equation is very accurate in estimating the current interest rate for hotel mortgages.

Consider the following interest rate formula:

$$Y = 3.279 + .741X$$

where Y = estimated hotel/motel mortgage interest rate, and X = actual AA utility bond yield. If the average, long-term yield on AA utility bonds is 13.4%, the calculated hotel mortgage interest rate, Y, would be $3.279 + .741 \times 13.4$, or 13.2%. This formula has a correlation coefficient of .973, which indicates its reliability. The regression equation should be updated quarterly with the most recent data from the American Council of Life Insurance.

Other sources of lending information include local banks and insurance companies, real estate investment trusts, mortgage brokers, and regulatory agencies. By comparing the rates used by several sources, the appraiser can estimate the mortgage interest components with relative accuracy.

The mortgage recapture component, which represents the return of the investment, is expressed in the rate of amortization. According to the American Council of Life Insurance, hostelry loans have typically been structured to be repaid over a 20- to 25-year term. The recapture component plus the interest component equals the yearly mortgage constant. The annual debt service is calculated by multiplying the mortgage constant by the original loan balance.

Many lenders are increasing their yields by adding mortgage "kickers" to the stated interest rate on hotel mortgages. These extra interest payments are generally based on a percentage of the total rooms revenue; they currently range 1%–3%. Some lenders structure their kickers on a percentage of rooms revenue above the stabilized amount. This allows a hotel to reach a specific operating level before paying the extra interest; with these stabilized formulas, however, the added kicker can be as much as 10%–25% of rooms revenue. The appraiser handles a mortgage kicker as if it were an ordinary expense and deducts it from the income before interest and depreciation.

The remaining 25%–40% of a hostelry investment is equity money. Like common stock, which is entitled to the residual earnings after all expenses, including debt services, have been paid, real estate equity investments normally provide returns higher than those demanded by the mortgage component. The yearly equity return is called the "equity dividend" by appraisers and the "cash-on-cash return" by hostelry investors.

To estimate the appropriate equity dividend for a particular hotel investment, the appraiser must be familiar with the current demands of hostelry owners and investors. A broad cross-section of active buyers must be observed because each is influenced by a variety of factors. Results based on a limited sample can produce misleading assumptions. For example, an investor in a high tax bracket may settle for a lower-than-market equity dividend if the shelter benefits are particularly attractive. An opportunity to resell a property after several years for an appreciated price may reduce a buyer's equity dividend demand. Because owning a hotel is associated with a certain degree of status, some buyers may be willing to accept a lower return.

An active hotel-motel broker, such as a member of the Motel Brokers Association of America, can often provide insight into current market demands for hostelry equity dividends. Over the past 10 years, most hostelry prices have been based on equity returns ranging from a high of 20%–25% to a low of 9%–12%. Good sources of equity information include typical hotel buyers and investors, lenders seeking equity participation and joint ventures, and hotel management companies.

Applying the Proper Discounting Procedure

There are several procedures for combining mortgage and equity data into a discount factor or capitalization rate that will transform projected net income into an indication of value. The selection of discount factors and capitalization rates depends on many elements, including: the length of the income projection period, the age of the property and its position in its life cycle, the nature of mortgage financing, and the sophistication of equity investors. The following discussion describes the various methods of developing discount factors and their proper application in the valuation process.

Discounting Each Year's Income Over a Full Life Cycle

The simplest form of valuation begins with a projection of the property's yearly net income (before interest and depreciation) over the full life of the improve-

Table 5.4

Year	Projected Income Before Interest and Depreciation	Discount Factor @ 16.75%	Discounted Net Income
1	$ 200,000	.8565	$ 171,300
2	680,400	.7336	499,141
3	1,096,416	.6284	688,987
4	1,360,489	.5382	732,215
5	1,632,587	.4610	752,623
6	1,895,433	.3949	748,506
7	2,094,674	.3382	708,419
8	2,330,801	.2897	675,233
9	2,443,228	.2481	606,164
10	2,558,726	.2125	543,729
11	2,633,888	.1820	479,368
12	2,704,701	.1559	421,663
13	2,769,987	.1336	370,070
14	2,828,409	.1144	323,570
15	2,878,450	.0980	282,088
16	2,918,396	.0839	244,853
17	2,946,311	.0719	211,839
18	2,960,014	.0616	182,336
19	2,957,054	.0527	155,836
20	2,934,677	.0452	132,647
21	2,889,793	.0387	111,834
22	2,818,947	.0331	93,307
23	2,718,270	.0284	77,199
24	2,583,444	.0243	62,777
25	2,409,649	.0208	50,121
26	2,191,512	.0178	39,009
27	1,923,052	.0153	29,423
28	1,677,493	.0131	21,975
29	1,294,066	.0112	14,493
30	7,276,792*	.0096	69,857
		Total	$9,500,582
		Value (Say)	$9,500,000

*Reversionary land value

ments. Multiplying each year's net income by the proper present value of a reversion of one factor and totaling all these discounted net income figures produces the overall property value.

This process is demonstrated in Table 5.4, using the 30-year flow of income in inflated dollars described in Table 5.2. A 16.75% discount factor was selected, based on 30-year return rates required by hotel investors.

This procedure is not very practical because preparing a 30-year projection of income before interest and depreciation is quite time-consuming and very long-term projections are extremely unreliable. Market support for the 16.75% discount factor is another area of concern. Although hotel investors are generally seeking long-term opportunities, very few can actually quantify their return requirements over a 30-year period. The 16.75% discount factor used in this example is totally unsupported. Therefore, due to the excessive projection period and the arbitrary nature of the discount factor, the process of discounting each year's net income over a full life cycle does not reflect the actions of typical hotel buyers and sellers and is rarely used in hotel-motel valuations.

Ten-Year Projection Using an Equity Yield Rate

To eliminate some of the uncertainties associated with excessively long-term net income projections, most appraisers currently use projection periods of 3–10 years.

The 10-year projection using an equity yield rate is similar to an Ellwood valuation approach, in which the yearly income to equity plus an equity reversion is discounted at an equity yield rate, and the income to the mortgagee is discounted at a mortgage yield rate. The sum of the equity and mortgage values is the total property value.

The benefits to the equity component include equity dividends from the income after debt service for the 10-year projection period and the gain or loss from the property's assumed resale. The resale or reversion benefits include the gain or loss caused by value appreciation or depreciation, plus any mortgage amortization. The benefits of the mortgage component are the interest kicker and amortization, plus repayment of the remaining mortgage balance at the end of ten years.

The following steps are required to perform a valuation with 10-year income projection using an equity yield:

1. Income before interest and depreciation (net income) is projected for an 11-year period using inflated dollars.
2. If a mortgage kicker is considered a typical financing requirement, an appropriate yearly amount is deducted from net income in the same manner as an operating expense would be deducted.
3. An equity yield rate is established.
4. The terms for typical financing are set forth, including the interest rate, amortization term, and loan-to-value ratio.

5. An overall capitalization rate (going-out rate) suitable for capitalizing the 11th year's net income into an assumed sale price is estimated.

6 A trial market value is hypothesized and the mortgage and equity components are calculated using the loan-to-value ratio.

7. Based on the initial mortgage balance determined in Step 6, the yearly debt service (interest and amortization) is deducted from each year's projected net income (after paying the mortgage kicker) to produce the equity dividend. The mortgage balance at the end of the 10th year is then calculated.

8. The property reversion value (assumed sale price) at the end of the 10th year is estimated by dividing the 11th year's net income by the overall capitalization rate.

9. The equity reversion equals the property reversion minus the mortgage balance and any expense involved in selling the property.

10. The equity dividend plus the equity reversion are discounted to the present value at the equity yield rate. The total is the equity value.

11. If the mortgage terms do not reflect the market rate, the interest, kicker, amortization, and 10th-year mortgage balance must be discounted to the present value at the mortgage yield rate. If the mortgage terms are market rate, this step may be disregarded because the discounted mortgage value equals the initial mortgage balance.

12. The equity value is added to the mortgage value to produce the property's market value. If the calculated market value equals the trial market value (Step 6), then the process is complete. If the calculated market value does not equal the trial market value, steps 6 through 12 must be repeated using a different hypothesized trial market value. Through the iterative process, the difference between the calculated and trial market values can be narrowed and eventually eliminated.

Naturally, the procedure described above is much easier with a computer that can perform many iterative processes rapidly.

The following calculations demonstrate how the 10-year projection using an equity yield is applied to data from the 30-year life cycle projection presented in the previous example.

1. Because a 30-year life cycle projection is difficult to compile and its accuracy decreases in the later years, hotel analysts typically project income and expenses until the year the facility attains its stabilized occupancy. From this point on, any gains in net income can generally be attributed to the impact of inflation. The subject hotel achieves its stabilized occupancy in Year 4, so any subsequent gains in the income before interest and depreciation

are assumed to be caused by inflation. Taking the first four years' income before interest and depreciation from the 30-year life cycle projection in Table 5.4, and inflating the 4th year's net income at a rate of 8% results in the data shown in the column on the following chart.

	1	2	3	4
Year	Projected Income Before Interest and Depreciation	Mortgage Kicker	Debt Service	Equity Dividend
1	$ 200,000	$ 15,000	$926,000	$ – 741,000
2	680,000	37,000	926,000	– 283,000
3	1,096,000	55,000	926,000	115,000
4	1,360,000	60,000	926,000	374,000
5	1,469,000	65,000	926,000	478,000
6	1,586,000	70,000	926,000	590,000
7	1,713,000	76,000	926,000	711,000
8	1,850,000	82,000	926,000	842,000
9	1,998,000	89,000	926,000	983,000
10	2,158,000	96,000	926,000	1,136,000
11	2,331,000	104,000	926,000	1,301,000

2. On the date of the appraisal, a mortgage kicker based on 2% of rooms revenue is considered an appropriate expense. A deduction for this additional interest is reflected in the second column of the chart.
3. An equity yield rate of 19.9% is established.
4. Typical mortgage finance terms for similar hotel properties are set: interest rate—12.7%, amortization—30 years, mortgage constant—12.99%, and loan to value ratio—75%.
5. The going-out overall capitalization rate is set at 12.5%.
6. A trial market value of $9,500,000 is then tested:

		Ratio
Mortgage	$7,125,000	75%
Equity	2,375,000	25
Total	$9,500,000	100%

7. The yearly debt service is calculated (Column 3):

$$\$7,125,000 \times .1299 = \$926,000$$

127

The mortgage balance at end of 10th year is $6,707,000.

8. Property reversion (assumed sale price) at the end of 10th year is:

$$\frac{\$2,331,000}{.125} = \$18,650,000$$

9. The equity residual is calculated:

Assumed sale price	$18,650,000
Less: Mortgage balance	− 6,707,000
Sale expenses	− 1,018,000
Equity reversion	$10,925,000

10. Equity dividends plus the equity reversion are discounted to present value at the equity yield rate:

Year	Equity Dividend and Reversion	Discount Factor @ 19.9%	Equity Value
1	$ − 741,000	.8339	$ − 618,000
2	− 283,000	.6954	− 197,000
3	115,000	.5799	67,000
4	374,000	.4836	181,000
5	478,000	.4033	193,000
6	590,000	.3363	198,000
7	711,000	.2804	199,000
8	842,000	.2339	197,000
9	983,000	.1950	192,000
10	1,136,000	.1627	185,000
11	10,925,000	.1627	1,777,000
		Total	$2,374,000
		Equity value	$2,375,000(rounded)

11. The market value of mortgage is $7,125,000.

12. The market value is then verified:

	Trial Value	Ratio	Calculated Value	Ratio
Mortgage	$7,125,000	75%	$7,125,000	75%
Equity	2,375,000	25	2,375,000	25
Total	$9,500,000	100%	$9,500,000	100%

128

The advantage of valuing a hotel with a 10-year projection using an equity yield rate is that the projection period is reduced to 10 years. Another benefit of this approach is that the value of the mortgage component can be substantiated from the market by obtaining current and comparable mortgage terms for similar lodging facilities; assuming a 75% loan-to-value ratio, 75% of the property's market value can be justified. The difficulty arises in quantifying the equity reversion and determining an appropriate equity yield rate.

Estimating a value as of the 11th year to derive a value as of the first year does not always appear logical. Substantiating the 10th year's going-out, overall capitalization rate is also extremely difficult. The major drawback in utilizing this approach in today's market, however, is the equity yield.

Many types of real estate are controlled by highly sophisticated investors, but hotel owners do not always appreciate the true meaning of an equity yield. For the most part, hotel investors and operators think in terms of cash on cash, or equity dividends. They usually have no intention of selling their properties after five or ten years. Reversionary benefits, such as property appreciation and mortgage amortization, that are incorporated into a yield calculation are inherently considered in an equity dividend rate. Because hostelry investors think as they do, hotel appraisers can easily obtain extensive data to justify equity cash on cash requirements, but there is almost no support for an equity yield. Because the appraiser must reflect the thinking and actions of typical buyers and sellers, the current investment rationale of hotel owners is an essential consideration.

Investor outlook is constantly changing. Several years ago, hotel buyers were projecting in constant, not inflated, dollars. They based decisions on one stabilized year, rather than a two- to four-year projection. In the future, hotel investors should display more sophistication; they may use a yield approach to equity return rather than a simple cash-on-cash method.

Two- to Five-Year Projection Using Equity Dividend

Hotel investors currently base their equity components on two- to five-year equity dividend rate projections; this generally takes the form of a cumulative preferred return to the limited, or money, partner.

The value of the equity is calculated by capitalizing the equity dividend for the stabilized year at the equity dividend rate, and discounting that value plus the equity dividends for each of the intervening build-up years to the initial year at the equity dividend rate. The sum of the discounted values is the equity. This procedure eliminates the need to estimate a resale; it deals with equity dividend rather than equity yields.

The following steps and data are required to perform a valuation with the two- to five-year projection using cash on cash:

1. Income before interest and depreciation (net income) is projected for a two- to five-year period using inflated dollars.
2. If a mortgage kicker is considered a typical financing requirement, an appropriate yearly amount is deducted from the net income just as an operating expense would be deducted.
3. An equity dividend rate is established.
4. The terms for typical financing, including the interest rate, amortization term, and loan-to-loan ratio, are set forth.
5. A trial market value is hypothesized and the mortgage and equity components are calculated using the loan-to-value ratio.
6. Based on the initial mortgage balance determined in Step 5, the yearly debt service (interest and amortization) is deducted from the projection of the income before interest and depreciation, but after the mortgage kicker, to produce the equity dividend.
7. The value of the equity is calculated by capitalizing the equity dividend for the stabilized year, and discounting that value plus the equity dividend for each of the intervening build-up years to the initial year at the equity dividend rate. The sum of the discounted values is the equity.
8. Assuming that the mortgage represents market terms, its value is added to the equity value calculated in Step 7 to produce the property's market value. If the mortgage does not reflect market terms, its discounted value must be used.
9. When the calculated market value equals the trial market value selected in Step 5, the process is complete.

Here again, a computer can assist in the iterative process to equalize the trial and calculated values.

Another way to produce the proper market value is to solve a simultaneous equation in Step 5. The following example demonstrates this process:

1. In the previous example, the hotel analyst projected income before interest and depreciation (net income) to a stabilized year and then continued the projection to the 11th year by simply increasing the stabilized net income at the inflation rate. The two- to five-year projection process does not project net income beyond the stabilized year. The first column of the following chart uses data from the 30-year life cycle projection, but it estimates the income before interest and depreciation only up to the stabilized year (Year 4):

| | 1 | 2 | 3 |
Year	Projected Income Before Interest and Depreciation	Mortgage Kicker	Net Income After Mortgage Kicker
1	$ 200,000	$15,000	$ 185,000
2	680,000	37,000	643,000
3	1,096,000	55,000	1,041,000
4	1,360,000	60,000	1,300,000

2. A mortgage kicker based on 2% of rooms revenue is deducted in the second column of data.

3. An equity dividend rate of 9% is considered appropriate, based on the current equity return requirements of numerous hotel investors.

4. Typical mortgage finance terms for similar hotel properties are: interest rate—12.7%, amortization—30 years, mortgage constant—12.99%, and loan-to-value ratio—75%.

5. Using the two equations in the simultaneous valuation formula developed by Suzanne Mellen of Hospitality Valuation Services, Inc., the property's trial market value is hypothesized. The following variables are assigned:

NI	=	net income
V	=	value
M	=	loan-to-value ratio
f	=	annual debt service constant
n	=	number of years in projection period
d_e	=	annual equity dividend
R_e	=	annual equity dividend rate
$1/S^n$	=	present value of $1 factor

SVF Equation 1. Calculation of Annual Cash Flow to Equity (Equity Dividend):

$$NI^1 - (f \times M \times V) = d_e^1$$
$$NI^2 - (f \times M \times V) = d_e^2$$
$$NI^3 - (f \times M \times V) = d_e^3$$
$$(NI^n - (f \times M \times V)) \div R_e = d_e^n$$

SVF Equation 2. Calculation of Equity as Sum of Discounted Cash Flows:

$$(d_e^1 \times 1/S^1) + (d_e^2 \times 1/S^2) + (d_e^3 \times 1/S^3) + \ldots + (d_e^n \times 1/S^{(n-1)}) = (1 - M)V$$

Simultaneous Valuation Formula. Combination of Equations 1 and 2 by substitution of d_e:

$$((NI^1 - (f \times M \times V))1/S^1) + ((NI^2 - (f \times M \times V))1/S^2) +$$
$$((NI^3 - (f \times M \times V))1/S^3) + \ldots +$$
$$(((NI^n - (f \times M \times V)) \div R_e)1/S^{(n-1)}) = (1 - M)V$$

The simultaneous valuation formula is applied to the subject property to solve for V (value). The equity dividend is first expressed as the net income after the mortgage kicker minus debt service. In the stabilized year, the equity dividend is capitalized at the equity dividend rate.

SVF Equation #1:

Year	Net Income After Mortgage Kicker	−	Debt Service	=	Equity Dividend and Reversion
1	$ 185,000	−	$(.1299 \times .75 \times V)$	=	d_e^1
2	643,000	−	$(.1299 \times .75 \times V)$	=	d_e^2
3	1,041,000	−	$(.1299 \times .75 \times V)$	=	d_e^3
Stabilized	$\dfrac{1,300,000}{.09}$	−	$(.1299 \times .75 \times V)$	=	d_e^4

Discounting the equity dividend at the equity dividend rate produces the value of the equity, or .25 V:

Year	Discount Factor @ 9%
1	.9174
2	.8417
3	.7722
Stabilized	.7722

SVF Equation #2:

$$(d_e^1 \times .9174) + (d_e^2 \times .8417) + (d_e^3 \times .7722) + (d_e^4 \times .7722) = .25V$$

Substituting the equity dividend equations for $d_e^1 - d_e^n$ expresses everything in terms of V.

132

Simultaneous Valuation Formula:

$(($185,000 - (.1299 \times .75 \text{ V})) \times .9174) + (($643,000 - (.1299 \times .75 \text{ V})) \times .8417) + (($1,041,000 - (.1299 \times .75 \text{ V})) \times .7722) + ((($1,300,000 - (.1299 \times .75 \text{ V})) \div .09) \times .7722) = .25 \text{ V}$

Combining the terms results in:

$-.0894 \text{ V} - .0820 \text{ V} - .0752 \text{ V} - (.0752 \text{ V} \div .09) + \$169,719 + \$541,213 + \$803,860 + (\$1,003,860 \div .09) = .25 \text{ V}$

Further combining yields:

$-1.0822\text{V} + \$12,668,792 = .25 \text{ V}$

$$V = \frac{\$12,668,792}{1.3322}$$

$V = \$9,509,677$

Value $= \$9,500,000$ (rounded)

		Ratio
Mortgage	$7,125,000	75%
Equity	2,375,000	25
Total	$9,500,000	100%

6. The yearly debt service is $7,125,000 \times .1299 = \$926,000$

Year	Net Income After Mortgage Kicker	Debt Service	Equity Dividend
1	$ 185,000	$926,000	$ −741,000
2	643,000	926,000	−283,000
3	1,041,000	926,000	115,000
4	1,300,000	926,000	374,000

7. The value of the equity is:

Stabilized (Year 4) value $= \dfrac{\$374,000}{.09} = \$4,156,000$

133

Year	Equity Dividend and Reversion	Discount Factor @ 9%	Equity Value
1	$ − 741,000	.9174	$ − 680,000
2	− 283,000	.8417	− 238,000
3	115,000	.7722	89,000
4	4,156,000	.7722	3,205,000
		Total	$2,376,000
		Equity value	$2,375,000 (rounded)

8. The values of the mortgage and equity are added to yield the total market value:

Market Value of Mortgage	$7,125,000
Calculated Value of Equity	2,375,000
Total Value	$9,500,000

The values derived from the 10-year projection using an equity yield and the two- to five-year projection using cash on cash are identical. Because hotel investors currently use equity dividends rather than equity yields to value the equity component, the simpler two- to five-year projection using cash on cash appears more appropriate. By eliminating the longer projection period, the going-out capitalization rate, and the unsupportable equity yield assumptions, the appraisal reflects the present investment rationale of typical hotel buyers and sellers.

This approach does not prohibit the appraiser from projecting out to the 11th year, assuming a resale, calculating an equity reversion, and solving for the internal rate of return. If the assumptions employed in the 10-year projection using equity yield were incorporated into the internal rate of return calculations, the following IRRs would result:

Component	Internal Rate of Return
Total Property	16.6%
Mortgage	13.5
Equity	19.9

Capitalize One Stabilized Year

Instead of projecting income before interest and depreciation two or more years into the future, a stabilized estimate of net income can be capitalized at an appropriate overall rate. A stabilized net income refers to a representative year or, more technically, to the average net income over the property's economic life. In estimating stabilized earnings, more weight is given to the income expected during the early years because this income is less affected by discounting.

Looking once again at the 30-year life cycle projection one would expect net income to stabilize between the third and fourth years of operation. Based on this analysis and other judgments, the stabilized income before interest and depreciation, but after a mortgage kicker, is estimated as $1,140,000.

One procedure for developing a capitalization rate is the band-of-investment (weighted cost of capital) technique. Combining the weighted average of the return demanded by the mortgage position of the investment with the dividend required by the equity component results in a capitalization rate that reflects the basic financial composition of a hostelry investment.

The same mortgage terms and equity dividend requirements used in the two- to five-year projection using cash on cash are also appropriate here:

Mortgage finance terms:
Interest rate:	12.7 %
Amortization:	30 years
Mortgage constant:	12.99%
Loan-to-value ratio:	75 %
Equity dividend	9 %

The band of investment is used to calculate the capitalization rate:

	Portion		Rate		Weighted Rate
Mortgage	.75	×	.1299	=	.0974
Equity	.25	×	.0900	=	.0225
	Overall Capitalization Rate			=	.1199

The capitalized value is:

$$\frac{\$1,140,000}{.1199} = \$9,507,923, \text{ say } \$9,500,000$$

135

The value can be proved as follows:

75% Mortgage	$7,125,000	×	.1299	=	$ 926,000
25% Equity	2,375,000	×	.0900	=	214,000
	$9,500,000				$1,140,000

The proof shows that the $9,500,000 value can be divided into a mortgage portion (75%) of $7,125,000 and an equity portion (25%) of $2,375,000. The yearly mortgage payments of interest and amortization are calculated by multiplying the original mortgage balance by the constant (.1299), which results in an annual debt service of $926,000. The equity dividend is established by multiplying the equity investment by the anticipated equity return (.09), which yields $214,000. The annual debt service plus the equity dividend equals the stabilized income before interest and depreciation.

Essentially, the band-of-investment technique works backwards, using the projected stabilized net income to calculate the value that will meet the demands of mortgage and equity investors.

The components that form the band of investment, such as mortgage terms and equity requirements, can be well documented and supported. However, the stabilized net income used in this approach is difficult to estimate accurately. To get a good indication of a property's net income potential, the analyst should project its income and expenses several years. Weighting the figures to estimate a stabilized net income is a purely judgmental process.

Another way to derive a capitalization rate is to analyze the terms and conditions of actual market sales. For example, consider an investor who recently purchased a motel for $3,000,000. An income analysis indicates that the property has a stabilized income before interest and depreciation of $359,700. The market-derived overall capitalization rate for this sale is:

$$\frac{\$\ 359,700}{\$3,000,000} = 11.99\%$$

With this or any other market-related approach, the appraiser should have a complete understanding of transaction and the motivations of the parties involved. Adjustment must be made for any unusual details so that the derived capitalization rate represents normal market conditions. Some questions that the appraiser might ask are:

136

1. Is the stated selling price the market value, or does unusual existing or purchase-money financing affect this value?
2. Is the price based on existing or anticipated income?
3. Is the buyer motivated by special factors, such as tax shelter, or referral benefits.
4. Does the property suffer from deferred maintenance that must be corrected by the buyer?
5. Did the transaction conform to the doctrine of a willing buyer and a willing seller, both with full knowledge of all circumstances?
6. Is the comparable property somewhat similar to the property being appraised with respect to size, location, market, and condition?
7. Does the market-derived overall capitalization rate contain a reserve for replacement? If it does not, the subject property's projected income before interest and depreciation should also exclude a reserve for replacement.

An appraiser is seldom able to obtain enough data from the sale of a comparable hostelry to derive a meaningful capitalization rate based on the market. Just understanding the motivations of the buyer and the seller requires more than a casual observation of the transaction.

After-Tax Analysis

Recent changes in income tax laws allow for shorter depreciable lives and other after-tax benefits, so hotel and motel investments are becoming more popular among tax-conscious investors. The various tax benefits received by an equity investor are built into the equity dividend rate, which has traditionally been a before-tax calculation. As investors become more sophisticated, however, the after-tax aspect of real estate investments has a definite impact on their purchase decisions.

The use of computer-assisted valuation procedures will continue to grow in years to come, particularly in the area of after-tax analysis. Through the application of computerized programs and models, both appraisers and investors will be able to simulate future events and develop various investment alternatives and strategies.

Estimating Hotel Land Values
With Comparable Ground Leases

Hotel appraisers are sometimes asked to estimate the value of a total property and then to break out a separate land value. To calculate the land value, the appraiser investigates the market for recent land transfers of vacant parcels with similar acreage, street frontage, location, and zoning. Any differences between the comparable property and the subject are then adjusted using an adjustment grid. In practice, this process can be difficult due to the lack of sufficiently comparable vacant land sales data and the complexity of estimating the necessary adjustments. The comparable ground lease method is an alternate approach, based on the premise that the value of land is tied directly to its capacity to generate income at its highest and best use.

Each year, a number of hotel transactions are structured using ground leases. Typical rental terms vary from simple flat payments with escalation of adjustments to formulas based entirely on gross revenues. If the appraiser wants to quantify the income attributed to the land alone, the net rental using a percentage of gross revenue is the logical choice.

The following example illustrates the comparable ground lease procedure for estimating hotel land values using rental terms of actual hotel-motel ground leases.

Subject Property:	Southeastern Highway Motor Hotel
Number of rooms:	200
Projected rooms revenue:	$1,915,000
Projected food revenue:	$1,150,000
Projected beverage revenue:	$ 575,000

Ground leases for eight motor hotels similar to the subject were found; their rental formulas are set forth in the chart below. The estimated ground rental for the subject is calculated using the comparable formulas and the subject's projected revenues.

			Percentage of Gross			
Comparable Number	Fixed Rental (Per Room)	Plus:	Rooms Revenue	Food Revenue	Beverage Revenue	Estimated Ground Rental
1	None		3%	1%	1%	$ 74,700
2	$257		3	—	—	108,850
3	None		7	—	—	134,000
4	72		4	2	—	114,000
5	149		2	1	1	85,350
6	None		5	—	3	113,000
7	None		4	1	1	93,850
8	None		5	—	—	95,750
					Average Estimated Ground Rental =	$102,437

138

If all the comparables were equally similar to the subject, the average ground rent of $102,437 would be a supportable estimate of the income attributed to land. The value of the land would then be calculated by capitalizing the subject's estimated ground rent by an appropriate land capitalization rate:

$$\frac{\$102,437}{.11} \ = \ \$931,245$$

$$\text{Land value} \ = \ \$930,000 \text{ (rounded)}$$

Summary

Of the three valuation approaches available to the appraiser, the income capitalization approach generally provides the most persuasive and supportable conclusions when valuing a lodging facility. The appraiser follows a three-step process to stimulate the investment rationale of a typical hotel-motel buyer:

1. Project income before interest and depreciation for one stabilized year or for a number of years.
2. Develop a discount factor or capitalization rate that reflects the various investment risk components.
3. Apply the proper discounting and/or capitalization procedure.

The resulting estimate of market value represents the actions of hostelry investors and provides a basis for comparing investment alternatives.

Developing capitalization rates and applying the proper discounting procedure is an important part of the income capitalization approach. The appraiser should always try to reflect the current rationale and actions of typical buyers and sellers in the marketplace. Although several of the capitalization and discounting procedures described in this chapter were criticized for being overly subjective and not representative of present investment thinking, the analyst should remember the axiom of change. The discounting procedure utilized by hotel buyers this year may not be suited to market and investment conditions next year. Therefore, appraisers must constantly update their appraisal procedures to reach supportable estimates of market value.

6
Projecting Income and Expenses

To develop a supportable estimate of value using the income capitalization approach, realistic projections of income and expenses must be made. Hotels and motels are unique forms of real estate with many unusual characteristics, such as an intensive use of labor, cost-of-goods-sold expense categories, and a retail product identity. Therefore, special knowledge and data are required to create an estimate of the future income of a hostelry. This chapter describes a step-by-step procedure for projecting income and expenses using data sources available to all appraisers.

Existing Facility vs. Proposed Facility

Valuing an existing hostelry generally requires less field work than valuing a proposed facility. The appraiser first reviews the local supply and demand situation and projects the subject's future revenue. Then, using the property's operating ratios from previous years' audited statements, various expense categories are estimated. These estimates should be compared to the operating results of similar properties, if available, or to national averages; any differences should be resolved. Discrepancies might occur for several reasons:

1. *Unusual property characteristics.* Some hostelries are more costly to operate than others. For example, seashore motels have higher maintenance expenses, motels located in the Northeast pay more for energy, commercial hotels have more credit card commissions, and airport hostelries have shuttle bus expenses.

2. *Assumed competent management.* Projected expenses reflect competent management, which may be better than, equal to, or less capable than existing management.

3. *Different levels of occupancy and average rate.* When comparing expense ratios for two properties, care must be taken to see that both operate at similar levels of occupancy and have similar average rates. Lodging facilities generally experience more efficient operating results as their rates and occupancies increase.

The final estimate of income and expenses for an existing hostelry should be a blend of past operating results and future expectations.

Assembling sufficient market and comparable data for a proposed facility requires more research. The primary objective of market analysis is to accumulate enough information to formulate an estimate of occupancy and average rate. Once these two factors are established, rooms revenue and other sources of income may be computed.

Because a proposed hostelry has no operating history on which to base an expense projection, the appraiser must either obtain data from existing comparable properties or use national averages. Statistics from either of these sources are processed to project income and expenses for the subject. Because national averages are available to all appraisers, they are used here to demonstrate the projection procedure.

National Averages

Each year, two national accounting firms compile operating statistics and ratios for hundreds of hotels and motels throughout the United States. This information is categorized according to property size, room rate, geographical location, and other characteristics. These data represent average operating results and typical management ability. They may be used to evaluate an existing operation or to project income and expenses for a proposed facility. The two data sources are:

142

Trends in the Hotel-Motel Business
Pannell, Kerr, Forster & Company
420 Lexington Avenue
New York, NY 10017

U.S. Lodging Industry
Laventhol & Horwath
1845 Walnut Street
Philadelphia, PA 19103

Uniform System of Accounts for Hotels

The data contained in *Trends in the Hotel-Motel Business* and *U.S. Lodging Industry* are arranged in accordance with the *Uniform System of Accounts for Hotels*. This system, which was established by the Hotel Association of NY City in 1926 and later adopted by the American Hotel and Motel Association, provides a simple formula for classifying the accounts used by hostelries of all types and sizes. The universality of the system enables appraisers to compare individual properties or groups of properties with similar characteristics. A revised edition of the *Uniform System,* designed to comply with recent changes in accounting practices, was issued in 1977.

A complete set of financial statements for a hotel or motel should include a balance sheet, a statement of income and expenses, a statement of changes in financial position, and any disclosures necessary to comply with generally accepted accounting principles. The appraiser is primarily interested in the data contained in the statement of income and expenses.

The following list is extracted from *A Uniform System of Accounts for Hotels* (1977), published by the Hotel Association of New York City, Inc., 141 West 51st Street, New York, NY 10019. It shows how various hotel activities are classified in income and expense statements.

- *Operated departments*
    Rooms
    Food and beverage
    Casino
    Telephone
    Garage-parking lot
    Golf course
    Golf pro shop
    Guest laundry
    Swimming pool-cabanas-baths

143

Tennis
Other operated departments
Rentals and other income
  Total operated departments
- *Undistributed operating expenses*
  Administrative and general expenses
  Marketing
  Guest entertainment
  Property operation, maintenance, and energy costs
    Total undistributed operating expenses
- *Total income before fixed charges*
  Rent, property taxes, and insurance
  Interest
  Depreciation and amortization
- *Income before income taxes and gain or loss of sale of property*
  Gain or loss on sale of property
- *Income before income taxes*
  Income taxes
- *Net Income*

The total income after expenses for each major revenue-producing department is listed separately. If there are other departments' revenues and expenditures, they too are enumerated. The expenses incurred by undistributed overhead departments and capital expenses are then listed. These listings are totaled to determine the property's income before taxes. Finally, state and federal income taxes are deducted to arrive at the net income.

Because this format does not suit the specific needs of the appraiser who must capitalize income after property taxes and insurance, but before interest, depreciation, and amortization, a slightly modified system is required:

Income before fixed charges
Less
  Property taxes
  Insurance

Income before interest and depreciation

Under the Uniform System of Accounts, salaries and wages are allocated to the individual departments and expense categories as follows:

- *Rooms*

Assistant managers
Front office
Housekeeping
Service (doorman, front)
House officers and watchmen
- *Food and beverage*
  Food preparation
  Food and beverage service
- Administrative and general
  Manager's office
  Accounting office
  Data processing
  Front office bookkeeping
  Night auditors
  Credit office
  Timekeepers
  Receiving clerks
  Employment office
  Employees' locker attendants
- *Marketing*
  Sales department
  Advertising
  Merchandising
  Public relations and publicity
  Research
- *Guest entertainment*
  Manager
  Entertainment director
  Stagehands
- *Property operation, maintenance, and energy costs*
  Chief engineer and assistant
  Engineers
  Painters and paperhangers
  Radio and television repair
  Grounds and landscape
  Office and storeroom

Income-Expense Relationships

To utilize the Uniform System of Accounts and national average statistics properly, the appraiser should be familiar with the system's various revenue and expense categories (e.g., rooms revenue, telephone expense, administrative and general expenses, and energy costs). Each category has a specific income-expense relationship that reflects the weighted effect of the individual items assigned to it. The relative impact of each of these items (accounts), its volume relationship, and the proper use of units of comparison are described.

The category definition identifies the individual revenue and expense items contained in each broad category. The relative impact is the percentage of the category ascribable to the individual item. The volume relationship is based on the concept that the total revenue for a lodging facility is determined by three variables: occupancy, average rate, and food and beverage volume. The expenses that are relatively unaffected by moderate shifts in these variables are fixed expenses; expenses that vary with changes in occupancy are occupancy-sensitive variable expenses. The volume of food and beverage also affects certain food and beverage-sensitive variable expenses.

To compare operating statistics from actual hotel financial statements (or national averages), the data should be arranged to provide five units of comparison:

1. Percent of total revenue
2. Percent of rooms revenue
3. Percent of food and beverage revenue
4. Per available room
5. Per occupied room

Each unit of comparison reflects a specific volume relationship. The appraiser must evaluate the weighted impact of the individual revenue or expense items comprising a particular category and understand how these accounts are affected by changes in occupancy, average rate, and food and beverage volume. The appraiser can then select the unit of comparison that provides the most appropriate basis for projecting future income and expenses. Table 6.1 shows the volume relationships reflected by various units of comparison.

This table should be used in the following manner. If the weighted impact of the individual items comprising a particular category tends to be fixed, the per available room unit of comparison would be the most appropriate. The percent of rooms revenue should be selected if the category is both occupancy and rate sensitive. A category that is food and beverage-sensitive would use a percent of food and beverage revenue.

National averages are usually categorized on the basis of several variables, such as geographical location, rate groups, and property size. Because all ex-

Table 6.1 Volume Relationships

Units of Comparison	Weighted Impact of Items within Categories
Percent of rooms revenue	Occupancy and rate sensitive
Percent of total revenue	Occupancy, rate, and food and beverage sensitive
Percent of food and beverage revenue	Food and beverage sensitive
Per available room	Fixed
Per occupied room	Occupancy sensitive

penses are somewhat rate sensitive (i.e., a high-rate property will typically spend more, dollar-for-dollar, than a low-rate property), it is important to compare statistics of comparable operations, especially with respect to average rate. Comparing hostelries with similar rate structures eliminates the need to consider items that are rate sensitive. Therefore, the appraiser can use a percent of rooms revenue if the volume relationship is only occupancy sensitive, and a percentage of total revenue if the volume relationship is occupancy and food beverage sensitive.

Revenue Categories

Tables 6.2 through 6.4 illustrate the breakdown of each revenue category.

Rooms Revenue

Rooms revenue is generated by the sale of guest rooms to individual travelers, groups such as tours and business meetings, and permanent guests who take rooms for extended periods of time (Table 6.2).

Table 6.2 Rooms Revenue

Category	Percent of Category	Fixed Revenue	Variable Revenue Occupancy Sensitive	Variable Revenue Rate Sensitive	Variable Revenue Food and Beverage Sensitive
Transient-regular	0–100	—	Highly	Highly	—
Transient-group	0– 75	—	Highly	Highly	—
Permanent	0– 25	—	Highly	Highly	—
Total	100	—	Highly	Highly	—

The percentage of business represented by these three segments varies according to the type of property and its location. Many motels, especially budget motels with little or no meeting space, derive 100% of their occupancy from transient-regular patrons. A convention-oriented facility may achieve a substantial group occupancy. Permanent occupancy generally accounts for only a minor portion of a hotel's revenue. Long-term guests often require special facilities, such as individual kitchens and living rooms, and nonstandard services, such as maid service on a weekly, rather than daily, basis.

As might be expected, rooms revenue is highly occupancy and rate sensitive. In fact, these are the two primary variables that interact to form the total rooms revenue:

$$\text{Percentage occupancy} \times \text{average rate} \times \text{number of available rooms/day} \times 365$$
$$= \text{total rooms revenue}$$

The projection of total rooms revenue provides a basis for estimating all other categories of income and expense. Previous sections of this monograph have described various procedures for quantifying the local demand, allocating the resulting room nights among competitive hostelries, and arriving at an estimated occupancy ratio for an appraised property. The projected occupancy may be for one stabilized year or for several years, depending on how much detail the appraiser wishes to include in documenting future trends.

The estimate of average rate is a function of several interrelated factors:

1. Room rates charged by competitive properties and local supply and demand relationships.
2. The class of facilities offered by the subject.
3. Constraints imposed by invested capital, anticipated debt service, and operating costs.
4. The amount of double occupancy.
5. The usage of special rates (e.g., commercial, convention, government, senior citizen)

The current rates charged by local competitive hostelries generally establish a range of attainable rate levels for a proposed facility. Although a new hotel can typically achieve an average rate that is higher than an existing comparable property, the supply and demand market relationship is still important. Forcing rates substantially higher than local market levels ultimately results in an erosion of occupancy and profits.

Most hotel operators try to achieve an average rate that approaches price resistance. For example, a 200-room motel is currently operating at 80% occu-

148

pancy with a $50 average rate; the rooms revenue is $80\% \times \$50 \times 200$ rooms $\times$ $365 = \$2,920,000$. The operator discovered that by gradually raising the average rate to $53, the occupancy fell to 75% and the rooms revenue was $75\% \times \$53 \times$ 200 rooms $\times 365 = \$2,902,000$. Although revenue declined by $18,000, the bottom line increased as a result of savings in occupancy-sensitive variable expenses, such as maid service, linens, rooms supplies, and energy costs. Further attempts to increase rates were met by customer resistance and sharply lower occupancies. When profits began to decline, the rate was rolled back to $53, which showed maximum profitability.

The obtainable average rate often determines whether a proposed lodging facility is economically feasible. Hotel developers generally rely on this rule of thumb: Every dollar of average rate will support $1,000 of property cost (land, improvements, and furnishings) per room. Thus, if the market will support an average rate of $50, the total property cost should not exceed $50,000 per room. However, because of the inflationary nature of today's market, an average rate of $1.25–$1.50 is generally required to support each $1,000 of property cost.

The average rate is calculated by dividing the total rooms revenue by the number of occupied rooms over a specified period of time. This figure represents the weighted average of the number of rooms sold at various rates (e.g., single, double, commercial, tour, on-season, off-season). The advertised or "rack" rates tend to set the upper limits of the average rate. The actual average rate can be significantly below posted rates if the property offers one or more discounted price structures. Therefore, the appraiser should use average, not posted, rates when comparing lodging facilities.

Food and Beverage Revenue

Food and beverage revenue is generated by a hotel's restaurants, lounges, coffee shop, snack bar, banquet rooms, and room service (see Table 6.3). Aside from operations with active lounges and banquet facilities that draw local residents, hotel guests generally represent a substantial portion of the food and beverage patrons.

The ratios of food to rooms and food to beverage depend on many factors including the size and type of facilities, availability in the local market, competition, entertainment policy, and management expertise. Basing an estimate of food and beverage volume on "typical," "national," or "industry" ratios that are not supported by actual comparable operating experience can result in misleading projections. Like occupancy and average rate, food and beverage revenue projections should come from the market and reflect local supply and demand relationships.

149

The preferred method of projecting food and beverage volume for properties with little or no operating history is the build-up cover and average check approach. One patron eating one meal constitutes a cover. An average check is the total food volume divided by the number of covers. Projecting the number of covers a food outlet will serve per period and multiplying this number by the expected average check produces an estimate of food volume. Beverage revenue can be forecast in a similar manner.

A lodging facility has two sources of food and beverage patronage—guests of the hotel and local residents. The number of guests at a hotel on a daily basis (house count) is calculated by multiplying the property's occupancy by its total available rooms times the average number of guests per room (double occupancy).

occupancy	×	available rooms	×	average guests per room	=	house count
.70	×	140	×	1.3	=	127

The number of in-house food and beverage patrons is estimated by projecting the percent capture for each meal period and multiplying this factor by the average daily house count. Although many variables influence in-house capture (e.g., menu, prices, type of travelers, competition, and location), the percentage typically falls within the following ranges:

Meal Period	In-House Capture (restaurant and room service)
Breakfast	50%–80%
Lunch	10%–40%
Dinner	30%–60%
Evening (cocktail lounge)	20%–60%

The average check should be based on the menu prices at local restaurants and hotel dining rooms offering food and service of comparable quality. It can also be determined by creating a hypothetical menu and establishing prices based on actual food and labor costs.

Estimating the amount of local food and beverage business requires a market survey like the one used to quantify the room demand. Hotel restaurants do not typically attract a significant number of local residents. The following chart indicates what might be considered good restaurant patronage from local residents based on a percentage of the expected in-house capture:

Meal Period	Local Restaurant Patronage as % of In-House Capture
Breakfast	0%–15%
Lunch	60%–150%
Dinner	30%–60%

In contrast, banquet and lounge business often consists almost entirely of local residents. The volume from banquets depends on the size and type of facilities, local market demand, and the hotel's ability to sell and service this type of patronage. Interviewing area groups and organizations and evaluating the banquet business of other lodging and catering facilities can help measure the potential banquet market. Total banquet revenue is estimated by projecting the number and size of groups that will utilize the facilities during the year and multiplying this figure by the average banquet check.

Lounge business is usually very difficult to forecast if there is no previous operating history. Lounge patrons tend to be fickle and may frequent a night spot because it has the best entertainment or is the latest "in" place. Shifts in popularity often occur overnight, and this can cause a radical change in the lounge revenue.

Food and beverage income from other sources, such as public room rentals, cover charges, and miscellaneous banquet revenue, is usually estimated as a percentage of total food and beverage revenue.

Combining the projections for all food and beverage outlets results in a fi-

Table 6.3 Food and Beverage Revenue

Category	Percent of Category	Fixed Revenue	Variable Revenue		
			Occupancy Sensitive	Rate Sensitive	Food and Beverage Sensitive
Food	60–85	—	Moderately	—	Highly
Beverage	15–40	—	Moderately	—	Highly
Other income					
Public room rentals	0– 2	—	Moderately	—	Slightly
Cover and minimum charges	0– 2	—	Moderately	—	Highly
Sundry banquet income	0– 2	—	Slightly	—	Highly
Total	100	—	Moderately		Highly

nal income total. Although the procedure described above may appear to be complicated, time-consuming, and subject to error, it generally produces a more reliable estimate than using an unsubstantiated percentage of the rooms revenue.

Telephone Revenue

Telephone revenue is derived from the charges to guests for local and long distance phone calls and from commissions or discounts granted by the phone company for placing these calls. Most of the telephone revenue from guests is offset by a corresponding toll charge from the phone company. When the cost of equipment and hotel-related business calls are added to the toll expenses, the telephone department usually operates at a loss.

As indicated in Table 6.4, telephone revenue is highly occupancy sensitive. An estimate of total income for this department should therefore be based on the revenue per occupied room or a percentage of rooms rented.

Table 6.4   Telephone Revenue

Category	Percent of Category	Fixed Revenue	Variable Revenue		
			Occupancy Sensitive	Rate Sensitive	Food and Beverage Sensitive
Local	25–60	—	Highly	—	—
Long Distance	25–60	—	Highly	—	—
Service Charges	0–10	—	Highly	—	—
Commissions— local	0–10	—	Highly	—	—
Commissions— long distance	0–10	—	Highly	—	—
Total	100	—	Highly	—	—

Rental and Other Income

Rental and other revenue is derived from the rental of store and office space; concessions such as barber shops, checkrooms, and valet service; and commissions from auto rental, photography, telegram, and vending services. Hotel store leases are typically based on a minimum rental against a percentage of sales. Concessions and commissions are earned in much the same way. These sources of revenue appear to be highly occupancy sensitive and slightly food and beverage sensitive. Therefore, a percentage of total gross revenue should be used to

152

estimate this category. Rental and other income is expressed as a net revenue, with no offsetting expenses.

Expense Categories

Tables 6.5 through 6.11 show the breakdown of each expense category.

Rooms Expenses

Rooms expenses consist of items relating to the sale and upkeep of guest rooms and public space. Salaries, wages, and employee benefits account for a substantial portion of this category. Although the wages paid to maids, housemen, and bellmen tend to be highly occupancy sensitive, they are somewhat offset by the relatively fixed payroll for front desk personnel, public area cleaners, the housekeeper and the assistant manager. Therefore, salaries, wages, and employee benefits are only moderately occupancy sensitive.

Commissions and reservation expenses are usually based on room sales and therefore are highly occupancy and rate sensitive. Charges for china, glassware, linens, operating supplies, uniforms, and other operating expenses are only slightly affected by changes in volume, and are classified as very slightly occupancy sensitive. Contract cleaning is a relatively fixed expense, but it comprises only a small portion of the total category.

The weighted effect of the individual items of rooms expenses indicates that this category is primarily occupancy sensitive (see Table 6.5). Therefore, when evaluating data from one or more sources, the proper unit of comparison would be a percentage of rooms revenue.

Food and Beverage Expenses

Expenses for the food and beverage department consist of items necessary for the operation of a hotel's food, beverage, and banquet facilities. Sales and payroll costs are moderately to highly food and beverage sensitive and comprise a substantial portion of this category. The costs of china, glassware, linen, operating supplies, uniforms, and other operating expenses are very slightly food and beverage sensitive. Although the other expense items are basically fixed, they represent a relatively insignificant factor.

As shown in Table 6.6, food and beverage expenses are moderately food and beverage sensitive. Nevertheless, using one overall unit of comparison based on total food and beverage revenue may produce inaccurate projections. Most

Table 6.5 Room Expenses

Category	Percent of Category	Fixed Expenses	Variable Expenses		
			Occupancy Sensitive	Rate Sensitive	Food and Beverage Sensitive
Salaries and wages	50–70	—	Moderately	—	—
Employee benefits	5–15	—	Moderately	—	—
China, glassware and linen	3– 8	—	Very slightly	—	—
Commissions	0– 3	—	Highly	Highly	—
Contract cleaning	1– 3	Moderately	—	—	—
Laundry and dry cleaning	7–12	—	Slightly	—	—
Operating supplies	1– 4	—	Very slightly	—	—
Other operating expenses	1– 4	—	Very slightly	—	—
Reservation expenses	0– 8	—	Highly	Highly	—
Uniforms	1– 3	—	Very slightly	—	—
Total	100	Very slightly	Moderately	Slightly	

sources of national averages provide a fairly comprehensive breakdown of food and beverage expenses and the appraiser can usually obtain detailed statistics pertaining to the cost of food and beverage sales. By estimating these two costs separately (first as a percentage of food sales, and then as a percentage of beverage sales), the effect of any variance in the ratio of food to beverage sales is eliminated.

If sufficient data are available, salaries and wages can also be allocated to the food and beverage outlets individually or combined with other operating expenses and compared on the basis of total food and beverage revenue.

Telephone Expenses

Although revenue from guest calls is highly occupancy sensitive (see telephone revenue), most of this income is offset by a corresponding toll charge from the phone company. Telephone usage by the hotel, equipment rental, and other operating expenses are relatively fixed.

To project telephone expenses, a factor for the fixed items is added to the previously estimated telephone revenue. This net cost figure is normally estimated per available room (see Table 6.7).

154

Table 6.6 Food and Beverage Expenses

Category	Percent of Category	Fixed Expenses	Variable Expenses		
			Occupancy Sensitive	Rate Sensitive	Food and Beverage Sensitive
Cost of food consumed	35–45	—	—	—	Highly
Cost of employee meals	1– 4	—	—	—	Moderately
Cost of beverage sales	20–30	—	—	—	Highly
Salaries and wages	25–35	—	—	—	Moderately
Employee benefits	2– 9	—	—	—	Moderately
Silver, glassware, china and linen	1– 4	—	—	—	Very slightly
Contract cleaning	0– 3	Moderately	—	—	—
Kitchen fuel	1– 2	Moderately	—	—	—
Laundry and dry cleaning	1– 2	—	—	—	Slightly
Licenses	1– 2	Moderately	—	—	—
Music and other entertainment	2– 7	Moderately	—	—	—
Operating supplies	1– 3	—	—	—	Very slightly
Other operating expenses	1– 3	—	—	—	Very slightly
Uniforms	1– 2	—	—	—	Very slightly
Total	100	Slightly	—	—	Moderately

Administrative and General Expenses

Administrative and general expenses include the salaries and wages of all administrative personnel who are not directly associated with a particular department. Expense items related to the management and operation of the property also are allocated to this category.

Most administrative and general expenses are relatively fixed. The exceptions are: cash overages and shortages; commissions on credit card charges; credit and collection charges; management fees and a provision for doubtful accounts, which are somewhat affected by the quantity of transactions or total revenue; and salaries, wages, and benefits, which are very slightly influenced by volume. If the property is under professional supervision, the management fee account is usually listed separately. This further increases the weighted effect of the fixed items.

Table 6.7   Telephone Expenses

Category	Percent of Category	Fixed Expenses	Variable Expenses		
			Occupancy Sensitive	Rate Sensitive	Food and Beverage Sensitive
Local calls	20–60	—	Moderately	—	—
Long distance calls	20–60	—	Moderately	—	—
Rental of equipment	0–30	Moderately	—	—	—
Salaries and wages	0–10	Moderately	—	—	—
Employee benefits	0– 4	Moderately	—	—	—
Equipment charges	0–10	Moderately	—	—	—
Other operating expenses	0– 5	Moderately	—	—	—
Printing and stationery	0– 5	Moderately	—	—	—
Uniforms	0– 2	Moderately	—	—	—
Total	100	Moderately	Slightly	—	—

Because these expense items are fixed and very slightly variable, administrative and general expenses might be projected per available room. However, a projection based on this unit of comparison may be influenced by other, more variable items, so data from properties of comparable size and occupancy must be used. The results should be checked using a percentage of total revenue. If the two estimates are significantly different, a more thorough evaluation of the various items within the category is needed.

Management fees are generally established by contract and, therefore, can be accurately projected (see Table 6.8, pages 158-59).

Marketing Expenses

The marketing category is unique in that all the expense items, with the exception of fees and commissions, are controlled by management. Most lodging facilities establish an annual marketing budget which includes all planned expenditures. If this budget is followed, total marketing expenses can be projected accurately.

When a property operates under a franchise agreement, a portion of the marketing expense goes toward franchise fees. These royalties are typically tied to a percentage of rooms revenue, so this expenditure is highly occupancy and rate sensitive.

Many hotel-motel marketing experts argue that total revenues increase as advertising, sales, and other marketing expenses increase. Because there is some truth to this theory, the appraiser should project these expenses per available room and as a percentage of total revenue.

Marketing expenditures are unusual because results are not realized immediately, but the benefits are often extended over a long period. Depending on the type and scope of the advertising/promotion program implemented, results may be seen in a few weeks or not for several years. In general, the positive results of an effective marketing campaign tend to linger, and a property may enjoy the benefits of a concentrated sales effort for many months (see Table 6.9).

When projecting marketing expenses, these unique characteristics must be understood:

1. Unless a new lodging facility has a marketing program before opening, the normal lag time can impede the build-up of occupancy and income.
2. The initial years of operation generally require greater marketing expenditures.
3. If an existing property has spent very little on marketing prior to the projection period, a larger-than-normal budget may be required to maintain or increase current sales. On the other hand, an extensive advertising and promotion program may be followed by a period of low spending without adversely affecting revenue.

A marketing projection should also reflect the type of facility and the local supply and demand relationship. Certain types of hostelries, such as convention and resort properties, generally operate with a sizable marketing budget. Lodging facilities with marginal locations, access problems, excessive competition, declining market demand, and seasonal occupancy fluctuations also must spend more for advertising and promotion.

Guest Entertainment Expenses

The guest entertainment category is used when the expense for music and entertainment is significant and is intended to attract business to other departments besides food and beverage. Like marketing, guest entertainment represents a budgeted expense. There should be a direct relationship between expenditures and revenue, but the lag time and cumulative benefits are minimal.

When projecting guest entertainment, it is best to create an actual budget based on the current cost of a desired package. Most hostelry managers are familiar with the prices and terms demanded by various types of entertainment groups.

157

Table 6.8 Administrative and General Expenses

Category	Percent of Category	Fixed Expenses	Variable Expenses		
			Occupancy Sensitive	Rate Sensitive	Food and Beverage Sensitive
Salaries and wages	15–35	—	Very slightly	—	Very slightly
Employee benefits	1– 8	—	Very slightly	—	Very slightly
Cash overages and shortages	0– 3	—	Moderately	Moderately	Moderately
Commission on credit card charges	3–10	—	Highly	Highly	Highly
Credit and collection charges	0– 3	—	Moderately	Moderately	Moderately
Data processing expense	0–10	Moderately	—	—	—
Donations	0– 2	Moderately	—	—	—
Executive office expenses	3–10	Moderately	—	—	—
Insurance (general)	1– 5	Moderately	—	—	—

Internal audit expense	1– 3	Moderately	—	—	—
Internal communicating systems	0– 2	Moderately	—	—	—
Loss and damage	0– 1	Moderately	—	Highly	Highly
Management fees*	20–40	—	Highly	—	—
Miscellaneous	1– 4	Moderately	—	—	—
Postage and telegrams	2– 8	Moderately	—	—	—
Printing and stationery	3–10	Moderately	—	—	—
Professional fees	2– 5	Moderately	—	—	—
Provision for doubtful accounts	1– 3	—	Moderately	Moderately	Moderately
Trade association dues	1– 2	Moderately	—	—	—
Trade publications	1– 2	Moderately	—	—	—
Traveling expenses	1– 8	Moderately	—	—	—
Trustees' and registrars' fees	0– 3	Moderately	—	—	—
Uniforms	0– 2	Moderately	Slightly	Slightly	Slightly
Total	100	Moderately	Slightly	Slightly	—

*Sometimes stated separately.

Table 6.9   Marketing Expenses

Category	Percent of Category	Fixed Expenses	Variable Expenses		
			Occupancy Sensitive	Rate Sensitive	Food and Beverage Sensitive
Salaries and wages	10–60	Budgeted	—	—	—
Employee benefits	2–10	Budgeted	—	—	—
Sales	20–60	Budgeted	—	—	—
Advertising	20–60	Budgeted	—	—	—
Merchandising	5–40	Budgeted	—	—	—
Public relations and publicity	5–30	Budgeted	—	—	—
Research	0–15	Budgeted	—	—	—
Fees and commissions	0–50	—	Highly	Highly	Highly
Other selling and promotion	5–20	Budgeted			
Total	100	Budgeted	Slightly	Slightly	Slightly

Property Operation and Maintenance Expenses

Property operation and maintenance is another expense category that is largely controlled by management. Although some repairs are necessary to keep the facility open and prevent damage (e.g., plumbing, heating, and electrical), most maintenance items can be deferred for varying lengths of time.

All expense items in this category are either relatively fixed or very slightly occupancy and food and beverage sensitive. Based on this characteristic and the fact that management can regulate these expenditures, an amount per available room checked against a percentage of total revenue would be the preferred units of comparison (see Table 6.10).

Maintenance is an accumulating expense. If management elects to postpone a required procedure, they have not eliminated or saved the money, but only deferred payment until a later date. A lodging facility that has operated with a lower-than-normal maintenance budget for one or more years has probably accumulated a considerable amount of deferred maintenance. The appraiser should consider the effects of deferred maintenance items by deducting the amount required to cure existing deficiencies from the final estimate of value.

The age of a lodging facility greatly influences the required level of maintenance. A new property is protected for several years by modern equipment and

160

Table 6.10 Property Operation and Maintenance Expenses

Category	Percent of Category	Fixed Expenses	Variable Expenses		
			Occupancy Sensitive	Rate Sensitive	Food and Beverage Sensitive
Salaries and wages	20–40	—	Very slightly	—	Very slightly
Employee benefits	3–10	—	Very slightly	—	Very slightly
Building	3–10	—	Very slightly	—	Very slightly
Curtains and draperies	1– 7	—	Very slightly	—	Very slightly
Electrical and mechanical equipment	5–25	—	Very slightly	—	Very slightly
Elevators	0– 5	Moderately	—	—	—
Engineering supplies	2– 7	—	Very slightly	—	Very slightly
Floor covering	1–10	—	Very slightly	—	Very slightly
Furniture	1–20	—	Very slightly	—	Very slightly
Grounds and landscaping	1–10	Budgeted	—	—	—
Operating supplies	1–10	—	Very slightly	—	Very slightly
Painting and decorating	4–25	—	Very slightly	—	Very slightly
Refrigeration supplies	1– 5	Moderately	—	—	—
Removal of waste matter	2– 8	Moderately	—	—	—
Uniforms	0– 5	—	Very slightly	—	Very slightly
Miscellaneous	2– 8	Moderately	Very slightly	—	Very slightly
Total	100	Moderately	Very slightly	—	Very slightly

manufacturers' warranties. However, as a hostelry becomes older, maintenance expenses escalate. A well-organized preventive maintenance system may help delay deterioration, but most facilities face higher property operation and maintenance costs each year, regardless of their occupancy. Therefore, care must be taken to select comparable data from properties of similar age.

Energy Expenses

The significance of energy costs to hotel operators has increased considerably over the past several years. The rapid acceleration of electricity and fuel rates has eroded many profit margins and created a thriving business for energy consultants. Hotel operators have learned that energy costs can be controlled, and many properties have instituted conservation programs.

Most of a hostelry's electric and fuel consumption is relatively fixed and varies little with changes in occupancy.

Restaurants, kitchens, public areas, and corridors must be lighted and heated or air conditioned whether the house is full or not. The energy cost of an additional occupied room (i.e., a few hours of lights, television, and heat or air conditioning) is minimal. Therefore, energy costs should be projected per available room and cross-checked using either a percentage of rooms revenue or a per-occupied-room formula. A percentage of total revenue may be appropriate if the property attracts a sizable banquet business that generates a variable energy demand (see Table 6.11).

Energy costs vary geographically. Thus far, the recommended procedure for projecting departmental expenses has been to use comparable data or national averages from properties with similar rate structures. When projecting power and fuel requirements, however, room rates become a secondary consideration. The appraiser should instead select statistics from locations with similar climates and energy sources.

Rent Expense

The rent expense category is divided into three types of rentals typically incurred by lodging facilities: real estate rentals, electronic data processing rentals, and other rentals.

Table 6.11   Energy Expenses

Category	Percent of Category	Fixed Expenses	Variable Expenses		
			Occupancy Sensitive	Rate Sensitive	Food and Beverage Sensitive
Electric current	—	—	Very slightly	—	Very slightly
Fuel	—	—	Very slightly	—	Very slightly
Steam	—	—	Very slightly	—	Very slightly
Water	—	—	Very slightly	—	Very slightly
Total	—	—	Very slightly	—	Very slightly

162

Real estate rentals include the leasing of land, improvements, furniture, fixtures, and equipment. Land and improvement leases typically take one of four forms:

1. Fixed rental at periodic intervals.
2. Fixed minimum rental plus a percentage of revenues.
3. Fixed minimum rental against a percentage of revenues.
4. Straight percentage of revenues.

Furniture, fixtures, and equipment leases are usually fixed monthly rentals with terms of five to 10 years.

To project fixed rental expense items, the appraiser must carefully review the proposed or actual lease and understand all its provisions. If the lease calls for a percentage of revenues, the appraiser should use the estimates derived from revenue projections.

Electronic data processing rentals are normally fixed monthly rentals with no volume sensitivity.

Other rentals include the rental cost of any other major items that would otherwise have been purchased and capitalized as fixed assets. Any projections should be based on the actual lease terms and provisions.

Property Taxes

Property taxes include both real estate and personal property taxes. Property taxation is one of the primary ways municipalities obtain capital for public expenditures such as highways, schools, parks, and government services. Real estate taxes allocate the municipal tax burden on the basis of real estate value, i.e., the higher a property's value, the larger the owner's share of the tax burden. A property's assessed value is established by the local taxing authority and must be based on some percentage (1%–100%) of market value. As long as all parcels within a given jurisdiction bear an identical market value relationship, the allocation can be considered equitable.

The appraiser may use one of several procedures to project real estate taxes on a proposed lodging facility.

Assessed value developed by local assessor. The logical starting point is to have the local assessor review the proposed improvements and develop an estimate of their assessed value. In many instances, however, the assessing authority is reluctant to suggest a preliminary value for fear that it will be bound to that estimate when the project is completed. When a value is developed for the appraiser, it tends to be somewhat high so that the owner will not object when a final (lower) value is rendered.

Assessed value developed by comparable assessments. Property assessments are public information. An estimated assessment for the subject can be developed by evaluating the assessed values of other lodging facilities within a given jurisdiction. The appraiser should use a common unit of comparison, such as the assessed value per room or assessed value per square foot, to equalize any size differences and adjust for variances in restaurant space, meeting rooms, and recreational facilities. At times it may be helpful to separate the land from the improvements and calculate independent values for each element.

Residual procedure. Because the assessed values within a particular taxing jurisdiction should bear a specific percentage relationship to market value, multiplying this percentage or equalization rate by the local tax rate creates a capitalization rate adjustment that includes the estimated real estate taxes.

Example

A proposed motel is to be located in a jurisdiction where the equalization rate is 30% and the tax rate has stabilized at approximately $55.55 per $1,000 of assessed value. The property's stabilized income before interest, depreciation, and real estate taxes is projected at $512,500. The indicated capitalization rate derived by using the band-of-investment procedure is 12%. The projected real estate tax can be calculated as follows:

Adjusted capitalization rate:

Band-of-investment rate	.12000
Plus real estate tax adjustment (.30 × .0555)	+ .01665
Equals adjusted capitalization rate	.13665

Estimated market value:

$$\frac{\$512,500}{.13665} = \$3,750,000$$

Estimated assessed value:

$$\$3,750,000 \times .30 = \$1,125,000$$

Projected real estate taxes:

$$\frac{\$1,125,000}{1,000} \times \$55.55 = \$62,500$$

Proof:

Income before interest, depreciation, and real estate taxes	$512,500
Less projected real estate taxes	− 62,500
Equals income before interest and depreciation	$450,000

Estimated market value:

$$\frac{\$450,000}{.12} = \$3,750,000$$

The residual procedure is based on the assumption that the equalization rate reflects the actual relationship between the area's assessed values and market values. The valuation procedures and projections used by the appraiser must closely resemble those employed by the assessor in order to obtain a similar opinion of market value. Unfortunately, these two premises are generally invalid, so the residual procedure is not very reliable.

The appraiser should investigate all three procedures for projecting taxes, but in most cases the greatest weight should be given to the real estate tax projection developed by comparable assessments.

Insurance Expenses

The insurance expense category includes the cost of insuring the building and its contents against damage or destruction from fire, weather, sprinkler leakage, boiler explosion, plate glass breakage, and so forth.

Insurance rates are based on many factors, including building design and construction, fire detection and extinguishing equipment, the local fire district, the distance from the fire house, and the area's fire experience. A local insurance agent can provide a fairly accurate estimate of insurance expenses based on either the facility's plans and specifications or the fire ratings of comparable lodging facilities in the area. If the appraiser must rely on national averages, the expense per available room would be the appropriate unit of comparison.

Expense Projections Using National Averages

The preceding section has described the income-expense relationship of each departmental category included in the *Uniform System of Accounts*. The individual items in each category were evaluated on the basis of their sensitivity to changes in volume. The overall sensitivity of the category was determined and an appropriate unit of comparison was recommended. This section will show how these units of comparison are actually used to develop expense projections based on the data available from national averages.

When using national averages, the first step is to select the property type that best resembles the lodging facility being appraised. Distinctions between transient hotels and motels and motor hotels with restaurants are based on both size and average rate. In some cases a visual interpolation of the two sets of statistics might be appropriate. For example, in appraising a 175-room facility with a high average rate, some of the rate-sensitive data for transient hotels might be used. Similarly, the appraisal of a 400-room economy property might take into account the statistics for motels and motor hotels with restaurants.

When identifying property type, the appraiser should also determine which characteristics within the type are most appropriate for the subject. National data are divided into several main classifications that are further broken down into subclassifications.

- *Geographical divisions*
    New England and Middle Atlantic
    North Central
    South Atlantic
    South Central
    Mountain and Pacific
- *Rate groups*
    Ranges that vary yearly and by property type
- *Size (rooms)*
    Ranges that vary by property type
- *Size of city*
    Large city
    Small city
- *All properties*
    Average of all subclassifications

The key to selecting the proper set of statistics is the summary description of the average property comprising the subclassification. The information contained in this description includes average size (number of rooms), percentage of occupancy, average rate, and ratio of food, beverage, and rooms sales.

The appraiser first finds the subclassifications containing average rates similar to the projected rate of the subject. The list of subclassifications with comparable rate structures may be narrowed by isolating properties that are approximately the same size. If this does not pinpoint one subclassification, the appraiser should look for similar occupancy levels and geographic locations. Again, some of the statistics for two subclassifications may be merged through visual interpolation. At this stage, the appraiser has isolated a set of statistics applicable to the subject, at least with respect to average rate and size. These data should then be arranged by expense category, as shown in Table 6.13.

Using the rooms, food, and beverage revenues previously developed, a similar table is constructed substituting the percentage and per-room amounts with estimates of the total dollar expense for each category (see Table 6.14). Each category will have four expense projections based on the four units of comparison. The preceding section described the expense categories in detail and recommended one or more units of comparison reflecting volume and rate sensitivity.

If the rate, occupancy, and size of the subject are similar to the average characteristics of the selected subclassification, and the expense estimate developed by the recommended unit of comparison is supported after cross-checking, the resulting figure is well-supported by national data. Any major variance between the recommended unit of comparison and the cross-check should be investigated. In most instances the difference can be attributed to an unusual volume relationship between food and beverage and rooms.

In many cases the selected subclassification will show a comparable average rate, but the projected occupancy or size may not be similar. Under these circumstances the subclassification's percentages and expenses per room must be adjusted to reflect the different volume relationship.

Occupancy adjustments. If the subclassification's occupancy is lower than that of the property being appraised, the expenses per available room are in-

Table 6.13   Expenses by Categories

Expense Category	Percentage of Total Revenue	Percentage of Rooms Revenue	Expense per Available Room	Expense per Occupied Room
Rooms department	N/A	27.8	$2,228	$3,406
Telephone—net cost	1.0	1.9	153	233
Administrative and general	8.0	14.3	1,145	1,750

N/A: Not Applicable

creased and the percentage factors for both rooms and total revenue are decreased. If the subclassification's occupancy is higher, the expenses per available room are decreased and the percentage factors for both rooms and total revenue are increased.

Size adjustments. If the number of rooms in the average property in the subclassification is less than the number in the property being appraised, the expenses per available room are decreased and the percentage factors for both rooms and total revenue are decreased. If the number of rooms in the average subclassification property is greater, the expenses per available room are increased and the percentage factors for both rooms and total revenue are increased.

Depending on the differences between the average property in the selected subclassification and the projected characteristics of the property being appraised, these adjustments may be minimal or quite significant. Although the type, direction, and reasoning behind each adjustment have been discussed here, the extent of change depends on a variety of factors, such as the composition of the expense category, the amount of disparity, the property type competition, local labor and operating costs, and the age of the data. At this point in the projection process, any mechanical manipulation of statistical data is futile and the appraiser must rely on personal experience.

Table 6.14   Dollar Expense Estimates

Category	Recommended Units of Comparison	Cross-Checked Against
Rooms expense	Percentage of rooms revenue	Per occupied room
Food and beverage expense	Percentage of food and beverage revenue	—
Telephone expense	Per available room	Percentage of rooms revenue
Administrative and general	Per available room	Percentage of total revenue
Marketing	Per available room	Percentage of total revenue
Property operation and maintainance	Per available room	Percentage of total
Energy costs	Per available room*	Per occupied room
Property taxes	Per available room	—
Insurance	Per available room	—

*Interpolate with the geographical subcategory.

Summary

Projecting income and expenses for a lodging facility is a step-by-step process that follows a logical sequence. The procedure is based on a well-documented estimate of occupancy and average rate, supported by the local supply and demand relationship. Food and beverage revenue is projected on a similar basis, after estimating the in-house capture and local restaurant patronage.

The expense categories identified by the *Uniform System of Accounts* exhibit different volume sensitivities, which influence the selection of an appropriate unit of comparison. When all the expense categories have been quantified, they are arranged like a standard income and expense statement. The resulting net income before interest and depreciation is then ready to be capitalized into an estimate of value.

Bottom line percentages of industrial property and office buildings generally fall into an acceptable range. Hotels and motels, however, have no standard profit percentage. Successful lodging facilities show bottom lines of anywhere from 5%–50% due to the widely different profit potentials of food and beverage revenue and rooms gross. A rooms-only business may show a bottom line of 30%–40%; a banquet-oriented facility will generate more dollar profits, but exhibit a small profit percentage. For this reason, using shortcuts or "rules of thumb" to eliminate some of the steps in the projection process tends to reduce the overall reliability of the final estimate.

A Word of Caution

The use of national averages in projecting income and expenses has been emphasized here for illustration and because these statistics are readily available to all appraisers. In appraising lodging facilities, national averages should be the "data of last resort," used only when there are no actual operating statistics from the subject and comparable properties in the area. The following case study concerns the proposed Sheraton Inn that was discussed in Chapters 2 and 3.

CASE STUDY

Projected Revenues

The revenue categories under the *Uniform System of Accounts* that are appropriate for the proposed Sheraton Inn are rooms, food and beverages, telephone, and other income.

Rooms Revenue

Based on the market study that examined the local demand for transient accommodations and the current supply of lodging facilities, the subject property should attract the following number of room nights for the first, second, and stabilized years.

Years	Projected Room Nights Captured	Room Nights Available	Projected Occupancy
1	43,801	73,000	60%
2	51,154	73,000	70
Stabilized	55,032	73,000	75

The average rates for all competitive lodging facilities within the market area are researched in the field. The following chart lists the average rates of the five hostelries:

Hotel	Average Rates
Days Inn	$29.00
Suncrest Motel	33.00
Holiday Inn	40.00
Hilton Hotel	48.00
Ramada Inn	38.00
Average	$39.27

The present average rate for the area is $39.27; the Hilton Hotel has the highest rate of $48.00.

In today's (current) dollars, the Sheraton Inn can expect to have an average rate slightly higher than the Hilton's because:

1. The Sheraton Inn will be a new facility, and new facilities generally achieve higher average rates.
2. The Sheraton Inn will occupy a prime location.
3. The Sheraton's facilities will be comparable to the Hilton.
4. The Sheraton will derive a smaller portion of its business from convention

patronage, which is generally discounted and tends to reduce a hotel's average rate.

Based on this analysis, the Sheraton Inn's average rate is estimated at $50.00 in today's dollars (development Year 0).

Because this projection of income and expenses should be made in inflated, not constant, dollars, an appropriate inflation rate must be determined. The appraiser can use an overall inflation rate for both income and expenses, a variable inflation rate that changes each year, different inflation rates for income and expenses, or different inflation rates for individual income and expense items. The inflation option employed depends on the future inflation expectations within the marketplace. This case study will use an overall inflation rate of 8% per year (compounded) for both income and expenses.

All estimates of revenue and expenses should be made in current dollars and inflated to the subject's opening date, and then inflated further to the stabilized year. The Sheraton's average rate per occupied room is calculated in the following chart:

Average Rate Per Occupied Room

Development Year	0	1	2	3	4	5
Operational Year	—	—	—	1	2	Stabilized
Basic average rate	$50.00	$54.00	$58.30	$63.00	$68.00	$73.45
Occupancy adjustment					+4%	+6%
Average rate				$63.00	$70.70	$77.85

The development year starts with Year 0, which is the date construction commences. The subject property is constructed in two years and opens in operational Year 1, which is the third development year. In Year 1 (the effective date of the appraisal) the Sheraton Inn's average rate is $63.00.

Inflation is not the only factor that affects a hotel's average rate. As occupancy increases, the average rate may rise faster than inflation because management can sell more higher-priced rooms during peak periods when lower-priced room are not available.

To reflect the subject's improved competitive position, a 4% occupancy adjustment is made in operational Year 2, and a 6% adjustment in Year 3.

Combining the projected occupancy with the average rate results in an estimate of rooms revenue as shown in the following chart.

Rooms Revenue

Years	% Occupancy		Average Rate		Available Rooms		Days Per Year		Rooms Revenue
1	.60	×	$63.00	×	200	×	365	=	$2,759,000
2	.70	×	$70.70	×	200	×	365	=	$3,613,000
Stabilized	.75	×	$77.85	×	200	×	365	=	$4,262,000

Food and Beverages Revenue

An investigation of the local demand for food, beverage, and banquet facilities indicates that area residents eat dinner at a full-service restaurant an average of two to three times per month. Very few dine at an area motel, except for an occasional banquet.

The closest restaurant that serves breakfast is a small diner, approximately one mile from the Sheraton Inn. Because the diner is beyond walking distance, the subject property should expect a fairly high in-house capture for breakfast. The only local market will be an occasional breakfast meeting between a motel guest and a local resident.

Interviews with tenants of the large office park directly across from the Sheraton reveal that there is a fair to good demand for executive luncheon business. The complex has a cafeteria that is popular among the clerical and middle-management personnel; but most business entertaining is done at one of several first-class restaurants located approximately three to four miles away. The Sheraton's in-house lunch capture should be low, because most of the commercial patrons will opt for different surroundings at one of the competitive restaurants. The local capture will generally consist of business luncheons generated by the office park.

Dinner will attract a greater proportion of in-house guests, particularly those who have just checked in or who are about to check out. The local capture will probably consist of area residents dining alone and those meeting with a guest of the motel.

The local market for banquet patronage appears to be good. Many of the office park companies expressed a need for a nearby facility at which to hold conferences, business meetings, and office parties. The surrounding community has few convenient meeting and banquet facilities to accommodate anniversary parties, association meetings, and fraternity gatherings. With a proper sales effort, the Sheraton should attract a steady flow of banquet revenue.

The following income analysis is based on the preceding market evaluation

172

and a review of the menu prices and facilities offered by competing restaurants and motels.

Restaurant Food Revenue

Based on the expected demand mix for the Sheraton Inn, a double occupancy of 1.3 guests per room is expected. The following chart shows the subject's estimated yearly house count.

Estimated Yearly House Count

Year	Rooms		Guests per Room		Occupancy		Days per Year		Yearly House Count
1	200	×	1.3	×	.60	×	365	=	56,940
2	200	×	1.3	×	.70	×	365	=	66,430
Stabilized	200	×	1.3	×	.75	×	365	=	71,175

The number of in-house food service patrons, or capture, is calculated by projecting the percentage of in-house capture for each meal period and multiplying this factor by the yearly house count. The Sheraton Inn is expected to capture 70% of its house count for breakfast, 20% for lunch, and 40% for dinner. The in-house food service capture by meal period is illustrated in the following chart:

Projected In-House Food Service Capture (Including banquet business from in-house groups)

	Yearly House Count		% In-House Capture		In-House Food Service Capture
Year 1					
Breakfast	56,940	×	.70	=	39,858
Lunch	56,940	×	.20	=	11,388
Dinner	56,940	×	.40	=	22,776
Year 2					
Breakfast	66,430	×	.70	=	46,501
Lunch	66,430	×	.20	=	13,286
Dinner	66,430	×	.40	=	26,572
Stabilized Year					
Breakfast	71,175	×	.70	=	49,822
Lunch	71,175	×	.20	=	14,235
Dinner	71,175	×	.40	=	28,470

Local Patronage Food Revenue

	In-House Food Service Capture		Average Check		In-House Food Revenue		Local Patronage as % of In-House Food Revenue		Local Patronage Food Revenue
Year 1									
Breakfast	39,858	X	$ 7.50	=	$ 298,900	X	.03	=	$ 9,000
Lunch	11,388	X	12.50	=	142,300	X	.40	=	57,000
Dinner	22,776	X	21.50	=	489,700	X	.30	=	146,900
Total					$ 930,900				$212,900
Year 2									
Breakfast	46,501	X	$ 8.05	=	$ 374,300	X	.05	=	$ 18,700
Lunch	13,286	X	13.40	=	178,000	X	.50	=	89,000
Dinner	26,572	X	23.20	=	616,500	X	.35	=	215,800
Total					$1,168,800				$323,500
Stabilized Year									
Breakfast	49,822	X	$ 8.55	=	$ 425,900	X	.05	=	$ 21,300
Lunch	14,235	X	14.30	=	203,500	X	.50	=	101,700
Dinner	28,470	X	24.95	=	710,300	X	.35	=	248,600
Total					$1,339,700				$371,600

Research of comparable restaurants and other lodging facilities provides a basis for estimating the Sheraton's average food check (exclusive of liquor) per cover (patron). Separate estimates are made for each meal period and an overall banquet average is calculated. Inflating today's dollars out five years produces the following chart.

Average Check

Development Year	0	1	2	3	4	5
Operational Year	—	—	—	1	2	Stabilized
Breakfast	$ 6.00	$ 6.45	$ 6.95	$ 7.50	$ 8.05	$ 8.55
Lunch	10.00	10.75	11.60	12.50	13.40	14.30
Dinner	17.00	18.40	19.90	21.50	23.20	24.95
Banquet	13.50	14.60	15.75	17.00	18.30	19.55

The local patronage food capture is based on a percentage of the in-house food revenue projection. This percentage can vary from year to year, depending on the local community's acceptance of the hotel's restaurant. The next chart calculates the Sheraton's in-house food revenue by multiplying the in-house food service capture for each meal period by the average check for the meal. The local patronage food revenue is then estimated by multiplying the in-house food revenue by the local patronage percentage. (See chart on page 174.)

Adding the in-house food revenue and the local patronage food revenue produces the total restaurant food revenue.

Restaurant Food Revenue

Year	In-House Food Revenue		Local Patronage Food Revenue		Total Restaurant Food Revenue
1	$ 930,900	+	$212,900	=	$1,143,800
2	1,168,800	+	323,500	=	1,492,300
Stabilized	1,339,700	+	371,600	=	1,711,300

Banquet Food Revenue

Banquet and lounge business often draws on local residents. The volume from banquets depends on the size and type of catering facilities, local market demand, and the hotel's ability to attract and service this type of patronage. Area groups and organizations are interviewed to determine the amount of banquet demand and the type of facilities required. Examining the current usage of local catering halls and other hotel banquet facilities also helps quantify banquet demand.

Based on an analysis of the local banquet market and the excellent catering facilities planned for the Sheraton Inn, a banquet demand of three functions per week averaging 110 people per banquet is projected. Multiplying the projected banquet demand by the average banquet check results in the following estimated banquet food revenue for the first three operational years.

Banquet Food Revenue

Year	Average Banquet Check		Average Size of Banquet		Estimated Banquets per Week		Weeks per Year		Banquet Food Revenue
1	$17.00	×	110	×	3.0	×	52	=	$291,700
2	18.30	×	110	×	3.0	×	52	=	314,000
Stabilized	19.55	×	110	×	3.0	×	52	=	335,500

Total Food Revenue

Total food revenue is the combination of food revenue from restaurant sales and banquet sales.

Total Food Revenue

	Year 1	Year 2	Stabilized
Projected restaurant food revenue	$1,143,800	$1,492,300	$1,711,300
Projected banquet food revenue	291,700	314,000	335,500
Projected total food revenue	$1,435,500	$1,806,300	$2,046,800
Rounded	$1,435,000	$1,806,000	$2,046,000

Beverage Revenue

Several area motels have active cocktail lounges that attract both motel guests and local residents. Based on interviews with nearby motel and restaurant managers, there is a consistent relationship between the ratio of food and beverage sales. Although a ratio analysis is not necessarily valid in every market area, there is sufficient evidence from facilities near the Sheraton Inn to indicate that beverage revenue should amount to approximately 40% of food revenue.

Beverage Revenue

Year	Total Food Revenue		Beverage to Food Ratio		Beverage Revenue
1	$1,435,000	×	.40	=	$574,000
2	1,806,000	×	.40	=	723,000
Stabilized	2,046,000	×	.40	=	818,000

Telephone Revenue

As a commercial-oriented lodging facility, the Sheraton Inn is expected to generate a high volume of local and long-distance telephone calls. According to the local telephone company, nearby lodging facilities are currently averaging $650–$675 per occupied room in yearly telephone revenue. Based on today's dollars, the Sheraton should produce $661 per occupied room. Inflating this factor at 8% per year produces the following estimate of telephone revenue per occupied room:

Telephone Revenue Per Occupied Room

Development Year	0	1	2	3	4	5
Operational Year	—	—	—	1	2	Stabilized
Telephone revenue	$661	$714	$771	$833	$900	$973

Telephone revenue is calculated by multiplying the average number of occupied rooms per day (occupancy × room count) by the projected telephone revenue per occupied room.

Telephone Revenue

Year	Occupied Rooms		Revenue Per Occupied Room		Telephone Revenue
1	120	×	$833	=	$100,000
2	140	×	900	=	126,000
Stabilized	150	×	973	=	146,000

Other Income

Other income is expected to be derived from vending machines, the game room, a small gift shop, commissions from auto rentals, and the check room. National averages show that similar hotels receive $320–$350 of income per occupied room after all expenses. The income per occupied room inflated at 8% is:

Other Income per Occupied Room

Development Year	0	1	2	3	4	5
Operational Year	—	—	—	1	2	Stabilized
Other income	$331	$357	$386	$417	$450	$487

Multiplying the average number of occupied rooms by the estimate of other income revenue provides the following chart.

Other Income

Year	Occupied Rooms		Revenue Per Occupied Room		Other Income
1	120	×	$417	=	$50,000
2	140	×	450	=	63,000
Stabilized	150	×	487	=	73,000

Summary of Revenues

Totaling the projected rooms, food, beverage, telephone, and other income revenue estimates produces this table of total revenue.

Summary of Total Revenues

	Year 1 $	%	Year 2 $	%	Year 3 $	%
Rooms	$2,759,000	56.1%	$3,613,000	57.1%	$4,262,000	58.0%
Food	1,435,000	29.2	1,806,000	28.5	2,046,000	27.9
Beverage	574,000	11.7	723,000	11.4	818,000	11.1
Telephone	100,000	2.0	126,000	2.0	146,000	2.0
Other income	50,000	1.0	63,000	1.0	73,000	1.0
Total	$4,918,000	100.0%	$6,331,000	100.0%	$7,345,000	100.0%

Projected Expenses

Because the Sheraton Inn is a proposed hotel with no operating history, and comparable income and expense data from nearby lodging facilities are unavailable, some of the projected expenses must be derived from national average statistics.

For the purpose of illustration, the ratios and statistics are presented in a manner similar to the national averages published each year by the accounting firms of Pannell Kerr Forster & Company and Laventhol & Horwath. The data, however, are hypothetical and designed to demonstrate the procedures for projecting expenses.

Because of its size, the subject property most closely resembles motels and motor hotels with restaurants. The statistics within this property type are divided into four main classifications and 12 subclassifications. The accompanying table describes the average property in each subclassification. (See page 180.)

Selecting the Most Comparable Data

When using national averages, the data that are most comparable to the property being appraised must be identified. The table presents a summary description of the average property in each subclassification. For example, under the geographical subclassification "South Central," there may be 85 hotels located in the South Central United States. Each of these hotels has different characteristics,

Summary Description

	Average Size (Rooms)	% of Occupancy	Average Rate	Food & Beverage to Rooms Ratio
All motels and motor hotels with restaurants	180	70.6	$46.30	.73
Geographical				
New England & Middle Atlantic	171	69.2	55.20	.70
North Central	205	73.8	50.25	.74
South Atlantic	190	70.3	45.30	.72
South Central	210	72.1	41.50	.71
Mountain & Pacific	196	79.0	49.40	.76
Average Rate				
Under $35	140	68.4	41.30	.75
$35–$50	188	72.8	46.50	.73
Over $50	230	74.6	65.40	.69
Size				
Under 150 rooms	140	68.0	39.10	.73
150–200 rooms	165	69.0	44.30	.76
Over 200 rooms	285	71.4	51.00	.74

but the average characteristic is a room count of 210 rooms, 72.1% occupancy, a $41.50 average rate, and a ratio of food and beverage to rooms of 71%. Matching the characteristics of the Sheraton Inn to one of the subclassifications pinpoints the national data most appropriate for making expense projections.

Selecting the proper subclassifications is based on the process of elimination and proceeds in the following order: average rate, size (number of rooms), occupancy, and geographic location. First, all hotels with dissimilar average rates are eliminated. Then, all properties with significantly different room counts are thrown out. If, at this point, the range has not been narrowed to one subclassification, all facilities with greatly differing occupancies are eliminated. The last selection criterion is geographic location.

As of its stabilized year of operation, the proposed Sheraton will have the following characteristics:

	Stabilized Projection
Number of rooms	200
Percentage of occupancy	75%
Average rate	$77.85
Average rate in current dollars	$55.00
Ratio of food and beverage to rooms	.67

Subclassification Selection

The average rates from the chart of subclassification characteristics range from $39.10 to $65.40. Three of the twelve subclassifications have average rates similar to the Sheraton's $50.00 rate. The other nine subclassifications have dissimilar rates, so they are eliminated. The subclassifications with similar average rates are:

North Central	$50.25
Mountain and Pacific	49.40
Over 200 Rooms	51.00

From these three subclassifications, properties of differing size are eliminated. The average property in the Over 200 Rooms subclassification has 285 rooms, so it cannot be compared to the Sheraton. The other two subclassifications have room counts similar to the subject.

North Central	205 rooms
Mountain and Pacific	196 rooms

Next, one of the two subclassifications must be eliminated based on occupancy. The North Central's occupancy of 73.8% is closer to the Sheraton's stabilized level of 75% than the Mountain and Pacific occupancy of 79%. This difference is significant enough to drop the Mountain and Pacific subclassification from further consideration.

Based on this selection procedure, the North Central subclassification provides the most comparable data for projecting many of the subject's expenses. Although the Sheraton Inn is not located in the North Central United States, rate, size, and occupany tend to affect operating expenses more than geographical location and should, therefore, be given greater weight when selecting comparable data.

The table on pages 184-85 shows the operating data for the North Central subclassification as they generally appear in national averages. This table will be referred to in the case study as the North Central Data Table.

Data from national averages are typically arranged as a percentage of total revenue, percentage of rooms revenue, percentage of food and beverage revenue, and a dollar amount per available room. The dollar amount per occupied room can be calculated by dividing the amount per available room by the average occupancy rate (73.8%) for the subclassification. The fixed and variable characteristics of an individual expense category determine which unit of comparison provides the most appropriate basis for the expense estimate.

Rooms Expense

Rooms expense is occupancy and rate sensitive, so the percentage of rooms revenue is the proper unit of comparison. The rooms expense percentage from the North Central Data Table is 24.8%. Using this percentage as a base, certain adjustments are made to bring the North Central data in line with the characteristics of the Sheraton. The following chart shows the two areas where minimal adjustments are needed.

	North Central Data	Sheraton Inn Projections
Occupancy	73.8%	75.0%
Average rate	$50.25	$50.00

The Sheraton's higher occupancy indicates a somewhat more efficient operation, which will probably lower expense percentages. Higher occupancies cause per-room units of comparison to increase; obviously, when occupancies decline, these units of comparison decrease.

The Sheraton's lower average rate tends to increase its percentage expense ratio, but has little impact on per room units of comparison.

Precise occupancy and rate adjustments to the North Central's rooms expense percentage are shown in the following chart.

Rooms Expense Adjustment

Unit of comparison:	Percent of Rooms Gross
North Central subclassification	24.8%
Adjustments:	
Subject's higher occupancy	moderately downward
Subject's lower rate	slightly upward
Adjusted unit of comparison	24.5%

The moderately downward adjustment for occupancy is somewhat offset by the slightly upward adjustment for average rate; therefore, the unit of comparison is lowered from 24.8% to 24.5%.

The rooms expense unit of comparison for the stablized years is 24.5%. Certain adjustments must be made to reflect the proper expense for operational Years 1 and 2. This is accomplished with a fixed and variable expense component analysis.

First, the rooms department expense for the stablized year is determined using the 24.5% expense ratio and the projected rooms revenue.

Stabilized Year

Rooms revenue-stabilized year	$4,262,000	
Rooms expense ratio	.245	
Rooms expense-stabilized year	$1,044,190	say, $1,044,000

Expenses are either fixed or variable. For lodging facilities, variable expenses are those that change with varying levels of occupancy or patronage in the restaurants and lounges. Fixed rooms department expenses include general management, housekeeper, linen, public area cleaning, and supplies. Variable expenses include maid service, laundry, reservations, supplies, and commissions.

Rooms expense is approximately 55% fixed and 45% variable. For the stabilized year, this would amount to: $574,000 in fixed expenses and $470,000 in variable expenses.

To determine the rooms department expense at lower occupancies, the fixed expenses are held constant and the variable expenses are reduced in proportion to the decline in volume. The effects of inflation must be considered by increasing the rooms revenue for Years 1 and 2 by the inflation rate of 8%, then all revenues are in stabilized year dollars.

183

North Central Data Table
Motels and Motor Hotels with Restaurants, North Central Subclassification

Average size (rooms), 205; percentage of occupancy, 73.8; average rate per occupied room, $50.25

	Percentage of Total Revenue	Percentage of Rooms Revenue	Percentage of Food or Beverage Revenue	Amount per Available Room	Amount per Occupied Room
Revenues					
Rooms	56.0%	100.0%		$13,536	$18,341
Food	29.6	52.8		7,147	9,684
Beverages	11.8	21.1		2,856	3,870
Telephone	2.0	3.6		487	660
Other income (net)	.6	1.1		149	202
Total revenues	100.0%	178.6%		$24,175	$32,757
Departmental costs and expenses					
Rooms	13.9%	24.8%		$ 3,357	$ 4,549
Food and beverages					
Cost of food sold	10.3	18.4	34.9%	2,494	3,379
Cost of beverages sold	2.5	4.4	20.9	597	809
Departmental expenses	19.3	34.6	46.8	4,681	6,343
Total food and beverages	32.1	57.4	77.7%	7,772	10,531
Telephone	2.7	4.8		644	873
Total costs and expenses	48.7	87.0		$11,773	$15,953
Total departmental income	51.3%	91.6%		$12,402	$16,804

Undistributed operating expenses				
Administrative and general	7.3%	13.0%	1,765	2,392
Marketing	3.3	5.9	795	1,077
Property operation & maintenance	4.6	8.1	1,100	1,491
Energy costs	3.9	7.0	950	1,287
Total undistributed expenses	19.1%	34.0%	$ 4,610	$ 6,247
Income before fixed charges	32.2%	57.6%	$ 7,792	$10,557
Fixed charges				
Property taxes	2.9%	5.2%	$ 700	$ 948
Insurance	.4	.7	100	135
Total fixed charges	3.3%	5.9%	$ 800	$ 1,083
Income before interest and depreciation	28.9%	51.7%	$ 6,992	$ 9,474

Rooms Revenue in Constant Stabilized Dollars

Rooms Revenue	Stabilized	Year 2	Year 1
Inflated dollars	$4,262,000	$3,613,000	$2,759,000
Inflation factor	—	× 1.08	× 1.167
Constant stabilized year dollars	$4,262,000	$3,902,040	$3,219,753
Decrease of rooms revenue from stablized year		.9155	.7550

The decrease of rooms revenue from the stabilized year represents the percentage change in rooms revenue attributed to the change in occupancy.

The rooms expense for Year 2 is calculated by taking the fixed expenses of $574,000 and adding the variable expenses ($470,000) multiplied by the percentage of change in rooms revenue from the stabilized year. This produces the rooms department expense in stabilized year dollars. Dividing this amount by an 8% deflation factor converts the Year 2 rooms expense to Year 2 dollars.

Year 2 Rooms Expense

Fixed	$ 574,000
Variable $470,000 × .9155 =	+ 430,000 (rounded)
Total (in stabilized year dollars)	$1,004,000
Deflation factor	÷ 1.08
Rooms expense (Year 2)	$ 930,000 (rounded)
Ratio to rooms revenue	25.7%

The same procedure is used for the Year 1 rooms expense.

Year 1 Rooms Expense

Fixed	$ 574,000
Variable $470,000 × .7550 =	+ 355,000 (rounded)
Total (in stabilized year dollars)	$ 929,000
Deflation factor	÷ 1.167
Rooms expense (Year 1)	$ 796,000 (rounded)
Ratio to rooms revenue	28.8%

The ratio of rooms expense to rooms revenue declines from 28.8% in Year 1 to 24.5% in the stabilized year, which is an appropriate reduction for the increase in occupancy.

The rooms expense can be cross checked by calculating the marginal expense of selling one additional room (in 1981 dollars.)

Marginal Expense of Selling One Additional Room

Rooms department expense	
Year 1	$ 796,000
Stabilized year	1,044,000
Rooms occupied per day	
Year 1	120
Stabilized year	150
Increase in occupied rooms	30

Adjust to current value dollars
Present value 5 years @ 8% = .6806 × $1,044,000   = $ 710,000 (rounded)
Present value 3 years @ 8% = .7938 × $ 796,000   =   632,000 (rounded)
Increase in rooms expense (current value $) $ 78,000
Added expense per room per day

$$\frac{\$78,000 \div 30}{365} = \$7.12$$

The rooms expense of selling one extra room per day is $7.12. It is composed of occupancy-sensitive variable expenses such as the maids' payroll, laundry, and operating supplies.

Food and Beverage Expenses

Food and beverage expenses are moderately food and beverage sensitive. Although data to estimate an overall food and beverage departmental expense are available, using one unit of comparison based on total food and beverage revenue may produce inaccurate projections. Most sources of national averages provide a fairly comprehensive breakdown of the food and beverage expense category. By estimating these two costs separately, the effect of any variance in the ratio of food to beverage is eliminated.

The indicated expense percentages for the North Central subclassification are as follows:

Food and Beverage Expense Adjustment

	Percentage of Revenue
Units of comparison:	
North Central	34.8% food cost
subclassification	20.9% beverage cost
Adjustments:	46.8% departmental
Volume per room	very slightly upward
Subject's lower rate	very slightly upward
Adjusted units of comparison	35.0% food cost
	21.0% beverage cost
	47.0% departmental

Like the rooms expenses, these expenses must be adjusted to eliminate any differences between the comparable and the subject. The North Central's ratio of food and beverage volume to rooms revenue is 73.9%; this is higher than the Sheraton's stabilized percentage of 67.2%. The Sheraton's lower food and beverage volume per room would warrant adjusting the comparable's expense percentages slightly upward.

It usually takes several years for food and beverage operations to generate sufficient gross revenues and operating efficiencies to achieve the expense ratios estimated above. Food and beverage expense projections for the first two years are based on the assumption that the subject property will build volume and establish the systems and controls necessary to keep costs and operating expenses in proportion. The previously calculated food, beverage, and departmental expenses can be further modified to reflect the lower volume and start-up costs in Years 1 and 2. The totals in the Food and Beverage Expenses chart have been rounded.

Telephone Expense

Current telephone regulations allow hotels to receive a 10%–15% commission on all local and long-distance calls. This rebate usually does not cover the cost of equipment rental, operators, and service. Therefore, the telephone department of a lodging facility generally operates at a loss. However, recent changes in the telephone tariffs will permit hotels and motels to add a surcharge to all calls; the amount of this surcharge will be determined by each individual hotel, so it is possible that the telephone department could become a profit center. For the pur-

Food and Beverage Expenses

	Appropriate Revenue Projection		Unit of Comparison		Food and Beverage Expenses	(Rounded)
Year 1						
Cost of food sold	$1,435,000	×	.38	=	$ 545,000	
Cost of beverages sold	574,000	×	.24	=	138,000	
Departmental expenses	2,009,000	×	.49	=	984,000	
Total					$1,667,000	
					(83%)	
Year 2						
Cost of food sold	$1,806,000	×	.36	=	$ 650,000	
Cost of beverage sold	723,000	×	.22	=	159,000	
Departmental expenses	2,529,000	×	.48	=	1,214,000	
Total					$2,023,000	
					(80%)	
Stabilized						
Cost of food sold	$2,046,000	×	.35	=	$ 716,000	
Cost of beverages sold	818,000	×	.21	=	172,000	
Departmental expenses	2,864,000	×	.47	=	1,346,000	
Total					$2,234,000	
					(78%)	

pose of this case study, it will be assumed that the telephone department is still operating under the current 10%–15% commission structure and showing a loss.

The net cost of the telephone department is termed telephone loss. According to the North Central Data Table, the net telephone loss on a per room basis equals the telephone revenue minus the telephone expense per room, which results in a loss of $157.

Telephone Loss

North Central Subclassification	Amount Per Available Room
Telephone revenue	$ 487
Telephone expenses	− 644
Telephone loss	($157)

189

A slight downward adjustment is necessary to reflect the subject's higher occupancy and the ability to spread more call revenue over the fixed expenses.

Telephone Expense Adjustment

	Loss Per Available Room
Unit of comparison:	
North Central Subclassification	$157
Adjustments:	
Subject's higher occupancy	slightly downward
Adjusted unit of comparison	$155

Applying the 8% inflation factor produces the following figures:

Telephone Loss Per Room

	0	1	2	3	4	5
Development Year	0	1	2	3	4	5
Operational Year	—	—	—	1	2	Stabilized
Telephone loss per room	$155	$167	$180	$195	$210	$230

The telephone loss per room is multiplied by the Sheraton's room count, and this figure is added to the telephone revenue to produce the total telephone expense.

Telephone Expense

	Year 1	Year 2	Stabilized
Telephone loss per room	$ 195	$ 210	$ 230
Number of rooms	× 200	× 200	× 200
Telephone loss	$ 39,000	$ 42,000	$ 46,000
Telephone revenue	100,000	126,000	146,000
Telephone expense	$139,000	$168,000	$192,000

Administrative and General Expenses

Administrative and general expenses are measured by the expense per room or as a percentage of total revenue. The second method will be used here.

According to the North Central Data Table, the administrative and general percentage of total revenue is 7.3%. Adjustments must be made for the subject's higher occupancy and lower rate. An upward adjustment is also required for the subject's lower food-and-beverage-to-rooms ratio because this ratio is based on a percentage of total revenue, which includes differences in food volume.

Administrative and General Expense Adjustments

	Percentage of Total Revenue
Unit of comparison: North Central Subclassification	7.3%
Adjustments:	
Subject's higher occupancy	slightly downward
Subject's lower rate	slightly upward
Subject's lower Food & beverage/rooms ratio	slightly upward
Adjusted unit of comparison	7.5%

The administrative and general expenses are adjusted from the stabilized year using the fixed and variable component method that was used to adjust the rooms department expense. In this instance, total revenue rather than rooms revenue will be utilized. The following tables outline this procedure. (For a more detailed explanation, see the section on room expenses). Once again the figures are rounded.

Total Revenue in Constant Stabilized Dollars

Total Revenue	Stabilized	Year 2	Year 1
Inflated dollars	$7,345,000	$6,331,000	$4,918,000
Inflation factor	—	× 1.08	× 1.167
Constant stabilized year dollars	$7,345,000	$6,837,000	$5,736,000
Decrease of total from stabilized year		.9308	.7809

Administrative and General Expense Calculation

Stabilized year

Total revenue—stabilized year	$7,345,000
Adm. & gen. expense ratio	.075
Adm. & gen. expense—stabilized year	$ 551,000

Fixed & variable components

Fixed component (70%)	$ 386,000
Variable component (30%)	$ 165,000

Decrease in total revenue from stabilized year

Year 2	.9308
Year 1	.7809

Year 2 adm. & gen. expense

Fixed	$ 386,000
Variable $165,000 × .9308 =	154,000
Total (stabilized year $)	$ 540,000
Deflation factor	÷ 1.08
Adm. & gen. expense (Year 2)	$ 500,000
Ratio to total revenue	7.9%

Year 1 adm. & gen. expense

Fixed	$ 386,000
Variable $165,000 × .7809 =	129,000
Total (stabilized year $)	$ 515,000
Deflation factor	÷ 1.167
Adm. & gen. expense (Year 1)	$ 442,000
Ratio to total revenue	9.0%

Management Fee Expense

The management fee is calculated as 3% of total revenue. The figures are rounded.

Management Fee Expense

Year	Total Revenue		Management Fee Percentage		Management Fee Expense
1	$4,918,000	×	3.0%	=	$148,000
2	6,331,000	×	3.0	=	190,000
Stabilized	7,345,000	×	3.0	=	220,000

Marketing Expense

The unit of comparison used to measure marketing expense is the amount per available room. The North Central Data Table shows a marketing expense of $795 per room.

The necessary adjustments include an upward adjustment for the Sheraton's projected higher occupancy, which will require a greater marketing effort, and a slight downward adjustment for the subject's lower, and probably more competitive, average rate.

Marketing Expense Adjustment

	Per Available Room
Unit of comparison:	
North Central Subclassification	$795
Adjustments:	
Subject's higher occupancy	slightly upward
Subject's lower rate	slightly downward
Adjusted unit of comparison	$800

Applying an 8% inflation factor and adding an extra marketing expenditure of 15% in Year 1 and 7% in Year 2 for increased start-up costs produce the following estimate of marketing expense per room:

Marketing Expense Per Room

Development Year	0	1	2	3	4	5
Operational Year	—	—	—	1	2	Stabilized
Marketing expense per room	$800	$864	$933	$1,088	$1,088	$1,175
Additional marketing				+15%	+7%	—
Marketing expense per room				$1,159	$1,164	$1,175

The total marketing expense is calculated by multiplying the marketing expense per room by the Sheraton's room count. Again, the expense figures are rounded.

Marketing Expense

	Year 1	Year 2	Stabilized
Marketing expense per room	$ 1,159	$ 1,164	$ 1,175
Number of rooms	200	200	200
Marketing expense	$232,000	$233,000	$235,000
Ratio to total revenue	4.8%	3.7%	3.2%

Property Operation and Maintenance Expense

The recommended unit of comparison for property operation and maintenance expense is the amount per available room. The North Central Data Table shows that property operations and maintenance normally costs $1,100 per available room.

A slight upward adjustment is made for the subject's higher occupancy, which means more wear and tear; a slight downward adjustment is made for the subject's lower food and beverage volume, and a moderate downward adjustment is made for the subject's age.

Property Operation and Maintenance Expense Adjustment

	Per Available Room
Unit of comparison:	
North Central Subclassification	$1,100
Adjustments:	
Subject's higher occupancy	slightly upward
Subject's lower food & beverage volume	slightly downward
Subject's age	moderately downward
Adjusted unit of comparison	$1,060

An 8% inflation factor is applied to the property's operations and maintenance expense. In addition, the per room expense is reduced by 35% in operational Year 1, and 10% in Year 2. This reduction is appropriate because hotels spend less on operations and maintenance in early years due to new equipment warranties, free service contracts, and the new condition of property components.

Property Operations and Maintenance Expense Per Room

Development Year	0	1	2	3	4	5
Operational Year	—	—	—	1	2	Stabilized
PO & M expense per room	$1,060	$1,145	$1,236	$1,335	$1,442	$1,558
Initial savings				− 35%	− 10%	—
PO & M expense per room				$ 868	$1,298	$1,558

Multiplying the Sheraton's property operations and maintenance expense per room by its room count produces the subject's projected property operations and maintenance expense. The figures are rounded.

Property Operations and Maintenance Expense

	Year 1	Year 2	Stabilized
P O & M expense per room	$ 868	$ 1,298	$ 1,558
Number of rooms	× 200	× 200	× 200
P O & M expense	$174,000	$260,000	$312,000
Ratio to total revenue	3.5%	4.1%	4.3%

Energy Expense

The unit of comparison used to estimate a hostelry's energy expense is the amount per available room. Because energy expense tends to be geographically sensitive, using the North Central subclassification might not produce a reliable estimate. Instead, the analyst should select statistics from locations with similar climates and energy sources. Energy costs for the New England and Middle Atlantic regions, where the Sheraton is located, currently average $950 per room. Adjustments are required for occupancy and food and beverage volume.

Energy Expense Adjustment

	Per Available Room
Unit of comparison:	
New England and Middle Atlantic Subclassification	$ 950
Adjustments:	
Subject's higher occupancy	Moderately upward
Subject's lower food & beverage volume	Slightly downward
Adjusted unit of comparison	$1,000

195

The $1,000 unit of comparison for energy expense relates to the stabilized year, when the Sheraton Inn will operate at 75% occupancy. The proper unit of comparison for operational Years 1 and 2, when the occupancy level is 60% and 70%, must be adjusted downward to deduct the marginal energy cost for these unoccupied rooms.

Energy expense in a hotel is basically fixed, but savings in the form of lower guest room power consumption can be realized when occupancy levels decline. With information from the local utility company, the actual cost of heat, light, power, and air conditioning for occupied and unoccupied guest rooms can be estimated. The difference between the occupied energy expense and the unoccupied energy expense is the marginal energy expense per occupied room.

For the Sheraton Inn, the marginal energy expense is estimated at $1.10. The following table shows the energy expense per room and the marginal energy expense per occupied room, adjusted for 8% inflation. Compared to the stabilized year, 30 fewer rooms will be occupied in operational Year 1, and 10 fewer rooms in Year 2. The marginal daily occupancy from the stabilized year is multiplied by the marginal energy expense per occupied room to produce the marginal daily energy expense. This daily factor multiplied by 365 shows the energy savings per year, or the proper occupancy adjustment. The figures are rounded.

Energy Expense Per Room

	0	1	2	3	4	5
Development Year	0	1	2	3	4	5
Operational Year	—	—	—	1	2	Stabilized
Energy expense per room	$1,000	$1,080	$1,166	$ 1,259	$1,360	$1,469
Marginal energy expenses per occupied room	$ 1.10	$ 1.19	$ 1:29	$ 1.39	$ 1.50	$1.61
Marginal daily occupancy from stabilized year				× 30	× 10	—
Marginal daily energy expenses				$ 41.70	$15.00	
Days per year				× 365	× 365	
Occupancy adjustment				$15,000	$5,000	

The total projected energy expense for the Sheraton Inn is calculated by multiplying the energy expense per room by the 200-room count and deducting the appropriate occupancy adjustment in Years 1 and 2. Again, the figures are rounded.

196

Energy Expense

	Year 1	Year 2	Stabilized
Energy expenses per room	$ 1,259	$ 1,360	$ 1,469
Number of rooms	× 200	× 200	× 200
Energy expense before occupancy adjustment	$252,000	$272,000	$294,000
Occupancy adjustment	− 15,000	− 5,000	—
Energy expenses	$237,000	$267,000	$294,000
Ratio to total revenue	4.8%	4.2%	4.0%

Property Taxes

The property tax assessments for the five competitive lodging facilities in the market area are taken from the property record cards in the local assessor's office. The following chart shows the total assessed value, and the assessed values on a per-room basis.

Property	Total Assessed Value	Assessed Value Per Room
Days Inn	$2,280,000	$15,200
Suncrest	2,160,000	16,000
Holiday Inn	5,632,000	25,600
Hilton Inn	9,600,000	32,000
Ramada Inn	4,440,000	24,000

The Sheraton's facilities will be most comparable to the existing Hilton Hotel. Although the subject's improvements will be newer than the Hilton's, the Hilton has slightly more meeting and public space on a per-room basis. All in all, the Sheraton's assessment should be similar to the Hilton's assessment on a per-room basis. Using a $32,000 per-room assessed value for the Sheraton Inn, the current property tax per room can be calculated.

Estimated Assessed Value and
Property Taxes for Subject

Assessed value per room	$ 32,000
Total assessment	$6,400,000
Current tax rate	$25.00 per $1,000
Current tax burden	$ 160,000
Current property tax per room	$ 800

Inflating the property taxes by 8% and multiplying the tax burden per room by the Sheraton's room count results in the following total property tax estimate.

Property Taxes Per Room

Development Year	0	1	2	3	4	5
Operational Year	—	—	—	1	2	Stabilized
Property taxes per room	$800	$864	$933	$1,010	$1,090	$1,175

Property Taxes

	Year 1	Year 2	Stabilized
Property taxes per room	$ 1,010	$ 1,090	$ 1,175
Number of rooms	× 200	× 200	× 200
Property taxes	$202,000	$218,000	$235,000
Ratio to total revenue	4.1%	3.4%	3.2%

Insurance Expense

The insurance requirements for the proposed Sheraton were reviewed by an agent familiar with hotel insurance. Based on the building construction and the local fire district, adequate coverage could be purchased for $20,000, or $100 per available room. This estimate was verified with national averages.

Inflating the per-room insurance expense by 8% and multiplying this figure by the Sheraton's room count results in the estimated yearly insurance expense.

Insurance Expense Per Room

Development Year	0	1	2	3	4	5
Operational Year	—	—	—	1	2	Stabilized
Insurance expense per room	$100	$108	$117	$125	$135	$145

Insurance Expense

	Year 1	Year 2	Stabilized
Insurance expense per room	$ 125	$ 135	$ 145
Number of rooms	200	200	200
Insurance expense	$25,000	$27,000	$29,000
Ratio to total revenue	.5%	.4%	.4%

Reserve for Replacement

A reserve for replacement equal to 2.5% of total revenue should be sufficient to maintain the capital improvements in a first-class manner. The figures in the following chart are rounded.

Reserve for Replacement

Year	Total Revenue		Reserve for Replacement Percentage		Reserve for Replacement
1	$4,918,000	×	2.5%	=	$123,000
2	6,331,000	×	2.5	=	158,000
Stabilized	7,345,000	×	2.5	=	184,000

Projected Income and Expenses

All the preceding projected revenues and expenses are combined in the income and expense statement for the proposed 200-room Sheraton Inn.

Projected Income and Expense Statement, Proposed 200-Room Sheraton Inn

	Year 1			Year 2			Stabilized		
	Amount Thou. $ (000)	% Total Revenue	Amount per Available Room	Amount Thou. $ (000)	% Total Revenue	Amount per Available Room	Amount Thou. $ (000)	% Total Revenue	Amount per Available Room
% of occupancy	60%			70%			75%		
Average rate per occupied room	$63.00			$70.70			$77.85		
Revenues									
Rooms	$2,759	56.1%	$13,795	$3,613	57.1%	$18,065	$4,262	58.0%	$21,310
Food	1,435	29.2	7,175	1,806	28.5	9,030	2,046	27.9	10,230
Beverages	574	11.7	2,870	723	11.4	3,615	818	11.1	4,090
Telephone	100	2.0	500	126	2.0	630	146	2.0	730
Other income (net)	50	1.0	250	63	1.0	315	73	1.0	365
Total revenues	4,918	100.0	24,590	6,331	100.0	31,655	7,345	100.0	36,725
Departmental Costs and Expenses									
Rooms	796	28.8[a]	3,980	930	25.7[a]	4,650	1,044	24.5[a]	5,220
Food and beverages									
Cost of food sold	545	38.0[b]	2,725	650	36.0[b]	3,250	716	35.0[b]	3,580
Cost of beverages sold	138	24.0[c]	690	159	22.0[c]	795	172	21.0[c]	860
Departmental expenses	984	49.0[d]	4,920	1,214	48.0[d]	6,070	1,346	47.0[d]	6,730
Total food and beverages	1,667	83.0[d]	8,335	2,023	80.0[d]	10,115	2,234	78.0[d]	11,170
Telephone	139	2.8	695	168	2.6	840	192	2.6	960
Total costs and expenses	2,602	52.9	13,010	3,121	49.3	15,605	3,470	47.2	17,350
Total departmental income	2,316	47.1	11,580	3,210	50.7	16,050	3,875	52.8	19,375

Undistributed Operating Expenses

Administrative & general	442	9.0	2,210	500	7.9	2,500	551	7.5	2,755
Management fee	148	3.0	740	190	3.0	950	220	3.0	1,100
Marketing	232	4.8	1,159	233	3.7	1,164	235	3.2	1,175
Property operations and maintenance	174	3.5	868	260	4.1	1,298	312	4.3	1,558
Energy costs	237	4.8	1,185	267	4.2	1,335	294	4.0	1,469
Total undistributed expenses	1,233	25.1	6,162	1,450	22.9	7,247	1,612	22.0	8,057
Income Before Fixed Charges	1,083	22.0	5,418	1,760	27.8	8,803	2,263	30.8	11,318
Fixed Charges									
Property taxes	202	4.1	1,010	218	3.4	1,090	235	3.2	1,175
Insurance	25	.5	125	27	.4	135	29	.4	145
Reserve for replacement	123	2.5	615	158	2.5	790	184	2.5	920
Total fixed charges	350	7.1	1,750	403	6.3	2,015	448	6.1	2,240
Income Before Interest and Depreciation	$ 733	14.9%	$ 3,668	$1,357	21.5%	$ 6,788	$1,815	24.7%	$ 9,078

[a] Percent of rooms revenue
[b] Percent of food revenue
[c] Percent of beverages revenue
[d] Percent of food and beverages revenue

Valuation by the Income Capitalization Approach

Based on an analysis of current hotel investor requirements, the most appropriate approach for valuing the Sheraton Inn seems to be the two- to five-year projection using equity dividend. The following steps show how the value estimate is developed.

1. Income before interest and depreciation is estimated.

Year	Income Before Interest and Depreciation
1	$ 733,000
2	1,357,000
Stabilized	1,815,000

2. An equity dividend rate is estimated. Discussions with hotel-motel investors and a review of numerous partnership agreements indicate that the anticipated equity dividend requirement for this type of lodging facility is approximately 12%.
3. Terms for typical financing are determined. Using the AA Utility Bond regression formula, the current hotel mortgage interest rate is estimated.

   Regression formula:

   $$Y = 3.279 + .7408 \, X$$

   Current AA utility bond yields (X): 13%

   Indicated hotel mortgage interest rate (Y):

   $$Y = 3.279 + .7408 \times 13$$
   $$Y = 12.91 \text{ (rounded)}$$

   Reviewing current lending conditions indicates that the Sheraton Inn should obtain the following mortgage terms:

Interest	12.91%
Amortization	25 years
Constant	.1344
Loan-to-value ratio	75%
Mortgage kicker	2% of rooms revenue

4. The projected income before interest and depreciation must be reduced by the mortgage kicker (2% rooms revenue). (The figures are rounded.)

Year	Income Before Interest and Depreciation	Rooms Revenue	Mortgage Kicker	Additional Interest	Net Income After Mortgage Kicker
1	$ 733,000	$2,759,000	2%	$55,000	$ 678,000
2	1,357,000	3,613,000	2	72,000	1,285,000
Stabilized	1,815,000	4,262,000	2	85,000	1,730,000

5. Using the simultaneous valuation formula, the trial market value is hypothesized.

Simultaneous valuation formula equation #1:

Year	Net Income After Mortgage Kicker		Debt Service	=	Equity Dividend and Reversion
1	$ 678,000	$-$	$(.1344 \times .75 \times V)$	=	$d_e{}^1$
2	1,285,000	$-$	$(.1344 \times .75 \times V)$	=	$d_e{}^2$
Stabilized	$\dfrac{1,730,000}{.12}$	$-$	$(.1344 \times .75 \times V)$	=	$d_e{}^3$

Year	Discount Factor @ 12%
1	.8929
2	.7972
Stabilized	.7972

Simultaneous Valuation Formula Equation #2:

$$(d_e{}^1 \times .8929) + (d_e{}^2 \times .7972) + (d_e{}^3 + .7972) = .25\,V$$

Filling the proper figures produces:

$$((678,000 - (.1344 \times .75V)) \times .8929) + ((1,285,000 - (.1344 \times .75V)) \times .7972$$
$$+ (((1,730,000 - (.1344 \times .75V)) \div .12) \times .7972) = .25V$$

Combining terms yields:

$$-.0900V - .0804V - (.0804V \div .12) + 605,386 + 1,024,402$$
$$+ (1,379,156 \div .12) = .25V$$

Combining terms further results in a final value indication.

$$-.8404V + 13,122,754 = .25V$$
$$V = \frac{\$13,122,754}{1.0904}$$
$$V = \$12,034,807, \text{ say } \$12,000,000$$

		Ratio
Mortgage	$ 9,000,000	75%
Equity	3,000,000	25
Total	$12,000,000	100%

6. Calculate debt service and net income to equity.

Year	Net Income After Mortgage Kicker		Debt Service		Equity Dividend
1	$ 678,000	–	$1,211,000	=	$-533,000
2	1,285,000	–	1,211,000	=	74,000
Stabilized	1,730,000	–	1,211,000	=	519,000

7. The value of the equity is calculated. (The figures are rounded.)

Stabilized value $= \dfrac{\$519,000}{.12} = \$4,325,000$

Year	Equity Dividend and Reversion	Discount Factor at 12%	Equity Value
1	$ -533,000	.8929	$ -476,000
2	74,000	.7972	59,000
Stabilized	4,325,000	.7972	3,447,000
	Total Equity Value		$3,030,000

8. The property value is estimated.

Market value of mortgage	$ 9,000,000
Calculated value of equity	3,030,000
Total value	$12,030,000 or $12,000,000

The value indication for the Sheraton Inn produced by the income capitalization approach is $12,000,000.

Internal Rate of Return

Using the value indicated by the income capitalization approach, the internal rate of return (IRR) can be calculated for the total property, the debt, and the equity. The following assumptions will be used in the internal rate of return calculations:

Inflation. Rooms revenue and net income will increase at an annual rate of 8% after the stabilized year.

Projection period. The IRR will be based on a 10-year projection with a sale taking place at the end of the 10th year, based on the 11th year's projected net income.

Reversion value. The 11th year's projected net income will be capitalized at 12.5% to estimate the residual value.

The following table shows the 11-year projection.

Year	Rooms Revenue	Income Before Interest Depreciation	Mortgage Kicker	Constant Debt Service	Total Debt Service	Equity Dividend
1	$2,759,000	$ 733,000	$ 55,000	$1,211,000	$1,266,000	$ – 533,000
2	3,613,000	1,357,000	72,000	1,211,000	1,283,000	74,000
3	4,262,000	1,815,000	85,000	1,211,000	1,296,000	519,000
4	4,603,000	1,960,000	92,000	1,211,000	1,303,000	657,000
5	4,971,000	2,117,000	99,000	1,211,000	1,310,000	807,000
6	5,369,000	2,286,000	107,000	1,211,000	1,318,000	968,000
7	5,798,000	2,469,000	116,000	1,211,000	1,327,000	1,142,000
8	6,262,000	2,667,000	125,000	1,211,000	1,336,000	1,331,000
9	6,763,000	2,880,000	135,000	1,211,000	1,346,000	1,534,000
10	7,304,000	3,111,000	146,000	1,211,000	1,357,000	1,754,000
11	7,889,000	3,359,000	158,000	1,211,000	1,369,000	1,990,000

The assumed sale at the end of the 10th year, or reversion value, is arrived at by capitalizing the 11th year's income before interest and depreciation at a going-out overall rate of 12.5%.

$$\frac{\$3,359,000}{.125} = \$26,872,000$$

The residual mortgage reversion value is the mortgage balance at the end of Year 10, or $8,008,000. The equity reversion value is the property reversion value minus the residual mortgage value.

$$\$26,872,000 - \$8,008,000 = \$18,864,000.$$

Using either a computer or financial calculator, the internal rates of return can be calculated as shown on the following page.

Internal Rate of Return

Total property	19.82%
Mortgage	13.92
Equity	27.40

The following tables verify the internal rates of return. The figures are rounded.

Total Property:

Year	Income Before Interest and Depreciation	Discount Factor @ 19.82%	Discounted Value
1	$ 733,000	.8346	$ 612,000
2	1,357,000	.6966	945,000
3	1,815,000	.5813	1,055,000
4	1,960,000	.4852	951,000
5	2,117,000	.4049	857,000
6	2,286,000	.3377	773,000
7	2,469,000	.2821	696,000
8	2,667,000	.2354	628,000
9	2,880,000	.1965	566,000
10	29,983,000*	.1640	4,917,000
		Total	$12,000,000

*$3,111,000 + $26,872,000

Mortgage:

Year	Total Debt Service	Discount Factor @ 13.92%	Discounted Value
1	$1,266,000	.8778	$1,111,000
2	1,283,000	.7705	989,000
3	1,296,000	.6763	877,000
4	1,303,000	.5937	773,000
5	1,310,000	.5211	683,000
6	1,318,000	.4574	603,000
7	1,327,000	.4015	533,000
8	1,336,000	.3525	471,000
9	1,346,000	.3094	416,000
10	9,365,000*	.2716	2,544,000
		Total	$9,000,000

*$1,357,000 + $8,008,000

Equity:

Year	Equity Dividend and Reversion	Discount Factor @ 27.40%	Discounted Value
1	$ – 533,000	.7849	$ – 418,000
2	74,000	.6161	46,000
3	519,000	.4836	251,000
4	657,000	.3796	250,000
5	807,000	.2979	240,000
6	968,000	.2339	226,000
7	1,142,000	.1836	210,000
8	1,331,000	.1440	192,000
9	1,534,000	.1131	173,000
10	20,618,000*	.0888	1,830,000
		Total	$3,000,000

*$1,754,000 + $18,864,000

The internal rate of return calculations are interesting because they show that, with the mortgage kicker, the mortgage is yielding approximately one point over the stated interest rate of 12.91%. The equity is yielding 27.4%, which is significantly higher than the 12% equity dividend that formed the basis for the value calculation.

Value Conclusion

In Chapter 2 the case study of a proposed Sheraton Inn was introduced and used to demonstrate the step-by-step procedure for quantifying the local demand for transient accommodations and allocating this demand among the competitive lodging facilities. Based on the supply and demand relationship developed in Chapter 3, the subject's occupancy was projected to reach a stabilized level in operational Year 3. Using national operating statistics adjusted to fit the specific characteristics of the Sheraton, a three-year projection of income and expense was made in this chapter. These forecasted future benefits were then converted into a value indication by discounting. Using the income capitalization approach, the final value indication for the proposed Sheraton Inn, as of the date it is complete and operational (assumed two years from now), is

$12,000,000
TWELVE MILLION DOLLARS

The appraiser should cross-check this value with the cost and sales comparison approaches when appropriate.

7
Valuations and Market Studies for Restaurants

(Written by Stephen Rushmore, MAI, and Steven Bram)

Growth and Development of the Restaurant Industry

Restaurants are high-risk, labor-intensive businesses whose values depend not only on the value of land, building, and equipment, but also on management's ability to operate a food-service establishment. Long hours, ownership aggravation, and volatile business cycles plague restaurateurs and cause high rates of failure. Food-service operators have tried to reduce these risks and operate restaurants profitably by introducing new types of outlets and using new technology. This chapter examines the many adaptations that have affected the food-service industry in the past and future trends that may be anticipated. The demand and supply of food-service operations will be evaluated and appropriate valuation procedures will be investigated. The restaurant case that accompanies this chapter illustrates various techniques for quantifying demand, projecting income and expenses, and estimating market value.

Historical Background
Early Egyptian merchants carried their food and cooking equipment with them.

Cooks and servants whose responsibility it was to prepare and serve the meals were part of the retinue. To avoid the burden and expense of traveling with food and staff, economy-minded merchants began looking for places to purchase meals along the road. The inns where the merchants slept were the logical places to serve these meals and soon became the earliest "roadside" restaurants.

When the Roman Empire established firm control over the civilized world, taverns and simple eating establishments appeared in major cities. When Mount Vesuvius erupted onto the resort towns of Pompeii and Herculaneum in 79 A.D., it preserved some of these eating establishments. Excavations have revealed that nearly every block of houses in Pompeii had its own tavern. Around Herculaneum, historians found numerous "snack bars," apparently owned by the same person, that served dates, figs, nuts, wine, cheese, and some hot foods. Like today's restaurant chains, these facilities probably benefitted from increased product recognition and reduced overhead with economies of scale.

The Roman Empire can also be credited with other innovations such as the "banq," a Roman bench used at banquets; cabarets, where Romans could find food, beverages, and gambling; and the "taberno meritorio," an early predecessor of the fine restaurant.

All this development ended with the fall of Rome in 476 A.D., and no new food services emerged during the following feudalistic era.

Restaurants in Modern Times

When western Europe moved away from feudalism in the 12th century, "cookhouses" developed where cooked fish, meat, and fowl could be purchased for consumption.

In 18th century London, more than 200 coffee houses existed, serving strong coffee and pastries. In fact, the French word for coffee gives us the term "cafe."

In 1765 a Frenchman named Monsieur Boulanger originated the term "restaurant." Because Boulanger did not have a trader's license, the sale of soup in his establishment was officially illegal. So instead of selling his soup as food, he called it a "magical restorer," and posted the following phrase over his door: "Come to me all of you whose hearts cry out in anguish, and I shall restore you." He described his product in Latin as, "le restaurant divin." Eventually, the Latin translation for a magical restorer became the common term for today's food establishments—restaurants.

In the American colonies, foot and horseback trails accommodated many stage-coach riders. Services for these travelers were provided by networks of inns and taverns offering both food and lodging. In 1734, Samuel Cole owned taverns around Boston that provided food, but did not take overnight guests; he is acknowledged as America's first restaurateur.

Most food in American restaurants and hotels was hearty and satisfying, but it tasted plain. Some people wanted more from a restaurant, and Delmonico's of New York City opened its doors in 1827 to serve them. John Delmonico, a Swiss sea captain, and his brother Peter, a confectioner, offered an elegant and complete menu, printed in both French and English. Their business earned a reputation for quality food and service that survived several moves and two major fires. The acclaimed restaurant closed in 1923 after 96 years of operation, but it still provides the standard by which top-quality restaurants are measured.

Early restaurants usually served meals in one sitting, offering only a set "table d'hote" menu with no variations. Parker's of Boston changed this by introducing the first "a la carte" menu in America. Customers then could eat when and what they wanted. Parker is also known for inventing the "Parkerhouse roll," a soft dinner roll of a distinctive shape.

The food-service industry took an unexpected turn in 1919 with the passage of Prohibition. It soon became evident that the loss of liquor sales greatly affected restaurants' overall profitability. Not only did liquor help attract patronage, but its high profit margin subsidized many fine food operations. Even today, states that restrict the sale of alcoholic beverages generally have few better-quality restaurants.

In examining the growth of restaurants, it is important to mention other forms of food-service establishments. When transportation by water and rail became popular among the wealthy, food-service systems were developed on both riverboats and railroad cars. With the proliferation of automobiles, drive-in restaurants soon flourished. Airlines started by feeding their passengers box lunches and today offer a variety of hot meals. All of these specialized food-service outlets provide the same necessities as the taverns of colonial times—food and rejuvenation for the traveler.

Restaurant Chains

Operating a restaurant is a high-risk business. According to statistics, 50% of all restaurants are out of business within a year of opening. Of those that make it through the first year, 33% are closed by the end of Year 2.

To combat the many operational and management problems that cause this high rate of failure, chains or groups of restaurants have developed. Through a standardized approach, restaurant chains help reduce the risks of business and lower the industry's failure rates.

Efficient production standardization and quality control are vital to the success of a food-service establishment. To reduce the cost of food products and services and to make their operations more profitable, most restaurateurs use a simplified format and serve easily prepared menu items. A familiar name also plays an important role in a restaurant's success. People prefer going to a food outlet where they know the product will be dependable. Entrepreneurs have used these ideas in developing restaurant chains that provide a standardized product that is easily produced and readily accessible to the customer.

In 1876 Fred Harvey began the first modern "chain" in railcars and stationary buildings. The Horn & Hardart chain started in 1888; in 1919, the A & W (Allen & Wright) Corporation began selling root beer. Marriott and Stouffer began their food chains in 1920, and Howard Johnson started business in 1925. All of these chains exist today, and more chains and franchises develop continually. In 1981, 38% of all restaurant sales were made through multi-unit chain operations.

Chains have provided the answer to some of the major problems in the restaurant industry. The risk in restaurant operations has been reduced with management training and other specialized knowledge that chains make available to their operators. Through standardization of products and simplification of duties, training, management, and control are all more effective. A restaurant's volume and overall profitability also may be expected to increase due to its chain affiliation.

Environmental Factors Affecting the Restaurant Industry

The food service industry has made major technological advances since the days of the first Roman restaurants. Computers have increased the accuracy and availability of restaurant reports; computerized point-of-sale terminals facilitate the collection of detailed statistics on sales, menu mix, server efficiency, and a host of other facts. Using computers with telephone link-ups, financial information can be sent to the company's headquarters daily for area-wide company statistics. By periodically reviewing operating statistics—particularly profit and loss statements—restaurant management can maintain close control over the operation and reduce theft, waste, and other problems that plague the industry.

Technological developments have resulted in many labor-saving devices such as microwave ovens, high-pressure steamers, and other sophisticated cooking equipment. More efficient freezers and refrigerators allow for greater use of frozen prepared foods. Also, bulk freezer storage now makes large-scale purchasing an option available to operators of small restaurants.

Labor is a significant factor in the food-service industry. Employee salaries are generally close to minimum wage, and periodic increases in this rate have major implications for a restaurant. Although many food-service operations have introduced labor-saving devices such as automatically timed, deep fat fryers, measured service soda dispensers, and conveyor broilers, restaurateurs have been unable to reduce their dependence on unskilled labor. Workers are still needed to take, prepare, and serve each order; it is not cost-efficient to automate this process completely.

The Future

The future of the restaurant industry depends on many interrelated components such as the profile of consumers, changing food tastes, neighborhood shifts, personnel, maintenance, and theft. Because these items directly affect an operation's net income, evaluating a restaurant involves a complete understanding of many factors.

Currently, the most influential restaurant consumers are the "baby boom" children, who are now reaching their early thirties. Most individuals in this age group have graduated from college and have relatively high disposable incomes. As these patrons age, their tastes have matured. Some say they are less interested in fast-service restaurants, and clean, inexpensive, sit-down outlets such as coffee shops. No one is sure in which direction the baby boom group is actually turning, but restaurant owners realize that their patronage will have a major impact on the food-service industry.

Senior citizens are also becoming an important consumer segment. In the 1940s, the average man lived to 62.8 and the average woman to 67.3. According to the U.S. Bureau of Census, men now reach an average age of 70.6 and women attain 78.3 years. The needs and desires of senior citizens are different from those of other age groups; as their buying power increases, new types of restaurants can be expected to develop.

The number of working women in the labor force has escalated due to the increased number of female heads of households, poor economic conditions, and greater career opportunities for women. In 1970 there were 31.5 million women in the work force; twenty years later, in 1990, that number is expected to increase to 43.6 million. The increase in working women means more working people eating lunch out and, more importantly, fewer meals eaten at home. Women have traditionally prepared breakfast and dinner for their families, but working women may not have time to cook, so more families eat more meals away from home.

The changing characteristics of restaurant patrons affect the life cycles of existing restaurants and dictate the types of operations that will be demanded in the future. Changes in food preferences and eating habits will cause restaurants either to alter their modes of operation or face deteriorating economic lives.

Residential populations tend to shift over time. In some areas, people move into the suburbs, while in other areas, urban revitalization has been the trend. Restaurateurs must be aware of these demographic changes in order to assess their market projections properly.

Maintaining a full staff of competent restaurant workers can prove difficult. Typical restaurant salaries are not competitive with other industries, and insufficient training causes rapid turnover. Because the food-service industry is labor-intensive, policies must be developed to attract and train qualified personnel on all levels.

Theft by both employees and patrons is becoming a major problem for restaurateurs. Many small items used in restaurants are easily stolen. Employees with access to food and equipment can easily pilfer company property. In the future, operators will have to establish better methods to control theft in order to maintain their operation's profitability.

To operate successfully, the restaurateur must recognize all these factors and be able to integrate them into a business plan. Solving or anticipating these problems may be costly and time-consuming, but a restaurant must respond to a changing environment.

Demand for Restaurants

Success in the food service industry depends on the restaurateur's ability to provide the food, service, and atmosphere desired by the dining public. A restaurant operator must understand customer preferences. What types of restaurants are most popular? When do people eat out—breakfast, lunch or dinner? Where do they dine—in fast-service or full-menu restaurants in urban or surburban areas? Why do customers prefer one restaurant over another? Why do they prefer to eat out, rather than at home? By answering these questions, a restaurateur can ascertain the needs of the market and determine how a particular food-service outlet will satisfy this demand.

Restaurant Demand and Customer Attitudes

The appraiser starts a restaurant valuation or market study by collecting data on restaurant trends and consumer attitudes. Because this demand information changes with patrons' needs and desires, market researchers are generally interested in trends over several years, rather than information for one isolated year.

According to the National Restaurant Association, in 1981 the food-service industry had sales of nearly $125 billion, which was nearly 5% of the U.S. gross national product. Although sales, adjusted for inflation, declined in 1979 and 1980 (the first major decline since World War II), a 0.4% growth was experienced in 1981 and a gain of 1.3% is expected in 1982.

Food service includes all retail sales of foodstuffs prepared and consumed outside the home. Food-service operators and the supermarket and grocery sector compete directly for the consumer's dollar. In 1981 approximately 37% of the total food dollar in the United States was spent in the food-service business, an increase of 33% from 1970. The average person consumes about 20% of his meals away from home.

Three sectors make up the food-away-from-home market—commercial feeding, institutional feeding, and military feeding.

Commercial feeding accounted for approximately 85% of all food-service sales in 1981. Of this commercial feeding demand, almost 80% was supplied by eating establishments, including fast-service, limited-menu, and table service restaurants. In 1982 the commercial feeding segment is expected to grow 1.7% in real terms.

The institutional segment, including schools, hospitals, community centers, and other public buildings, contributed 14% of the total sales in the food-service industry. Continued budget cutbacks are expected to reduce sales in this segment in the near future.

Military feeding, the third segment, made up only .6% of the total sales in this market. Although this segment is expected to grow slightly in 1982, recent declines in the domestic military population will affect this area.

Sales in the three segments for 1980 and 1981 as well as projected sales for 1982 are shown in the chart on page 216.

Between 1970 and 1980, sales in the commercial feeding segment rose at an average annual rate of 10.4% in current dollars, or about 3% in constant dollars. Real sales (adjusted for inflation) fell slightly in 1974 because of the recession, then advanced rapidly in the mid-1970s, and slowed again in the late 1970s. Sales in the 1980s have shown growth, which is expected to continue. The first table on page 217 shows the fluctuation in the commercial feeding segment since 1971 in both current and constant dollars.

The growth of restaurant sales is expected to be strongest in the Sun Belt and mountain areas; the eastern and north central areas will show the smallest sales growth. The second table on page 217 shows this trend.

One of the most useful sources of information on restaurant sales is "Consumer Reports on Eating Share Trends," known as the CREST report. The report contains detailed trend information about meals sold in chain and indepen-

Food-Away-From-Home Market (Billions of Dollars)

Market	1980	1981	Percent of Change 1980-1981		1982 Estimated	Percent of Change 1981-1982	
			Current Dollars	Constant Dollars		Current Dollars	Constant Dollars
Commercial feeding	$ 96.2	$105.7	9.8%	0.5%	$118.3	11.9%	1.7%
Institutional feeding	17.2	18.4	7.0	(0.2)	19.7	7.0	(0.7)
Military feeding	0.6	0.6	0	0	0.7	insignificant	0
Total	$114.0	$124.7	9.4%	0.4%	$138.7	11.2%	1.3%

Source: U.S. Department of Commerce

Eating and Drinking Place Sales 1973-1981

	Sales in Billions of Current Dollars	Annual Percent of Change	
		In Current Dollars	In Constant Dollars
1972	$36.8	5%	1%
1973	37.9	12	2
1974	41.9	11	(2)
1975	47.5	13	4
1976	57.2	10	3
1977	63.3	11	3
1978	70.7	12	3
1979	79.6	13	2
1980	86.6	9	(1)
1981	94.1	10	1

Source: "Restaurant Trends and Analysis," Dean Witter Reynolds, Inc., June 1982.

dent restaurants. According to CREST, customer counts rose in 1981 after declining in 1980. In 1981 traffic increased 6.2% at family restaurants and 3.3% at fast-service restaurants. At the same time, however, customer counts fell 4.8% at cafeterias and 1.8% at coffee shops. Experts expect traffic counts to remain relatively stable in the early 1980s.

Eating Place Sales By Region (Projected)
(in Billions of Dollars)

Region	1981	1982	Increase
New England	$ 4.21	$ 4.55	8.0%
Middle Atlantic	11.84	12.83	8.4
South Atlantic	13.62	15.15	11.2
East North Central	16.11	17.50	8.6
West North Central	6.44	7.17	11.2
East South Central	4.08	4.52	10.7
West South Central	8.84	10.02	13.3
Mountain	4.43	4.98	12.4
Pacific	14.85	16.49	11.1
Total	$84.42	$93.21	10.7%

Source: National Restaurant Association, *Nation's Restaurant News,* Jan. 4, 1982

Restaurant Expenditures in Relation to Disposable Income (Dollar Amounts in Billions)

| | Personal Disposable Income | Food Consumption Away From Home | |
		Amount	Percentage of Income
1960	$ 352.0	$14.2	4.0%
1961	365.8	15.0	4.1
1962	386.8	16.1	4.2
1963	405.9	17.0	4.2
1964	440.6	18.0	4.1
1965	475.8	19.0	4.0
1966	513.7	20.2	3.9
1967	547.9	21.0	3.8
1968	593.4	23.3	3.9
1969	638.9	25.3	4.0
1970	695.3	27.7	4.0
1971	751.8	29.1	3.9
1972	810.3	31.8	3.9
1973	914.5	35.7	3.9
1974	998.3	40.2	4.0
1975	1,096.1	45.8	4.2
1976	1,194.4	51.2	4.3
1977	1,311.5	57.3	4.4
1978	1,462.9	64.2	4.4
1979	1,641.7	73.3	4.5
1980	1,821.7	80.4	4.4

Source: U.S. Department of Commerce and Survey of Current Business (revised).

Expenditures on food away from home tend to be highly income-elastic. In a Department of Agriculture study entitled "Income of Household Size and Income on Food Spending Patterns," the authors concluded that a 10% rise in income produced, on the average, an 8% increase in food purchased outside the home.

The above table shows the consistent relationship between personal disposable income and the amount of food purchased outside the home.

Motivated by the weak economy and new attitudes toward families and marriage, many women have entered the employment market. The increased number of women in the work force has had a positive effect on the food-service industry, because more women and families are eating meals away from home on a regular basis. The table shows the increase in working women.

218

Women in the Labor Force

Age	Numbers of Women (in Millions)			Average Annual Percent of Change	
	1970	1975	1980	1974	1980
16-19	3.2	4.0	4.3	5.0%	1.5%
20-24	4.9	6.1	7.1	4.9	3.3
25-34	5.7	8.5	11.8	9.8	7.8
35-44	6.0	6.5	8.6	1.7	6.5
45-54	6.5	6.7	7.0	.6	.8
55-64	4.2	4.2	4.6	0	1.9
65 and over	1.1	1.0	1.1	(2)	2.0
Total	31.6	37.0	44.5	3.5%	4.1%

Source: "Handbook of Labor Statistics," U.S. Bureau of Labor Statistics.

Consumer preferences and attitudes are the key to determining where people will go and how much they will spend in food-service establishments. By examining the incidence and frequency of restaurant patronage for each type of meal, the restaurateur can direct marketing efforts at the specific group most likely to produce sales. In a consumer attitude survey from the late-1970s, entitled "Consumer Reactions Toward Restaurant Practices and Responsibilities," the weekly frequency for restaurant patronage nationwide was:

Breakfast	.46
Lunch	1.23
Dinner	.89

Twenty percent of the respondents said they eat breakfast away from home on an average of 2.32 times a week. About 50% purchase lunch at restaurants 2.45 times a week; and 37% go out for dinner 1.18 times a week. The survey also revealed that males eat out more often than females especially at breakfast and lunch. Men eat lunch out 1.60 times a week, compared to women's .88 times; males eat breakfast out .61 times a week compared to females' .32 times.

As people near retirement age, fewer patronize restaurants, and those who do, go less often. On the other hand, the incidence and frequency of restaurant visits increase as income increases. Size-of-household statistics show that people living alone tend to eat breakfast out more often, and the most frequent patrons for lunch and dinner are from three- or four-member households. Residents of the Pacific region are most likely to visit restaurants, while people in the South

Central region are the most infrequent patrons. Complete details of this survey are enumerated in Table 7.1. (See pages 222-23.)

The same survey found that the characteristics considered most important in choosing or returning to a particular restaurant were cleanliness, quality and preparation of food, and courtesy of personnel. Other characteristics considered important were categorized by the type of restaurant. Price and location were important to patrons of quick-service restaurants; menu variety and price ranked high with customers of moderate-service restaurants; and full-service restaurants patrons wanted menu variety and atmosphere. Least important were the availability of a nonsmoking section, reservations, and liquor. The accompanying chart summarizes the complete findings by restaurant type:

Summary of Rankings

Order of Importance	Quick-Service	Moderate-Service	Full-Service
1	Cleanliness	Cleanliness	Food quality/ preparation
2	Food quality/ preparation	Food quality/ preparation	Cleanliness
3	Price	Menu variety	Menu variety
4	Location	Price	Courtesy/friendliness
5	Courtesy/friendliness	Courtesy/friendliness	Type of atmosphere
6	Speed of service	Speed of service	Price
7	Menu variety	Location	Nutrition of meals
8	Nutrition of meals	Nutrition of meals	Location
9	Type of atmosphere	Type of atmosphere	Speed of service
10	Choice of portion sizes	Choice of portion sizes	Individual preparation of meals
11	Individual preparation of meals	Individual preparation of meals	Choice of portion sizes
12	No-smoking section	No-smoking section	Reservations
13	Reservations	Reservations	Liquor
14	Liquor	Liquor	No-smoking section

Source: National Restaurant Association

Quick-service restaurants are self-service, have low per-meal costs, and use disposable plates and flatware. Moderate-service restaurants have table or counter service, employ food servers or helpers, and charge under $7.00 per meal. Full-service restaurants provide waiters or waitresses, tablecloths, and atmosphere; their per-meal costs are over $7.00. These definitions correspond to those used in the CREST report.

The demographic classifications of sex, marital status, age, income, household size, and geographical region are also used to identify people who eat a certain meal at a given type of restaurant—quick, moderate, or full service. This information is important in determining what type of restaurant is demanded by various groups at each particular meal period. These data are shown in Table 7.2. (See pages 224-25.)

The demand for restaurant menu items differs for males and females. The following survey was taken during the winter and spring of 1981; it shows the menu preferences of males and females.

Restaurant Item Demand

	Males	Females
Beverages		
Soft drinks	49.3%	50.7%
Diet	35.9	64.1
Regular	51.3	48.7
Alcoholic beverages	57.7	42.3
Beer	76.2	23.8
Cocktails	48.3	51.7
Wine	45.5	54.5
Menu items		
Fish or seafood	48.2	51.8
Chicken	46.9	53.1
Steak	55.5	44.5
Hamburgers	53.2	46.8
French fries	53.1	46.9
Salads	47.0	53.0
Sandwiches		
Hamburger	53.2	46.8
Cheeseburger	54.2	45.8
Roast beef	53.7	46.3
Fish	46.4	53.6
Chicken	42.0	58.0

Source: NDP Research Inc., CREST Family Diary Panel.

Breaking down the popularity of various food items by age group is also helpful in defining the demand characteristics of a particular market area. The figures in the Demand for Sandwiches by Age Group table are taken from a 1981 survey and show the age profile for four types of sandwiches (see page 226).

Table 7.1

	Eaten in Restaurant in Past Week			Average Number of Times Eaten Out in Past Week (Total Sample)			Average Number of Times Eaten Out (Those Eating) In Past Week		
	Breakfast %	Lunch %	Dinner %	Breakfast % No.	Lunch % No.	Dinner % No.	Breakfast % No.	Lunch % No.	Dinner % No.
Total	20	50	37	.46	1.23	.89	2.32	2.45	1.18
Sex									
Male	23	52	44	.61	1.60	1.01	2.70	3.05	1.33
Female	17	48	31	.32	.88	.77	1.83	1.82	1.03
Marital Status									
Not married	23	52	36	.59	1.49	.90	2.37	2.66	1.23
Married—wife employed	21	56	43	.56	1.39	.99	2.72	2.69	1.28
Married—wife not employed	16	45	35	.32	.96	.83	2.04	2.13	1.09
Age									
Under 25	25	69	41	.85	1.88	1.05	2.92	2.68	1.17
25-34	24	58	40	.56	1.29	.88	1.73	1.69	.90
35-44	19	45	40	.39	1.30	.98	1.97	2.74	1.22
45-54	19	51	38	.51	1.33	.91	4.63	4.36	2.10
55-64	16	43	37	.35	.85	.89	1.51	1.42	.94
65-74	13	36	27	.21	.88	.69	1.00	1.62	.67

Income									
Under $6,000	15	37	20	.32	.93	.53	2.31	2.62	1.12
$6,000-$9,999	17	48	36	.47	1.17	.92	2.81	2.56	1.39
$10,000-$14,999	24	53	40	.54	1.32	.93	2.59	2.92	1.42
$15,000-$24,999	21	57	47	.52	1.40	1.04	1.72	1.80	.87
$25,000 or more	22	58	49	.49	1.47	1.24	2.36	2.68	1.23
Household Size									
One	27	50	39	.72	1.51	1.04	2.52	2.69	1.35
Two	16	50	38	.41	1.18	.98	2.41	2.21	1.14
Three-Four	20	53	40	.39	1.18	.82	1.93	2.21	1.10
Five	17	42	29	.36	1.05	.64	2.76	3.30	1.24
Geographic Region									
New England	29	40	31	.55	.89	.69	1.90	3.28	1.21
Mid Atlantic	19	53	46	.52	1.44	1.04	2.59	2.66	1.27
North Central	26	52	39	.52	1.33	.98	1.81	2.33	1.15
South Atlantic	17	49	36	.52	1.27	.88	3.04	2.59	1.04
South Central	5	41	20	.12	.96	.49	2.82	2.19	.85
Mountain	18	58	37	.40	1.26	.83	2.94	3.27	1.64
Pacific	23	54	50	.56	1.12	1.08	2.60	1.89	1.36

Source: National Restaurant Association

Table 7.2 Percentage of Meals Purchased in Each Restaurant Type (By Type of Meal)*

	Breakfast				Lunch				Dinner			
	Quick Service	Moderate Service	Full Service	Total	Quick Service	Moderate Service	Full Service	Total	Quick Service	Moderate Service	Full Service	Total
Total	32%	55%	13%	(100%)	40%	49%	11%	(100%)	19%	37%	44%	(100%)
Sex												
Male	27	60	33	(100)	34	54	12	(100)	16	38	46	(100)
Female	43	44	13	(100)	48	41	11	(100)	23	37	40	(100)
Marital Status												
Not married	41	48	11	(100)	42	47	11	(100)	18	41	41	(100)
Married—wife employed	33	56	11	(100)	42	48	10	(100)	18	37	45	(100)
Married—wife not employed	24	61	15	(100)	34	53	13	(100)	20	35	45	(100)
Age												
Under 25	48	41	11	(100)	54	32	14	(100)	30	35	35	(100)
25-34	23	59	18	(100)	45	49	6	(100)	23	37	40	(100)
35-44	29	58	13	(100)	42	45	13	(100)	18	42	40	(100)
45-54	37	58	5	(100)	35	56	9	(100)	14	33	53	(100)
55-64	30	37	33	(100)	35	49	16	(100)	16	41	43	(100)
65-74	6	83	11	(100)	17	66	17	(100)	15	44	41	(100)

Income

Under $6,000	49	43	8	(100)	37	52	11	(100)	22	45	33	(100)
$6,000-$9,999	37	47	16	(100)	48	48	4	(100)	21	34	45	(100)
$10,000-$14,999	30	52	18	(100)	45	47	8	(100)	21	39	40	(100)
$15,000-$24,999	27	64	9	(100)	33	50	17	(100)	14	40	46	(100)
$25,000 or more	11	81	8	(100)	32	50	18	(100)	13	27	60	(100)

Household Size

One	37	48	15	(100)	44	48	8	(100)	16	45	39	(100)
Two	27	61	12	(100)	31	55	14	(100)	18	35	47	(100)
Three-Four	37	49	14	(100)	48	41	11	(100)	21	36	43	(100)
Five	24	69	7	(100)	32	56	12	(100)	20	33	47	(100)

Geographic Region

New England	56	44	—	(100)	33	50	17	(100)	17	29	54	(100)
Mid Atlantic	45	49	6	(100)	42	47	11	(100)	19	30	51	(100)
North Central	19	68	13	(100)	38	52	10	(100)	14	44	42	(100)
South Atlantic	44	34	22	(100)	47	45	8	(100)	22	43	35	(100)
South Central	47	18	35	(100)	26	52	22	(100)	24	37	39	(100)
Mountain	15	75	10	(100)	53	42	5	(100)	17	39	44	(100)
Pacific	22	70	8	(100)	37	53	10	(100)	23	32	45	(100)

*Percentages are calculated horizontally for this table.

Source: National Restaurant Association

Demand for Sandwiches by Age Group

Age Group	Hamburger	Chicken Sandwich	Roast Beef Sandwich	Fish or Seafood Sandwich
Under 12	23.4%	7.1%	5.4%	8.9%
13-17	8.3	5.4	2.5	3.9
18-24	9.5	8.7	5.3	6.1
25-34	18.6	24.7	16.4	17.0
35-49	19.6	29.2	23.3	23.5
50-64	14.1	17.2	28.9	26.0
65 and over	6.5	7.7	18.2	14.6

Source: NDP Research Inc., CREST Family Diary Panel.

The following macro trends can be deduced from these tables.

1. Men are more likely to order hamburgers, cheeseburgers, and roast beef sandwiches, while women prefer fish and chicken sandwiches.
2. The selection of entree items is affected by age group. People over 50 prefer steak, roast beef, fish or seafood, and veal; ethnic foods such as pizza and Mexican dishes are preferred by individuals 25–34 years old.
3. Women are more diet-conscious and order more salads and low-calorie items.
4. Children under 12 years of age especially like ice cream.
5. Breakfast items such as eggs, sausage, and bacon are more apt to be ordered by males than females.
6. Coffee, milkshakes, regular soft drinks, and beer are preferred by men; women order more tea, diet soft drinks, and wine.

Patrons' meal habits differ depending on the type of service provided by the restaurant. In quick-service restaurants, hamburgers tend to be the most popular food item. Customers are usually alone for breakfast (47%) and lunch (32%), but families with children comprised the largest group for dinner (49%). Couples were least likely to frequent quick-service restaurants.

Moderate-service restaurant customers prefer full-menu establishments, without a preference for a particular meal period—breakfast (59%), lunch (52%), and dinner (43%). Customers tended to be alone for breakfast (30%) and lunch (25%), and with their families and children for dinner (35%).

In full-service restaurants, customers most often preferred full-menu establishments with no preference for breakfast (74%), lunch (56%), or dinner (58%). A complete table of this information follows.

226

Meal Habits of Restaurant Customers

Food Speciality	Quick-Service			Moderate-Service			Full-Service		
	BR	**LU**	**DI**	**BR**	**LU**	**DI**	**BR**	**LU**	**DI**
Hamburgers	59%	71%	67%	6%	13%	5%	**	4%	1%
Chicken	4	7	8	0	4	6	**	5	2
Ethnic/foreign	2	3	1	1	4	6	3%	**	11
Pancakes	15	**	**	22	**	1	3	**	**
Donuts	7	0	**	2	**	0	**	**	**
Steak	**	4	9	6	8	17	14	6	13
Pizza	**	**	6	**	3	8	**	**	**
Fish/seafood	**	**	6	1	7	11	3	7	11
Hot dogs	**	3	1	**	1	**	**	2	**
Ice cream	**	**	**	**	**	**	**	1	**
Pie	**	1	**	**	**	**	**	**	**
Full menu	9	4	3	59	52	43	74	56	58
Roast beef	4	4	**	**	3	1	**	**	2
Other	**	**	2	3	2	2	3	4	1
No answer	**	1	**	**	2	**	**	1	1
Type of Group									
Alone	47	32	14	30	25	10	19	4	7
With spouse—no children	9	12	17	12	14	23	25	13	24
With date	**	1	3	2	2	6	**	**	9
With friend(s)—No couples	7	15	10	13	17	11	6	27	14
With couples	2	2	2	5	4	7	7	12	12
With business colleague	7	6	1	8	15	1	**	20	2
With family—children	21	28	49	22	15	35	31	11	21
With family—adults	7	4	3	8	6	6	12	12	10
Don't know/no answer	**	**	1	**	2	1	**	1	1

** Less than 5%.
Source: National Restaurant Association.

Since 1970, the number of senior citizens, i.e., people 65 years of age or older, has risen three times faster than the total population. Today, seniors represent 11% of the population and that figure will increase to 12.3% by 1990. Restaurant operators regard seniors as a significant market, and they are planning their operations accordingly. Seniors prefer to eat in full-menu restaurants, as the following table indicates.

Where Seniors Eat

Restaurant Category	Senior Citizens	Total U.S. Population
Full menu	42%	31%
Hamburger	11	20
Cafeteria	9	6
Hotel	7	5
Department/variety store	5	4
Fish	4	3
Budget steak	4	3
Ice cream	3	5
Other steak	2	2
Chicken	2	3
Pizza	1	5
Pancake	1	1
Mexican	1	2
Chinese	1	1
Donut	1	2
Other sandwich	1	2
Not specified	5	5
Total	100%	100%

Source: NRA Consumer Attitude Survey of Senior Citizen Eating Out Behavior.

Senior citizens also differ from the total population in the menu items they order.

10 Most Popular Menu Items

Ordered This Food Item	Senior Citizens	Total U.S. Population
Coffee	55%	24%
Potatoes	37	36
Salad	35	24
Vegetables	17	9
Hamburger	15	20
Fish and other seafood	13	9
Desserts/ice cream	18	15
Hot or iced tea	10	9
Chicken	9	8
Soft drinks	9	26

Source: NRA Consumer Attitude Survey of Senior Citizen Eating Out Behavior.

Knowledge of consumer preferences and attitudes toward the food-service industry helps the appraiser determine a restaurant's potential demand.

Restaurant Market Indexes

When evaluating the restaurant demand in a certain area, it is useful to know how the eating habits of that area compare to those of the average U.S. consumer and how these habits have changed over time. Since 1968, Market Statistics, a division of Bill Communications, Inc., has published this information each September in *Restaurant Business,* published at 633 Third Avenue, New York, NY 10017. The information is summarized in two indexes, the Restaurant Activity Index (RAI) and the Restaurant Growth Index (RGI). Statistics for over 300 U.S. metropolitan areas are tabulated annually.

Restaurant Activity Index

The RAI is the ratio of an area's restaurant sales, expressed as a percentage of total U.S. restaurant sales to the area's food store sales, expressed as a percentage of total U.S. food store sales. The calculation is performed as follows:

Food Sales (Figures Expressed in Millions of Dollars)

Description	Area X	Total U.S.
Restaurant	$3,000	$ 75,000
Food store sales	$5,000	$140,000

$$\frac{\substack{\text{Restaurant sales of Area X as a percentage of U.S. restaurant sales}}}{\substack{\text{Food store sales of Area X as a percentage of U.S. food store sales}}} = \frac{\dfrac{\text{Restaurant sales of Area X}}{\text{restaurant sales of U.S.}} = \dfrac{\$\ 3,000}{\$\ 75,000} = 4.00\%}{\dfrac{\text{Food store sales of Area X}}{\text{Food store sales of U.S.}} = \dfrac{\$\ 5,000}{\$140,000} = 3.57\%} = 1.12$$

The 1.12 is translated into an index with a base of 100, therefore, 1.12 indicates an RAI of 112. The following table summarizes the RAI for each region of the United States.

Restaurant Activity Index

Region	Population % U.S.	Food Store Sales % U.S.	Restaurant Sales % U.S.	RAI
New England	5.6167	5.8454	5.7214	98
Middle Atlantic	16.8811	17.0116	13.9985	82
East North Central	18.8020	18.1680	19.4230	107
West North Central	7.7948	6.6043	6.8401	104
South Atlantic	15.9175	15.7131	17.1664	109
East South Central	6.4128	6.3439	5.1030	80
West South Central	10.1373	10.6388	10.3641	97
Mountain	4.7599	4.7021	4.1401	88
Pacific	13.6779	14.9728	17.2434	115
United States	100.0000	100.0000	100.0000	100

Source: *Restaurant Business 1979.*

In Area X, the RAI index of 112 means that the ratio of restaurant to food store sales is 12% higher in this area than the national average. There are many reasons why a restaurant activity index might be greater than 100. In many urban areas, local citizens eat out more than the national average. A high index might also indicate that local restaurants receive nonlocal patronage from transient traffic, hotel guests, conventioneers, or residents of nearby communities.

An index may be lower than 100 in a rural area because local citizens eat out less often than the national average. Sometimes an insufficient number of restaurants in one area forces people to travel into neighboring metropolitan areas. A low index might also result if traveling distances to local restaurants are long or bad weather forces potential patrons to stay home.

The RAI index reflects the current level of restaurant activity, but it does not determine the cause of changes in activity. The index is calculated from a ratio, so it is also possible that changes in food stores sales, the denominator, would affect the index. The prices of food store items in relation to restaurant prices would affect the index too.

Restaurant Growth Index (RGI)

Restaurant demand can be traced to daytime and nighttime populations. The daytime population includes the commuting work force and transient population; the nighttime population consists of area residents. The weighted average of these two groups is the DNP.

To find the restaurant growth index, the DNP of an area as a percentage of

230

the total U.S. population is compared to the area's restaurant sales, expressed as a percent of total U.S. restaurant sales.

$$\frac{\text{Weighted average of daytime and nighttime population as a percent of total U.S. population}}{\text{Restaurant sales as a percent of total U.S. restaurant sales}} = \text{RGI}$$

The restaurant growth indexes for some major metropolitan areas are:

Metro Area	Resident Population as a % of U.S. Total	Daytime & Nighttime Population as a % of U.S. Total	Restaurant Sales as a % of U.S. Total	RGI
Los Angeles	3.2355	3.7586	4.7398	79
Miami	.6759	1.1233	1.0986	102
New York	4.3621	5.8915	4.2456	139

Source: *Restaurant Business*

The high RGI for New York City suggests that the restaurant market is underdeveloped and a new food-service operation would have less competition here than in Los Angeles.

Using Market Activity Indexes

When projecting revenues for a particular restaurant, the appraiser should know if area people tend to eat out more or less than average. The RAI facilitates such a comparison, but local factors must be included in the analysis. Some variation certainly could be expected between the dining habits of people in rural Maine and urban Dallas. Using the RGI, the analyst can determine if there is an unmet demand or an oversaturation of restaurants in a given area.

Combining the RAI and RGI indexes yields further information. The indexes for hypothetical metropolitan markets are listed below.

Metro Area	RAI	RGI
Market A	99	95
Market B	130	83
Market C	84	126
Market D	116	101

In market A, both the RAI and RGI are near 100, so demand for eating out is good (RAI = 99) and there is a large enough population to support the existing restaurant sales (RGI = 95).

A restaurateur in market B might not be so lucky. Although demand is strong, the indexes show a very competitive market. Market B residents exhibit a great propensity for eating out (RAI = 130) which may suggest a college or tourist area. The low RGI (RGI = 83), however, suggests that there are presently more restaurants in the area than needed.

Market C is in the opposite position and shows good growth potential. Currently, the population of Market C tends to eat at home more often. A restaurant in Market C would have a good chance for success if there are no constraints such as inclement weather half the year, an unreasonably high tax on restaurants, or a large supply of inexpensive food (e.g., from local farms). With an RGI of 126, this area does not have enough restaurants to support demand.

Market D presents a unique situation. Although its population has a very high tendency to eat out (RAI = 116), there appears to be the normal amount of restaurant sales for the daytime and nighttime populations (RGI = 101). This may indicate that Market D is a developed tourist area where a large transient population patronizes the eating establishments. Continued demand can be expected so long as nothing affects the area's drawing power.

The restaurant activity index and the restaurant growth index evaluate current and past trends, and help the analyst determine the future restaurant potential of a given area.

Over the years, multi-unit chain restaurants have developed specific demographic requirements for site selection. The criteria can be as simple as a population factor, or as complicated as a multiple regression formula that incorporates population, age, sex, income, occupation, traffic counts, office space, and other factors. Every type of restaurant draws from a specific market segment that is influenced by many factors.

The appraiser should be familiar with customer attitudes and the basis on which a restaurant site is selected. This information is matched against the attributes of the property under study to justify the local demand.

CASE STUDY

This case study is presented to illustrate the procedures for performing a market demand and supply analysis. The analysis is needed to develop the economic projections that are used in the income capitalization approach to restaurant valuation. The study will demonstrate how data are collected and how market value is estimated.

The property being appraised is a 150-seat steak restaurant located in Binghamton, New York. The various techniques used to quantify the demand for this particular restaurant and project its income and expenses are generally applicable to all types of restaurants. The information presented is realistic, but hypothetical. Because each restaurant appraisal assignment is unique, the methods used to collect and process the data into an estimate of value will probably vary.

Background Information

A 150-seat steak restaurant is proposed for a location at the State Street exit of Route 81, where it splits with Route 17 near the junction of Routes 7 and 434. The site is visible from half a mile away to travelers eastbound and from 300 feet away to travelers westbound on Route 81. Route 81 is a major, three-lane highway in upstate New York; Route 117 is a smaller, two-lane highway branching off to the Finger Lakes area. The site is just outside downtown Binghamton, which is the largest of the "Triple Cities"—Binghamton, Johnson City, and Endicott. The populations of these cities are:

	1970	1980	Percent of Change
City of Binghamton	64,123	55,860	(12.9)
Village of Endicott	16,556	14,457	(12.7)
Village of Johnson City	18,023	17,126	(5.0)

The Binghamton SMSA (standard metropolitan statistical area), which includes New York's Broome and Tioga counties and Pennsylvania's Susquehanna County, has a population of 212,661, according to the 1980 census. Although the population of the Triple Cities has declined over the past 10 years, the Binghamton SMSA has remained stable, indicating a normal population movement from the city to the suburbs.

Binghamton is located at the junction of the Susquehanna and Chenango Rivers. It has prospered since 1837, when the Chenango Canal was constructed to link the coal regions of Pennsylvania with the Erie Canal at Utica. Binghamton's many industries are described in the following table.

Name	Product or Process	Number of Employees
IBM	data processing equipment	20,000
Singer Co.—Link Flight Simulation Div'n	simulators and trainers	2,900
Endicott Johnson Corp.	shoes and accessories	2,500
General Electric Co.	aircraft electronic equipment	1,800
Universal Instruments	electronics industry production machinery	1,430

Source: Broome County Chamber of Commerce.

The total number of retail establishments in Broome County, which includes Binghamton, Johnson City, and Endicott, has fluctuated over the past 20 years, as shown below:

	Retail Establishments
1963	1,953
1967	1,868
1972	1,961
1977	1,950

The latest restaurant activity and growth indexes show that the Binghamton area has a low demand (RAI = 90), but a need for more restaurants (RGI = 115). This is a favorable market for a proposed food-service operation.

The subject property is eight blocks away from the central downtown area of Binghamton, where many offices, banks, and insurance companies are located. Sufficient parking is available, so people can drive to restaurants for lunch. Approximately 12,000 people work in downtown Binghamton. The major manufacturing plants are located on the rivers, about four miles from the proposed restaurant.

Most of the population lives no further than eight miles from downtown Binghamton, in the suburban areas of Binghamton, Endicott, and Union.

The Project

The developer of the project is a local citizen who has managed a major steak house chain. A group of local professionals will finance the project.

The restaurant will have 150 restaurant seats and 50 lounge seats. Entertainment will be provided on weekends, and the dining room can be converted into lounge seating after dinner. Parking for 100 cars is available.

The menu will offer four types of grilled steaks, prime rib, chicken, lamb chops, pork chops, and some grilled fish items. The restaurant will also feature a salad bar, a soup bar, and homemade breads. At lunchtime, smaller portions will be offered, along with steak and hamburger sandwiches. The average lunch check, without a beverage, has been projected at $7.00; and the average dinner check will be $14.50. Beer prices will start at $1.25, and mixed drinks will cost $1.75. Drinks made with the better brands of alcohol (call labels) will cost $2.25 or more.

Lunch will be served from 11:30 a.m. to 2:30 p.m. five days a week, and dinner will be served from 5:30 to 10 p.m. seven days a week.

The construction and decor will be first class; dark wood and antiques will be used throughout the restaurant. The outside of the building will be faced with used brick in a Tudor mansion style, and the service staff will wear Old English costumes. The subject restaurant is expected to be completed in 12 months and will open in Year 2 of the projection period.

Quantifying Demand

There are two methods that may be used to quantify the demand in a given restaurant area—the build-up approach based on an analysis of demand generators and the build-up approach based on an analysis of restaurant activity.

Using the build-up approach based on an analysis of demand generators, total restaurant demand can be calculated from thorough information on area inhabitants (demand generators). Information on the local population, can be obtained through interviews and from statistical marketing research. The demand of each appropriate market segment, e.g., young and old people, shoppers, business people, students, families, and single people, is measured by determining the overall size of the segment and how often the people comprising that segment dine away from home. This approach is generally used by restaurant chains who have developed specific criteria and profile information about their customers.

Quantifying demand based on an analysis of restaurant activity involves adding together the existing demand in each of the area's restaurants. The total demand of all the competitive restaurants would represent the area's total demand, except for peak times such as Friday and Saturday evenings or weekdays at noon when some customers may be turned away.

The approach based on restaurant activity is generally employed by independent restaurateurs who do not have the resources to document the local restaurant demand and develop specific customer criteria. For demonstration purposes, the build-up approach based on restaurant activity will be used in this case study.

Build-Up Approach Based on an Analysis of Restaurant Activity

There are six steps in the build-up approach based on an analysis of restaurant activity; these steps must be repeated for each meal segment.

1. Establish a trading area.
2. Identify competition within the trading area.
3. Determine the number of patrons per week (ppw) for competitors.
4. Convert ppw into a weekly competitive index.
5. Add any unmet peak demand.
6. Adjust for economic rates of change to find the total future demand.

Each of these steps will be explained and demonstrated using the proposed steak restaurant property.

Trading Area

The radius of a trading area is the distance from which approximately 80% of the potential customers come to dine at a particular restaurant for a certain meal.

The size of the area is affected by its population density, the surrounding competition, the type of meal being served, travel patterns, and the reputation of the restaurant. In a downtown metropolitan area, the trading area usually is only two or three blocks; in the suburbs, it might be 10–15 miles, and in rural areas the trading area could be up to 30 miles. A fast-service restaurant generally will have a smaller trading area than a deluxe, white tablecloth restaurant.

A trading area can be delineated using a survey, asking customers where they have come from as they leave the restaurant; this usually means a residence for dinner patrons and an office for lunch customers. Breakfast patrons may be asked where they live, where they work, and the route they travel between the two. The information is plotted on a map using dots; connecting the dots in a circle around the subject restaurant indicates the trading area.

236

Before the trading area can be established, it is important to determine if area residents will be attracted to the subject restaurant. For the subject steak house, two distinct customer segments have been identified—those for lunch and those for dinner. A separate trade area must be determined for each group. To estimate the existing total demand for each of these customer segments, the weekly patronage at similar establishments are totalled.

By interviewing lunch patrons at competitive luncheon establishments, it is discovered that patrons will drive up to eight minutes for lunch. The trading area for dinner is determined to be different. People are willing to drive farther for dinner because they can spend more time in the restaurant once they get there. The dinner trading area is determined to encompass a 20-minute driving area.

The Competition

After the trading area has been delineated, the competitive food service operations should be identified. Restaurants are competitive if they appeal to the same audience at the same meal. More specifically, a competitive restaurant offers the same type of meal and service in the same price range.

In a small trading area, all competitive restaurants should be visited and examined closely. To identify a restaurant as competitive, its average check should fall into the same price category as the subject's. The subject restaurant expects an average lunch check of $7.00 (without beverage) and an average dinner check of $14.50. Within the respective trade areas, four restaurants appear to compete with the subject for business at each meal.

Comparable restaurants with lunch checks of $6–$8 are:

1. Steak & Ale
2. Mama Josefino's
3. The Golden Goose
4. Steak Shot

The subject property competes for dinner customers with other steak restaurants with average checks of $12–$17. These restaurants are:

1. Steak & Ale
2. Bob's Steak House
3. Chenango Inn
4. Holiday Inn Dining Rom

Competitor's Patrons Per Week

Once the competition has been identified, the appraiser determines the number of seats in each restaurant and estimates the number of patrons per week (ppw) for each meal period. This information can be gathered by interviewing management or from personal observation.

By interviewing cashiers and service staff in the competitive restaurants, the ppw counts for three of the four lunch restaurants and two of the four dinner restaurants are determined. The results are as follows:

	Seats	ppw
Lunch		
Steak & Ale	106	1,590
Mama Josefino's	210	3,150
The Golden Goose	120	not available
Steak Shot	50	550
Dinner		
Steak & Ale	106	1,380
Bob's Steak House	100	not available
Chenango Inn	120	not available
Holiday Inn Dining Room	90	970

The ppw counts for the remaining restaurants, (The Golden Goose, Bob's Steak House, and the Chenango Inn) must be calculated through observation. First, the appraiser estimates how long it takes to "turn a cover," i.e., have a patron finish a meal. Then he or she walks through the restaurant counting the number of guests during a particular meal period. (Empty seats may be easier to count than occupied seats.)

For example, a patron at the Golden Goose takes an average of one and one-quarter hours to eat lunch, which is served between 11:30 a.m. and 2:30 p.m. Starting half an hour after opening and at intervals of one and one-quarter hours, the appraiser counts the number of patrons. On a typical weekday lunch, the following observations are made:

	Number of Patrons
Open at 11:30 a.m.	
Count at noon	60
Count at 1:15 p.m.	115
Count at 2:30 p.m.	20
Count at 2:30 p.m.	

238

To calculate the total number of patrons served at that meal, the counts from each observation period are added: $60 + 120 + 20 = 200$. Because lunch is served at this restaurant six days a week, the total ppw is 200×6 or 1,200. Through observations, the ppw counts for the two remaining dinner restaurants can also be calculated.

Bob's Steak House (average patron turnover every 1.5 hours)		Chenango Inn (average patron turnover every 1.75 hours)	
		Open at 6 p.m.	
Open at 5 p.m.		Count at 6:30 p.m.	40
Count at 5:30 p.m.	25	Count at 8:15 p.m.	50
Count at 7 p.m.	65	Count at 10 p.m.	20
Count at 8:30 p.m.	50	Close at 10:30 p.m.	
Count at 10 p.m.	20	Total daily	110
Close at 10:30 p.m.		Total ppw ($\times 6$)	660
Total daily	160		
Total ppw ($\times 6$)	960		

The total ppw count for the trading area at each meal period can now be established:

	ppw
Lunch	
Steak & Ale	1,590
Mama Josefino's	3,150
The Golden Goose	1,200
Steak Shot	550
Total lunch ppw	6,490
Dinner	
Steak & Ale	1,380
Bob's Steak House	960
Chenango Inn	660
Holiday Inn Dining Room	970
Total dinner ppw	3,970

To estimate the ppw count for some restaurants, the appraiser might have to make observations both on an average weekday evening and on a weekend evening. Sometimes a multiplier factor based on the number of cars in the parking lot may be used instead of a seat count. Occasionally, it is possible for an appraiser or restaurateur to estimate a restaurant's ppw count from personal experience in that particular market.

Competitive Index

A weekly competitive index is defined as the number of patrons served per seat per week for each meal period in a given restaurant. The competitive index indicates the restaurant's productivity and popularity; it is calculated by dividing the patrons per week at each meal by the number of seats available.

	ppw	Seats	Competitive Index
Lunch Segment			
Steak & Ale	1,590	106	15
Mama Josefino's	3,150	210	15
The Golden Goose	1,200	120	10
Steak Shot	550	50	11
Dinner Segment			
Steak & Ale	1,380	106	13
Bob's Steak House	960	100	10
Chenango Inn	660	120	6
Holiday Inn Dining Room	970	90	11

Unmet Peak Demand

All available seats are occupied at some time during most meal periods. Rather than wait, some customers may decide to eat a prepared convenience item from a store or street vendor; others may skip the meal altogether. This situation is common at lunchtime because most people take lunch between noon and 1:00 p.m. when most restaurants are busy.

Because a new restaurant is being added to the market, patrons will be redistributed among the existing restaurants, and some of this unmet demand will be accommodated. The unmet demand for lunch is estimated to be 10% of existing sales; it is believed that all demand is presently being served for dinner, so there is no unmet demand. For the subject lunch and dinner markets, the total unmet demand for the base year is:

Segment	Present ppw	Unmet Demand%	Unmet Demand
Lunch	6,490	10%	650
Dinner	3,970	0%	0

240

This unmet demand will not actually be realized until Year 2, when the subject restaurant opens.

Rates of Change

Based on the demand factors described in this chapter, the rate of growth or decline in demand should be established for each meal period. For example, it is estimated that total demand for lunch will increase 2% a year for the next three years and then stabilize at 1% growth; dinner demand is expected to increase 1.5% for the next six years. For the market segments involved in this case study, the potential restaurant demand for a food service outlet similar to the subject property could be charted as follows:

Restaurant Demand

Segment	Year 0	Year 1	Year 2	Year 3	Year 4	Year 5
Lunch						
Growth rate	—	2%	2%	2%	1%	1%
Demand	6,490	6,620	7,428*	7,577*	7,653*	7,730*
Dinner						
Growth rate	—	1.5%	1.5%	1.5%	1.5%	1.5%
Demand	3,970	4,030	4,090	4,131	4,193	4,256

*Includes unmet demand.

Supply of Restaurants

All restaurants operating within a given market area are somewhat competitive with one another. The appraiser should understand the dynamics of an area's restaurant supply in order to predict how a new operation will perform in the marketplace. A review of past changes in the nation's macro restaurant supply can indicate future trends in the food-service industry.

Between 1967 and 1977, the number of restaurants within the United States declined by approximately 10%. Most of the decrease occurred in the number of smaller operations with annual sales of less than $100,000. The number of restaurants in the $500,000–$1,999,000 sales category increased significantly during this period. The following chart illustrates these changes.

Number of Restaurants by Annual Sales
(Establishments Operated All Year with Payroll)

Annual Sales	Number of Establishments			Average Annual Percent of Change	
	1967	1972	1977	1972	1977
More than $5,000,000	25	33	89	6.0%	34.0%
$2,000,000–$4,999,000	156	265	788	14.0	39.0
$1,000,000–$1,999,000	774	1,505	5,324	19.0	50.0
$500,000–$999,000	1,686	7,563	20,754	70.0	35.0
$300,000–$499,000	7,132	13,738	26,489	19.0	19.0
$100,000–$299,000	41,911	66,121	85,841	12.0	6.0
$50,000–$99,000	62,601	72,314	66,917	3.0	(2.0)
$30,000–$49,000	58,405	59,916	39,086	.5	(11.0)
$20,000–$29,000	42,332	33,776	20,381	(5.0)	(13.0)
$10,000–$19,000	66,638	35,686	17,041	(17.0)	(22.0)
Less than $10,000	41,948	25,411	9,666	(12.0)	(33.0)
Total	325,608	316,328	292,376	(1.6)%	(0.6)%

Source: U.S. Department of Commerce, Bureau of Census, Census of Retail Trade, Subject Statistics.

Much of the industry growth over the past 10 years has been in the area of fast-food, self-service operations. This trend is evident in the following chart, which shows the growth in the number of restaurant establishments with no waiter/waitress service.

Number of Restaurants by Waiter/Waitress Service

Firms	1972	1977	Annualized Percent Change
Establishments with waiter/waitress service	143,474	142,585	0.1%
Establishments with no waiter/waitress service	50,194	75,669	10.0
Total	193,668	218,254	

Source: U.S. Department of Commerce, Bureau of Census, Census of Retail Trade, Subject Statistics.

Although the number of waiter/waitress-serviced establishments in the 1970s seems to have remained stable, the number of self-service restaurants increased at an average rate of 10% per year. This upward trend can be attributed to the tremendous growth of franchised fast-food operations.

Classifications

Studying the supply of restaurants can be very complicated because there are many different restaurant types and classifications. The factors that appraisers use to classify restaurants include location, meal price, the type of food served, and the method of service.

A food-service operation classified by its location might be found on a highway, in a downtown area, on a boat or a train, in a hotel, or in a residential shopping area.

Restaurant types may also be differentiated by meal price. The clientele of an inexpensive, fast-service restaurant generally differs from that of an expensive, table service restaurant.

Some people prefer to classify restaurants by the type of food served—either by specific menu items (e.g., hamburgers, chicken, fish) or by its ethnic association (e.g., American, Japanese, Mexican, Italian, Indian). This method of classification can be helpful in determining if a market will be saturated with a given food in the future.

Another means of classifying restaurants is the service method. The four standard methods of service are: fast service, or "fast food", coffee shop, specialty/family, and full service/atmosphere. Restaurants respond differently to the changing economic market, and their response reflects the type of service offered. This method of classification is used in many forms of analysis because a restaurant's type of service has the greatest impact on its operation and profitability.

At a fast-service, "fast-food" restaurant, the customer places an order with a counter worker, who receives and records the order, gives the food to the customer, and collects the money. Some fast-service restaurants delegate these tasks to a number of employees. The customer finds a table in the typically small seating area furnished with hard seats. In a modified fast-service restaurant, an employee may deliver the food to the table after the customer has ordered and paid at the service counter.

Coffee shop service originated in California and has spread throughout the country. Here, counter and table service are available in a bright and gaily decorated atmosphere; coffee shops have many windows, high ceilings, and unobstructed floor plans. The menu is varied, offering more than fast-service restaurants but not as much as full-service restaurants. Coffee shops are inexpensive and patronized primarily by families with children and senior citizens. Some major coffee shop chains include Penny's, Sambo's, JoJo's, and Big Boy. In the East, diners may also be considered coffee shop-style restaurants.

Specialty/family restaurants charge higher prices than coffee shops and may have more limited menus. They specialize in a particular type of food, such as Spanish, Oriental, Italian, steak, or seafood. Although their prices are higher than those of coffee shops, they can accommodate children—some may even have child-sized portions. Atmosphere and design can range from spartan to deluxe, but the major characteristic is the specialized food type.

In a full-service/atmosphere restaurant, an entree may be quite complicated and include many courses. Decor will be plush, with fewer seats per square foot. Meals are expensive and take more time to prepare and eat. Children are not typically found in these restaurants. Menus may vary, but they are often European or continental in style. This type of restaurant is usually independently owned.

Generally, restaurants only compete with other food-service operations in the same service class. Although diners may vary their selections of service from day to day and meal to meal, in most instances a restaurant selected for one specific meal period is chosen from a group of similar establishments.

Multi-Unit Operations

Franchised restaurants, or chains, have dramatically affected the food-service industry in recent years. The following charts show the growth of restaurant chains in recent years.

	Franchisee-Owned		Company-Owned		Total Chain Units	
Year	No. of Units	Percent	No. of Units	Percent	No. of Units	Percent
1972	26,219	81%	6,319	19%	32,538	100%
1974	29,726	75	10,107	25	39,833	100
1976	34,307	73	12,860	27	47,167	100
1978	39,802	72	15,510	28	55,312	100
1980	42,113	70	17,826	30	59,950	100
1981*	44,849	71	18,691	29	63,540	100

*Estimated.

Source: U.S. Department of Commerce, Bureau of Industrial Economics, "Franchising in the Economy," Table 56; and *Restaurant Business*.

The five largest franchisers in 1981 are listed in the following table.

244

Franchise Restaurant Systems—1981

Franchise System	Franchisee-Owned		Company-Owned		Total Chain Units	
	No. of Units	Percent	No. of Units	Percent	No. of Units	Percent
McDonald's	4,993	74%	1,746	26%	6,739	100%
Kentucky Fried Chicken	5,161	81	1,196	19	6,357	100
Burger King	2,571	85	451	15	3,022	100
Wendy's	1,481	66	748	34	2,229	100
Pizza Hut	2,055	51	2,005	49	4,060	100

Source: U.S. Department of Commerce, Bureau of Industrial Economics, "Franchising in the Economy," Table 56; and *Restaurant Business*.

The average sales for company-owned stores are about 15% higher than for franchisee-owned stores. The average 1982 estimate is $584,000 for company-owned stores and $505,000 for franchise-owned stores.

The table on the following page shows sales and unit statistics for the 25 largest chains in the country.

Chains account for a large proportion of the total sales figures for eating places in the United States.

Year	Chains (Multi-Units) Sales ($000,000)	Total Eating Places Sales ($000,000)
1979	$24.8 (35%)	$70.3
1980	$27.9 (37%)	$76.3
1981	$31.5 (38%)	$83.9

Source: U.S. Department of Commerce, Bureau of Census and Bureau of Industrial Economics, "Franchising in the Economy."

Restaurants that are not affiliated with chains are called "single-unit" eating places; this includes small "mom and pop" operations, medium-sized operations, and large, famous, single-unit dining establishments. The next table lists the top 25 independent restaurants in the country. The sales per unit for these single-unit operations averaged about $193,000 nationwide (versus $527,000 for all chain operations).

Top 25 Franchise Systems

Franchise System	Sales (Millions of dollars)		Number of Units	
	1976	1981	1976	1981
McDonald's	$3,030.0	$7,128.6	4,000	6,739
Kentucky Fried Chicken	1,600.0	2,490.0	3,989	6,357
Burger King	750.9	2,135.0	1,603	3,022
Wendy's	168.0	1,424.2	520	2,229
Pizza Hut	375.0	1,247.0	855	4,060
International Dairy Queen	684.0	1,125.0	4,792	4,805
Big Boy	550.0	845.0	937	1,180
Hardee's	324.0	843.6	953	1,379
Arby's	209.0	525.0**	568	1,146
Church's	180.0*	512.0	700*	1,363
Ponderosa	250.0	487.1	550	698
Howard Johnson's	370.0*	472.0*	900*	844
Taco Bell	120.0	464.4*	732	1,396**
Long John Silver's	156.3	463.9*	621	1,125
Dunkin Donuts	203.4	390.0	830	1,155
Bonanza	239.7	374.8	645	630
Burger Chef	300.0	340.0	925	725
Sizzler	120.8	295.7	287	478
Sonic Drive-Ins	136.8	285.0	567	1,046
Perkin's 'Cake & Steak	150.0*	266.0	260*	341
Mr. Donut	100.0*	243.5	575*	891
International House of Pancakes	148.0	224.5*	386	501
A & W	289.0	218.0	1,803	1,100
Pizza Inn	113.0	213.4**	525	734
Roy Rogers	80.0*	208.1*	200*	335

*Estimated by *Restaurant Business* or author.
**Company estimate.
Source: *Restaurant Business*.

A wide variety of foods are served in chain restaurants, but hamburgers, franks, and roast beef remained the most popular, with 50% of total chain sales in 1980. The number of chain units and total chain store sales, estimated to 1982, can be broken down by food type. (See table on page 248.)

Although chains have had a significant impact on the nation's industry, the appraiser performing a market study and valuation is primarily interested in information pertaining to the local market area. The proposed steak house described earlier will be used to illustrate how local, competitive food-service operations affect the allocation of the area's restaurant demand.

25 Largest Independent Restaurants

Name	City	Years in Operation	Total Sales (In Thousand $)
Windows on the World	New York City	3	$15,800
Tavern on the Green	New York City	4	11,000
Spenger's Fish Grotto	Berkeley, CA	50	9,219
"21" Club Inc.	New York City	50	8,600
Mai-Kai Restaurant	Ft. Lauderdale	24	7,439
Zehnder's	Frankenmuth, MI	124	6,565
Rainbow Room	New York City	45	6,500
Frankenmuth Bavarian Inn	Frankenmuth, MI	30	6,487
Rascal House	Miami Beach	26	6,190
Maxwell's Plum	New York City	13	5,800
Tangier Restaurant & Cabaret	Akron	25	5,560
Carson City Nugget	Carson City, NV	10	5,400
Pam Pan East	San Francisco	11	5,100
Grand Concourse	Pittsburgh	2	5,000
Joe's Pier 52 Seafood	New York City	12	5,000
Legal Sea Foods	Chestnut Hill, MA	5	5,000
Webers Inc.	Ann Arbor, MI	43	4,600
Columbia	Sarasota		4,500
Columbia	Tampa		4,300
Pea Soup Andersen's	Buellton, CA	56	4,185
Nick's Fishmarket	Chicago	2	4,050
Daphne's	Elizabeth, NJ	4	4,048
Daphne's	Miami	3	3,978
Bishop's	Lawrence, MA	30	3,950
Anderson's Cajun's Wharf	Nashville	2	3,900

Source: *Restaurant Business.*

CASE STUDY

Allocating Demand Among Supply

Using the build-up approach based on an analysis of restaurant activity, the total area restaurant demand is found and expressed in patrons per week (ppw). This total demand must then be allocated among the area restaurants based on the competitive nature of the supply.

Six steps are followed to allocate demand among the supply of restaurants:

Number of Chain Stores

Food Type	1972 No. of Units	1972 % of Total	1977 No. of Units	1977 % of Total	1982 (estimated) No. of Units	1982 (estimated) % of Total	Annualized 10-Year Growth
Chicken	4,561	14%	6,437	12%	8,197	12%	8%
Hamburgers, franks, roast beef, etc.	19,324	59	24,822	47	30,989	45	6
Pizza	2,385	7	6,759	13	10,251	15	43
Mexican (tacos, etc.)	906	3	2,147	4	3,639	5	40
Seafood	487	2	2,347	5	2,722	4	56
Pancakes	735	2	1,353	3	1,447	2	20
Steak, full menu	3,893	12	7,253	14	9,883	14	23
Sandwich/other	247	1	854	2	2,009	3	81
Total	32,538	100%	51,972	100%	69,137	100%	21%

Source: U.S. Department of Commerce, Bureau of Census, Bureau of Industrial Economics, "Franchising in the Economy," and *Restaurant Business*

1. List the supply of competitive restaurants in the trading area, including the proposed subject property.
2. List each restaurant's competitive index.
3. Calculate the overall competitive index.
4. Determine each restaurant's fair market share based on the overall competitive index.
5. Compare each restaurant's actual market share, based on its competitive index, to its fair share.
6. Calculate the number of patrons per meal period per week for the subject property.

Using this process, the appraiser not only finds out exactly how many patrons the subject restaurant should attract, but also how this number compares to what its fair share would be if all the restaurants were equally popular.

Restaurant Supply

The restaurants within the trading area that compete with the subject for customers represent the supply of restaurants. The restaurants competing with the proposed steak house and their respective seat counts are listed on the following page.

248

Supply of Competitive Restaurants—Number of Available Seats

	Base Year	Year 1	Year 2	Year 3	Year 4	Year 5
Lunch						
Steak & Ale	106	106	106	106	106	106
Mama Josefino's	210	210	210	210	210	210
Golden Goose	120	120	120	120	120	120
Short Stop	50	50	50	50	50	50
Subject Steak House	—	—	150	150	150	150
Total	486	486	636	636	636	636
Dinner						
Steak & Ale	106	106	106	106	106	106
Bob's Steak House	100	100	100	100	100	100
Chenango Inn	120	120	120	120	120	120
Holiday Inn Dining Room	90	90	90	90	90	90
Subject Steak House	—	—	150	150	150	150
Total	416	416	566	566	566	566

Competitive Indexes

The patrons per week (ppw) are calculated for the existing restaurants, and the competitive index is determined by dividing the ppw by the number of seats available at that meal. Essentially, the competitive index represents the number of patrons served per seat in one week.

Competitive Index of the Competition

	ppw	Competitive Index
Lunch Segment		
Steak & Ale	1,590	15
Mama Josefino's	3,150	15
The Golden Goose	1,200	10
Steak Shot	550	11
Dinner Segment		
Steak & Ale	1,380	13
Bob's Steak House	960	10
Chenango Inn	660	6
Holiday Inn Dining Room	970	11

The competitive indexes are known for the existing restaurants, but the appraiser must estimate the competitive index for the proposed restaurant. The appraiser should determine if, and how, the competitive indexes for the existing restaurants will change when the new restaurant enters the market.

Many factors affect the competitive index to varying degrees. Breakfast trade is affected by price, speed of service, quality, and accessibility (near business, near home, or en route).

The factors that affect luncheon business are food quality, service quality, atmosphere (conducive to business lunch), proximity to businesses, ample parking, personalized service, price, and speed of service. Dinner trade is affected by food quality, service quality, reputation, entertainment, popularity of food type, and price.

To estimate the competitive index for the proposed subject restaurant, the appraiser must evaluate how these factors interact and influence the customers' selection. The proposed subject property's competitive index will presumably fall within the same range as the competing properties; the exact index depends on the restaurant's ultimate popularity, as evidenced by its ability to meet customers' desires.

The subject steak house competes for lunch clientele with four restaurants that have indexes ranging from 10 to 15. The appraiser should study how the competing restaurants satisfy lunch customers' preferences and how these preferences affect their indexes. Based on these conclusions, the appraiser rates the proposed subject in each category and calculates its competitive index.

Rating Analysis of Factors Affecting the Competitive Index (1 = low; 10 = high)

	Steak & Ale	Mama Josefino's	Golden Goose	Short Stop	Subject Steak House
		Lunch Segment			
Food quality	8	8	7	7	8
Service quality	8	8	5	4	8
Atmosphere	5	10	2	5	7
Parking	10	5	8	8	10
Personalized service	10	6	6	6	7
Price	6	9	10	8	7
Speed of service	10	8	8	7	8
Competitive index	15	15	10	11	14*

*Estimated.

250

Comparing the above ratings for the competitive restaurants with the estimates for the subject restaurant indicates that a competitive index of 14 is reasonable. Because it generally takes only a short time for a restaurant's reputation to become established, the proposed steak house is expected to reach its goal for the lunch segment in three years.

Subject Steak Restaurant
Estimated Competitive Index

Lunch Segment
	Index
Year 2	12
Year 3	13
Year 4	14
Year 5	14

Through a similar analysis, the competitive index for the dinner segment is projected as follows:

Subject Steak Restaurant
Estimated Competitive Index

Dinner Segment
	Index
Year 2	11
Year 3	11
Year 4	12
Year 5	12

Any factors considered appropriate for the market segment may be used in the rating analysis. For instance, local preferences might include entertainment, size of portions, a famous owner, or menu selections.

Simply knowing the competitive indexes of the subject property and its competitors does not make the outcome completely predictable. All restaurants go through cycles, and the competitive index of an operation can change over time. Any anticipated changes in competitive indexes should be included in the analysis.

Overall Competitive Index

An overall competitive index is used as a basis to judge competing restaurants. It is essentially an average competitive index determined with the following formula.

$$\frac{\text{Total patrons per meal per week in trading area}}{\text{Total seats available per meal in trading area}}$$

$$= \text{Overall competitive index}$$

For the subject trade area of Binghamton, New York, the overall competitive indexes for Years 1 through 5 are as follows.

Overall Competitive Indexes

| | Binghamton Trade Area | | | | | |
	Base Year	**Year 1**	**Year 2**	**Year 3**	**Year 4**	**Year 5**
Lunch						
Total ppw	6,490	6,620	7,428	7,577	7,653	7,730
Total seats	÷ 486	÷ 486	÷ 636	÷ 636	÷ 636	÷ 636
Competitive index	13.4	13.6	11.7	11.9	12.0	12.2
Dinner						
Total ppw	3,970	4,030	4,090	4,131	4,193	4,256
Total seats	÷ 416	÷ 416	÷ 566	÷ 566	÷ 566	÷ 566
Competitive Index	9.5	9.7	7.2	7.3	7.4	7.5

Fair Share

A restaurant's fair share is the amount of business it would capture if all the restaurants had the same overall competitive index, i.e., all restaurants are equally popular and productive. The fair share percentage for a given restaurant is calculated as:

$$\frac{\text{Total seats in restaurant}}{\text{Total seats in area}} = \text{fair share percentage}$$

252

The fair shares for the competitive restaurants at each meal period are listed.

Fair Share Percentages

| | Binghamton Market Area | |
	Base Year/Year 1	Years 2–5
Lunch		
Steak & Ale	22%	17%
Mama Josefino's	43	33
Golden Goose	25	19
Short Stop	10	8
Subject Steak House	0	23
Dinner		
Steak & Ale	25%	19%
Bob's Steak House	24	18
Chenango Inn	29	21
Holiday Inn Dining Room	22	16
Subject Steak House	0	26

Actual Market Share

A restaurant's actual market share is determined using the competitive indexes of all the restaurants. It is calculated with the following formula:

$$\frac{\text{Restaurant A's number of seats} \times \text{Restaurant A's competitive index}}{\begin{array}{c}(\text{Restaurant A's number of seats} \times \text{Restaurant A's competitive index}) \\ + \\ (\text{Restaurant B's number of seats} \times \text{Restaurant B's competitive index}) \\ + \\ (\text{Restaurant C's number of seats} \times \text{Restaurant C's competitive index}) \\ + \\ (\text{Restaurant D's number of seats} \times \text{Restaurant D's competitive index})\end{array}} = \text{Actual market share}$$

For example, Steak & Ale's actual market share at lunch in Year 1 is calculated

$$\frac{106 \times 15}{(15 \times 106) + (15 \times 210) + (10 \times 120) + (11 \times 50)} = \frac{1,590}{6,490} = 24.5\%$$

When the subject steak house opens in Year 2, its number of seats, multiplied by its competitive index, must also be included in the denominator. Actual market shares for the subject area are calculated in the following table.

Actual Market Shares

	Binghamton Market Areas											
	Base Year		Year 1		Year 2		Year 3		Year 4		Year 5	
	Index	MS	Index	MS	Index	MS	Index	MS	Index	MS	Index	MS
Lunch												
Steak & Ale	15	24.5%	15	24.5%	15	19.2%	15	18.8%	15	18.5%	15	18.5%
Mama Josefino's	15	48.5	15	48.5	15	38.0	15	37.3	15	36.7	15	36.7
Golden Goose	10	18.5	10	18.5	10	14.5	10	14.2	10	14.0	10	14.0
Short Stop	11	8.5	11	8.5	11	6.6	11	6.5	11	6.4	11	6.4
Subject Steak Restaurant	0	0.0	0	0.0	12	21.7	13	23.1	14	24.4	14	24.4
Dinner												
Steak & Ale	13	33.7%	13	33.7%	13	24.0%	13	24.0%	13	23.4%	13	23.4%
Bob's Steak House	10	24.5	10	24.5	10	17.4	10	17.4	10	17.0	10	17.0
Chenango Inn	6	17.6	6	17.6	6	12.6	6	12.6	6	12.2	6	12.2
Holiday Inn Dining Room	11	24.2	11	24.2	11	17.2	11	17.2	11	16.8	11	16.8
Subject Steak Restaurant	0	0.0	0	0.0	11	28.8	11	28.8	12	30.6	12	30.6

Market Share versus Fair Share—Comparison and Cross-Check

	Base Year	Year 1	Lunch Segment Year 2	Year 3	Year 4	Year 5
Steak & Ale						
Market share	24.5%	24.5%	19.2%	18.8%	18.5%	18.5%
Fair share	22.0	22.0	17.0	17.0	17.0	17.0
Market share as a percent of fair share	111	111	113	111	109	109
Mama Josefino's						
Market share	48.5	48.5	38.0	37.3	36.7	36.7
Fair share	43.0	43.0	33.0	33.0	33.0	33.0
Market share as a percent of fair share	113	113	115	113	111	111
Golden Goose						
Market share	18.5	18.5	14.5	14.2	14.0	14.0
Fair share	25.0	25.0	19.0	19.0	19.0	19.0
Market share as a percent of fair share	74	74	76	75	74	74
Short Stop						
Market share	8.5	8.5	6.6	6.5	6.4	6.4
Fair share	10.0	10.0	8.0	8.0	8.0	8.0
Market share as a percent of fair share	85	85	82	81	80	80
Subject Steak House						
Market Share	0	0	21.7	23.1	24.4	24.4
Fair share	N/A	N/A	23.0	23.0	23.0	23.0
Market share as a percent of fair share	0	0	94	100	106	106

Each restaurant's fair share and actual market share for each meal period can now be compared to show which establishment has the largest share of business for a given year. This type of comparison also serves as a check to ensure that all the indexes are within the proper range.

Patrons Per Meal

The purpose of this supply and demand review is to forecast the number of patrons per week for the subject property in order to estimate food and beverage

Market Share versus Fair Share—Comparison and Cross-Check

	Base Year	Year 1	Dinner Segment Year 2	Year 3	Year 4	Year 5
Steak & Ale						
Market share	33.7%	33.7%	24.0%	24.0%	23.4%	23.4%
Fair share	25.0	25.0	19.0	19.0	19.0	19.0
Market share as a percent of fair share	135	135	126	126	123	123
Bob's Steak House						
Market share	24.5	24.5	17.4	17.4	17.0	17.0
Fair share	24.0	24.0	18.0	18.0	18.0	18.0
Market share as a percent of fair share	102	102	97	97	94	94
Chenango Inn						
Market share	17.6	17.6	12.6	12.6	12.2	12.2
Fair share	29.0	29.0	21.0	21.0	21.0	21.0
Market share as a percent of fair share	60	61	60	60	58	58
Holiday Inn Dining Room						
Market share	24.2	24.2	17.2	17.2	16.8	16.8
Fair share	22.0	22.0	16.0	16.0	16.0	16.0
Market share as a percent of fair share	110	110	108	108	105	105
Subject Steak House						
Market share	0	0	28.8	28.8	30.6	30.6
Fair share	N/A	N/A	26.0	26.0	26.0	26.0
Market share as a percent of fair share	0	0	111	111	118	118

revenues. The subject property's patrons per week may now be calculated as:

Total segment patrons per week × actual market share = ppw

Projection of Restaurant Revenues and Expenses

The income capitalization approach to restaurant valuation is based on antici-pated future revenues and expenses. The demand is converted into a projected revenue flow and all appropriate expenses are deducted, leaving the net income.

Projected Patrons Per Week—Subject Steak House

	Year 2	Year 3	Year 4	Year 5
Total trading area ppw lunch demand	7,428	7,577	7,653	7,730
Actual market share	21.7	23.1	24.4	24.4
Lunch capture	1,612	1,750	1,867	1,886
Total trading area ppw dinner demand	4,090	4,131	4,193	4,256
Actual market share	28.8	28.8	30.6	30.6
Dinner capture	1,178	1,190	1,283	1,302

This section presents a step-by-step process to calculate a restaurant's net income using either actual operating data or readily available national averages.

Existing versus Proposed Restaurants

The projection technique for valuing an existing or a proposed restaurant is the same, except that the demand for the proposed facility must be quantified. Earlier sections described how the appraiser reviews the local supply and demand situation to project future revenues for a proposed property. For an existing restaurant, similar market analysis is used to verify whether actual revenues are close to those projected and if these revenues represent competent management. Using these estimated revenues, the figures reported for comparable properties and national averages as guides, expected expenses can be calculated. The actual expenses reported for an existing property should also be compared with national averages to confirm their accuracy.

National Operating Averages

The most readily available restaurant operating data and statistics are the national operating averages compiled each year by the National Restaurant Association. This information is available in a publication entitled *Restaurant Industry Operations Report*. Copies of the report may be obtained by writing the research department of the National Restaurant Association at 311 First Street N.W., Washington, D.C. 20001, or by calling 202-638-6100.

The national averages are arranged in a standard format known as the Uniform System of Accounts for Restaurants.

According to this system, a chart of accounts for a restaurant income statement is arranged as follows:

Statement of Income and Expenses

- Sales
  - Food
  - Beverage
    - Total sales
- Cost of sales
  - Food
  - Beverage
    - Total cost of sales
- Gross profit
- Other income
    - Total income
- Controllable expenses
  - Payroll
  - Employee benefits
  - Direct operating expenses
  - Music and entertainment
  - Advertising and promotion
  - Utilities
  - Administrative and general
  - Repairs and maintenance
    - Total controllable expenses
- Income before occupancy costs
- Occupancy costs
  - Property taxes and insurance
- Income before interest and depreciation

When using national averages, the appraiser should be familiar with the main categories of revenues and expenses. The following summary describes each account that appears in a restaurant's statement of income and expense.

Expense Items

Food sales. Food sales include sales of all food items. This account is projected by multiplying the estimated number of patrons per week (ppw) by the anticipated average check times 52 weeks.

Beverage sales. Beverage sales vary among restaurants, depending on the type of operation. They will generally be a relatively constant percentage of food sales.

Cost of sales—food. The food cost is the amount of raw food products consumed by a restaurant operation. It is calculated by taking the beginning inventory, adding purchases, and deducting the ending inventory.

Food cost is usually reported as a percentage of food sales. This number is used to judge restaurant efficiency. When estimating a food cost percentage, data from similar menu categories should be compared. For example, a normal food cost for a Mexican restaurant may be 34%, but a steak house does well to operate at 40%.

Cost of sales—beverage. Beverage cost includes all liquors, wines, beers, and waters served in both the bar and restaurant areas. Like the food cost percentage, beverage cost can be affected by pricing, portion sizes, and the type of restaurant operation.

Other income. Only items associated with the operation of a restaurant are included in this category. Other income items include lounge cover charges, minimum food or beverage charges, banquet room rentals, nonfood sales (e.g., gum, cigarettes), rental of shops, concessions, or display areas, and cash discounts.

Payroll. Under the Uniform System of Accounts for Restaurants, the entire restaurant payroll is in one category. (For hotels, the payroll is apportioned to each department.) Regular salaries and wages, extra wages, overtime pay, vacation pay, commissions, and bonus payments are included.

The placement of the manager's salary sometimes causes confusion. In a proprietorship or partnership, where the owner is also the manager, a salary is usually taken in a form of cash drawing or net profit and does not appear on the payroll. In a restaurant organized as a corporation, the manager generally is paid from the payroll account. An owner-manager's salary may be more or less than the benefits received by the operation, so the income statement should be adjusted to reflect the actual value of the managerial services rendered.

Employee benefits. Employee benefits vary among restaurants, depending on management's payroll policies. Some typical employee benefits are social security tax (FICA), state and federal unemployment taxes, workmen's compensation insurance premiums, health and life insurance premiums, pension plan payments, complimentary employee meals (at cost), employee training, and staff parties.

Direct operating expenses. Direct operating expenses are the costs of services rendered to the customer. Some examples of direct operating expenses are uniforms, laundry, linen or linen rental, china, glassware, silverware, kitchen utensils, cleaning supplies, paper supplies, guest supplies, menus and drink lists, dry cleaning, contract cleaning, flowers and decorations, auto or truck expense, and licenses and permits.

A separate reserve account is sometimes used for linen, china, glassware, silver, and utensils. The direct operating expense account would be unfairly skewed if replacement of these items were expensed when purchased because they are bought periodically in bulk; therefore, a certain amount is accounted for in each period and then credited to a reserve for replacement account.

Music and entertainment. Some of the items listed under music and entertainment include expenses for musicians, entertainers, taped music, and meals served to musicians and entertainers.

Advertising and promotion. Advertising and promotion expenses are costs incurred for promoting, creating, and maintaining sales in the restaurant. Items included in this category are newspaper advertising, magazine advertising, flyers, brochures, postcards, direct mail expenses, postage and telephone expenses, and agency fees.

Utilities. Utility costs have become important to management because electric and gas rates have increased. These costs are generally fixed but can be controlled somewhat through proper conservation methods.

Administrative and general expenses. Administrative and general expenses are costs associated with the daily operation of the business, but not directly related to providing food service or comfort.

Most administrative and general expenses are relatively fixed. The exceptions are the provision for doubtful accounts and cash shortages, which are moderately variable, and the fees on credit card accounts, city sales tax, and management fees, which are usually highly variable.

Administrative and general expenses include office stationery, printing, and supplies, postage and telephone, management fees, executive office expenses, insurance, fees to credit-check organizations, provision for doubtful accounts, cash shortages, professional fees, protective services, royalties, franchise fees, sales taxes, and personnel expense.

Repairs and maintenance expenses. Repairs and maintenance expenses are controlled by management to some extent. The expenses in this category tend to be fixed but an increased number of patrons per week will affect the wear of items slightly and repairs will be needed in certain areas.

Property taxes. Real and personal property taxes are based on the assessed value established by the municipality and the tax rate.

Insurance expense. The insurance expense category includes the cost of insuring the building and its contents against damage or destruction from fire, weather, sprinkler leakage, boiler explosion, plate glass breakage, and so forth.

260

Reserve for replacement. Furniture, fixtures, and equipment are essential to restaurant operation and their quality often influences the status of a property. Included in this category are all nonreal estate items that are normally capitalized, not expensed. A reserve for replacement is usually not included in a restaurant's income and expense statement, but it should be recognized as a cash expense for valuation purposes.

Variations in Income and Expense Items

Certain revenue and expense categories fluctuate with changes in related elements such as the number of patrons and the average check. In analyzing changes in each category, the appraiser should be familiar with three relationships:

1. Category name. The category or subcategory that is presently being analyzed.
2. Relative impact. Because different expenses may have more or less effect on the total picture, variations should be weighted.
3. Volume relationship. A restaurant's revenue is determined by two factors—the number of patrons per week and the average check. Some expenses do not vary with volume and are termed fixed expenses. Expenses that do vary with changes in the number of patrons per week are called volume-sensitive expenses; those that change with the average check amount are called price-sensitive variables.

Appraisers use a number of techniques to evaluate changes in restaurant expenses based on the relationship between the amount of revenue expense per seat (restaurant seats and/or beverage seats) and the percentage of total sales. By understanding which elements contribute to changes in these two statistical units of comparison, the appraiser can forecast future movements. The amount of expense per seat indicates a fixed cost, but the percentage of total sales is used for variable costs because it depends on the number of patrons and the average check.

For example, a change in the number of total patrons will affect the payroll, which, in turn, will change the figures calculated as a percentage of total sales. On the other hand, a change in the number of total patrons will not affect the numbers calculated as a percentage of utility expenses because they are not sensitive to changes in the number of patrons. This concept is very useful in forecasting the effects of business changes on income statements. The following case study examines the proposed steak house described earlier in this chapter.

CASE STUDY

Projecting Revenues and Expenses

The patrons per week (ppw) demand at lunch and dinner has already been determined using a supply and demand forecast. Now, the revenues and expenses of the subject steak restaurant can be projected using operating data from actual restaurants with comparable menus, service, and facilities or the national averages published by the National Restaurant Association.

Revenues

The management of the subject steak house estimates average food checks of $7.00 at lunch and $14.50 at dinner in today's dollars. This was determined after looking at comparable restaurants and pricing out a sample menu.

The number of patrons per week has been projected as:

| | Patrons Per Week | | | |
	Year 2	Year 3	Year 4	Year 5
Lunch capture	1,612	1,750	1,867	1,886
Dinner capture	1,178	1,190	1,283	1,302

Because restaurants generally build up volume rapidly, an income and expense forecast based on a stabilized year is appropriate. Operational Year 2, which is three years from today, appears to be representative and will be used for the stabilized projection.

The annual revenue for each meal period is calculated by inflating the average check up to the stabilized year at an assumed annual inflation rate of 8%. The inflated average check is then multiplied by the stabilized number of patrons per week times 52 weeks. (See first table on following page.)

For the purpose of this case study, assume that national averages are the only data available. The classifications used here are similar to those used in the National Restaurant Association national averages publication, but the data are hypothetical.

First, the appraiser must determine in which classifications the subject steak house best fits. The most appropriate subclassifications are shown on the following page.

262

	Revenue Per Year				
	Year 0	**Year 1**	**Year 2**	**Stabilized**	
Lunch					
Average check	$ 7.00	$ 7.56	$ 8.16	$	8.82
Patrons per week					1,750
Weeks per year					52
Lunch food revenue				$	802,620
Dinner					
Average check	$14.50	$15.66	$16.91	$	18.27
Patrons per week					1,190
Weeks per year					52
Dinner food revenue					$1,130,547
Total food revenue					$1,933,167
					$1,930,000 (rounded)

Classification	Subclassification Selected
Years in business	Under five years
Type of restaurant	Full menu—table service
Region	Northeast
Location	Suburban
Affiliation	Single-unit independent
Sales volume	$1,500,000–$3,000,000
Menu theme	Steak

Beverage Revenue

The national averages of beverage sales, expressed as a ratio to food sales, show the following percentage data for each subclassification:

Subclassification	Beverage Sales as a Percentage of Food Sales
Under five years	38%
Full menu—table service	39
Northeast	37
Suburban	40
Independent	35
Sales of $1.5–$3.0 million	36
Steak	39

Reviewing these statistics, the appraiser looks for the percentage relationship that best represents the subject steak house. In estimating beverage volume, the type of restaurant (full menu—table service, 39%), location (suburban, 40%) and menu theme (steak, 39%) are the determining factors. Based on these percentages, it is estimated that 39% of food sales can be attributed to beverage sales. Therefore, beverage revenue and total revenue are estimated as follows:

	Stabilized Year
Food revenue	$1,930,00
Beverage percentage	39%
Beverage revenue	$ 750,000 (rounded)
Total revenue	$2,680,000

Cost of Sales—Food and Beverage

Food and beverage costs are extremely variable, so the proper unit of comparison is the ratio to total sales.

Subclassification	Food Cost as a Percent of Total Cost	Beverage Cost as a Percent of Total Cost
Under five years	41%	26%
Full menu—table service	41	27
Northeast	44	32
Suburban	40	31
Independent	39	28
Sales of $1.5–$3.0 million	39	24
Steak	45	32

Reviewing these food cost data, the two most important subclassifications for the subject steak house are location and menu theme, with the greatest weight given to the latter. As a result, food cost is estimated at 44% of food sales. Beverage cost does not seem to be as affected by these two factors, it appears to be equally affected by all the elements. Beverage cost is therefore estimated at 29%.

Expenses

Controllable Expenses

Of the subject steak house's expenses, payroll and direct operating expenses will

264

vary directly with sales volume. Portions of the employee benefit expenses will change with sales, while other parts remain fixed. These three categories are therefore projected as a percentage of total sales.

		As a Percent of Total Sales	
Subclassification	**Payroll**	**Employee Benefits**	**Direct Operating Expenses**
Under five years	25%	4%	6%
Full menu—table service	30	6	5
Northeast	26	5	5
Suburban	26	3	6
Independent	28	3	6
Sales of $1.5–$3.0 million	28	5	8
Steak	26	4	5

The payroll of a restaurant is most directly influenced by the type of restaurant, the region, the location and the menu theme. Based on these factors, a payroll percentage of 27% of total sales appears appropriate.

The factors that have most control over employee benefits, such as the type of restaurant, type of service, and region, suggest an estimate of 5% of sales for this category. The final number will be checked using a per-seat calculation.

Direct operating expenses are projected at 5% of sales, which is reasonable given the type of service and the menu plan presented by management.

Some restaurant expenses remain relatively fixed despite changes in volume. To compare these expenses for different restaurants, an index based on the expense per seat is used. The fixed expenses shown on page 267 are projected using this unit of comparison.

Other Income
Other income typically ranges .5%–2% of total sales, depending on the facilities at the restaurant. Because the subject steak house has no banquet space, entertainment lounge, concessions, or displays, other income will be low, about .5%.

Total Income
Total income is calculated as follows:

	Stabilized Year	Percentage
Sales		
Food	$1,930,000	72.0%
Beverage	750,000	28.0
Total sales	2,680,000	100.0
Cost of sales		
Food	849,000	44.0*
Beverage	217,000	29.0**
Total cost of sales	1,066,000	39.8
Gross profit	1,614,000	60.2
Other income	13,000	0.5
Total income	$1,627,000	60.7%

*Percent of food sales
**Percent of beverage sales

Expenses for music and entertainment at the subject steak house will be low because only taped music will be provided. Restaurants with entertainment expenses of over $175 per seat are probably supplying some type of live entertainment. Therefore, looking at subclassifications with expenses below $175, an entertainment expense of about $105 per seat is estimated for the subject restaurant. This amount must be inflated out at 8% for three years to estimate the music and entertainment expense as of the stabilized year: $105 × 1.26 = $132 per seat.

Advertising and promotion are needed to establish a firm base of business. Statistics for restaurants under five years old with full menus and steak specialties indicate current advertising budgets of approximately $255 per seat. Applying the 8% inflation factor to this estimate results in the following projection of advertising and promotion: $255 × 1.26 = $321 per seat.

Management has minimal control over utilities, although it can institute conservation programs. The management of the subject steak house has no plans to install extensive energy conservation machinery, so utility expenses will probably be near the $336 average for restaurants in the Northeast. Inflating this amount at 8% yields: $336 × 1.26 = $423 per seat.

Administrative and general expenses vary based on the style of management and the organization of the restaurateur. The subject's manager believes that a successful restaurant must be run like a business, with complete administrative office control and the necessary personnel. An estimated $730 per seat will be

Dollar Amount Per Seat

Subclassification	Music and Entertainment	Advertising and Promotions	Utilities	Administrative and General	Repairs and Maintenance
Under five years	$160	$255	$235	$632	$230
Full menu—table service	200	191	302	705	264
Northeast	95	318	336	900	341
Suburban	100	170	184	608	264
Independent	175	191	142	583	186
Sales of $1.5 to $3.0 million	250	244	268	705	326
Steak	105	276	201	730	279

spent for administrative and general expenses. Applying the 8% inflation factor yields: $730 × 1.26 = $920 per seat.

Because the building will be new, repairs and maintenance are projected at only $230 per seat; this figure is obtained from the subclassification of restaurants under five years old. Using the 8% inflation factor, the figure becomes: $230 × 1.26 = $290 per seat.

Occupation costs include property taxes and insurance. The national averages are:

| | Amount Per Seat | |
	Property Taxes	Property Insurance
Full menu—table service	$110	$55
Suburban	90	58
Northeast	100	50

Reviewing these data, $100 per seat, or $15,000 per year in today's dollars, appears adequately to account for property taxes. The Broome County tax assessor was consulted to verify this estimate. Inflating this estimate to the stabilized year: $100 × 1.26 = $126 per seat.

Property insurance is very location sensitive, so a local insurance agent was consulted. Mr. B. Safe, of Tri Cities Insurance Company, submitted an estimate of $7,800 per year for property insurance, which translates to $52 per seat. This is within the range of the national averages. Inflating this estimate to the stabilized year: $52 × 1.26 = $66 per seat.

A reserve for replacement of 1%–2% of total sales is usually sufficient to provide for timely replacement of furniture, fixtures, and equipment. Because the subject steak house is a new property, it is believed that 1% of total revenue will be enough.

The table on page 269 reflects the income and expenses for the stabilized year of operation.

The Valuation of Restaurants

This analysis of the supply, demand, and income components of the restaurant industry provides the basis for estimating market value.

Restaurants are retail businesses that create and dispense a product from a specific location. The elements that make up an operating restaurant include

Proposed 150-Seat Subject Steak House Statement of Income and Expenses for Stabilized Year

	Amount	Percent	Calculation
Sales			
Food	$1,930,000	72.0%	
Beverage	750,000	28.0	
Total sales	2,680,000	100.0	
Cost of sales			
Food	849,000	44.0	
Beverage	217,000	29.0	
Total cost of sales	1,066,000	39.8	
Gross profit	1,614,000	60.2	
Other income	13,000	0.5	$917,000 × 0.5%
Total income	1,627,000	60.7	
Controllable expenses			
Payroll	724,000	27.0	$2,680,000 × 27%
Employee benefits	134,000	5.0	$2,680,000 × 5%
Direct operating expenses	134,000	5.0	$2,680,000 × 5%
Music and entertainment	20,000	0.8	150 × $132
Advertising and promotion	48,000	1.8	150 × $321
Utilities	63,000	2.4	150 × $423
Administrative and general	138,000	5.1	150 × $920
Repairs and maintenance	44,000	1.6	150 × $290
Total controllable expenses	1,305,000	48.7	
Income before occupation costs	$ 322,000	48.7	
Occupation costs			
Taxes	19,000	0.7	150 × $126
Insurance	10,000	0.4	150 × $66
Reserve for replacement	27,000	1.0	$2,680,000 × 1%
Total occupancy cost	56,000	2.1	
Income before interest and depreciation	$ 266,000	9.9%	

land, building(s), furniture, fixtures, and equipment, business, and operating supplies. The appraiser must first identify the elements to be included in the valuation and determine how they affect the valuation process.

Land and Building

The land and building elements of a restaurant operation are sometimes owned by two different interests, i.e., the restaurant has a ground lease. Or the land and building may be owned by one party and leased to a second party, the restaurant operator. According to the National Restaurant Association, some form of lease structure is used by approximately 60% of all food operations in the United States.

Because restaurant leases often encumber the real property component, a logical way to value these two elements would be to capitalize the anticipated market rental.

Furniture, Fixtures, and Equipment

The furniture, fixtures, and equipment of a restaurant include not only the tables, chairs, and kitchen equipment but also items of decor. A typical restaurant lease, incorporating both land and building, provides the tenant with a basic shell in which a restaurant must be constructed. In many instances, tenant improvements can be substantial, depending on the style and atmosphere desired. The net income remaining after payment of all operating expenses and market rent for the land and building elements represents a return on the furniture, fixtures, and equipment and the going-concern value of the business.

Business

A restaurant contains an element termed the business component. Like any retail operation, a restaurant has business value, good will, and owner's profit that cease to exist when the restaurant closes. This business element is part of the real property income component that remains after the market rent is deducted from a restaurant's income.

Operating Supplies

A restaurant's inventories of unused food, beverages, and supplies do not add to the property's overall value because they are normally treated as a dollar-for-dollar adjustment upon closing.

The Three Approaches

Once the appraiser determines which elements are to be included in the valuation, the traditional three approaches to value are used—the cost, sales comparison, and income capitalization approaches.

The appraiser using the cost approach estimates the current replacement cost of the building, furniture, fixtures, and equipment, and deducts any loss in value from all forms of deterioration and obsolescence. The value of the land is then added to the depreciated replacement cost to find the value of the property.

Of the three approaches, the cost approach probably yields the least reliable indication of a restaurant's value. Restaurants, like hotels, are income-producing properties purchased to realize future profits, so reproduction cost often bears little relation to a restaurant's value. Furthermore, the cost approach provides no basis for estimating the restaurant's business value, which is related to its earnings capability, not its cost.

Using the sales comparison approach, the appraiser bases the estimate of market value on the actual sales prices of comparable restaurants, incorporating appropriate adjustments for differences in property location, size, decor, condition, and other attributes. This approach will provide a reliable indication of value if sufficient data on similar properties are available. The restaurants compared should be similar in affiliation, size, location, and mode of operation so that a minimum of adjustments is required.

The common units of comparison for a restaurant are value per restaurant and value per seat.

When valuing restaurants by the sales comparison approach, the appraiser should be sure that the components of the comparables (e.g., land, building, furniture, fixtures, equipment, and business) are the same as those of the subject.

The income capitalization approach generally is preferred for valuing income-producing properties because it reflects the usual rationale of investors. In this approach, market value is estimated by capitalizing a projected stabilized income stream using a capitalization rate that reflects both the cost of capital and the relative risk of the investment.

Applying the cost and sales comparison approaches to a restaurant involves the same valuation procedures used for all types of properties. However, the application of the income capitalization approach to a food-service operation is unique, as will be demonstrated in the following case study.

CASE STUDY

The previous case study concluded with a projection of the proposed steak house's income and expenses for the stabilized year of operation.

Applying the income capitalization approach to a restaurant operation, the appraiser values the real property components (land and building) separately from the personal property (furniture, fixtures and equipment) and business elements. Independent values are established for real and personal property components because they embody different risks. The real property components, in most instances, can be adapted to other uses if the food-service operation fails. Restaurant furniture, fixtures, equipment, and items of decor can sometimes be reused, but once they have been used, they depreciate rapidly. The restaurant has practically no business value if its operation is terminated. Because the risks associated with the furniture, fixtures, equipment, and business components of a restaurant are significantly higher than those of the real property components, different discount and capitalization rates are employed for these two components.

First, the restaurant's land and building components are valued based on their market rental. In today's dollars, lessors of restaurant real estate typically demand an 11%–15% return on a ground lease, and a 13%–17% return if the lease includes the land and building. The economic rent, or the income attributed to the real property (land and building), is calculated with a common restaurant rental formula, which is typically based on a percentage of gross revenue.

Percentage rents for restaurant leases are negotiated on the basis of factors such as mix of food and beverage sales, estimates of total sales, the expected profitability of the restaurant, the location and cost of construction, and the lessor's expenses (e.g., real estate taxes, insurance, and repairs). A percentage rent generally is expressed in one of two ways—a percentage of food gross (4%–6%) plus a percentage of beverage gross (8%–12%), or a percentage of total gross (6%–7%). The rent usually is a gross rent before real estate taxes, insurance, and structural repairs.

By estimating the total revenue of a restaurant and applying the appropriate percentage rent, the appraiser can project a market rent to be capitalized into real estate value.

The market rent, or income attributed to the real property (land and building) for the proposed steak house restaurant is based on a rental of 5% of total food sales and 10% of total beverage sales. The lessor is responsible for property taxes and insurance.

Sales	Stabilized Year	Percentage Rental	Market Rent
Food	$1,930,000	5%	$ 96,500
Beverage	750,000	10	75,000
Total	$2,680,000		$171,500
Income to lessor (economic rent)			$171,500
Less: Property taxes		$19,000	
Insurance		10,000	$ 29,000
Net to lessor:			$142,500

The appropriate capitalization rate is based on the risks associated with the restaurant's leased fee position and on factors such as financing, the terms of the lease, the quality of the tenant, and the cost of capital. A 15% overall capitalization rate was selected for this case study. The value of the real property elements (land and building) is estimated:

$$\frac{\$142,500}{.15} = \$950,000 \text{ real property value}$$

The income to the restaurant operator after payment of the market rent is calculated as follows:

Income before occupation costs		$322,000
Less: Market rent	$171,500	
Reserve for replacement	27,000	198,500
Operator's income		$123,500

The operator's income represents the income attributed to the furniture, fixtures, equipment, and business elements. As mentioned previously, the return requirements for the nonreal property components are significantly higher than the land and building returns.

Capitalization rates for a restaurant's invested capital typically fall into one of three areas: for an efficient, profitable operation with new equipment, a capitalization rate of 20%–25% is typical; for an operation with average profitability and older, well-maintained equipment, 25%–33% is appropriate; and for an inefficient operation with old, poorly maintained equipment, the rate should be 33%–50%.

Assuming that the subject restaurant will have new equipment and offer normal operational risks, an operator's income capitalization rate of 25% was selected.

$$\frac{\$123,500}{.25} = \$494,000 \text{ or } \$500,000 \text{ furniture, fixtures, equipment, and business}$$

The value of the proposed steak house restaurant is the combination of the two property components:

Real property (land and building)	$ 950,000
Furniture, fixtures, equipment, and business	500,000
Total restaurant value	$1,450,000

This value indication is checked against the indications derived using the cost and sales comparison approaches.

Index

276